The Son Who Learned Obedience

The Son Who Learned Obedience

A Theological Case Against the
Eternal Submission of the Son

D. Glenn Butner Jr.

☞PICKWICK *Publications* • Eugene, Oregon

THE SON WHO LEARNED OBEDIENCE
A Theological Case Against the Eternal Submission of the Son

Copyright © 2018 D. Glenn Butner Jr.. All rights reserved. Except for brief quotations in critical publications or reviews, no part of this book may be reproduced in any manner without prior written permission from the publisher. Write: Permissions, Wipf and Stock Publishers, 199 W. 8th Ave., Suite 3, Eugene, OR 97401.

Pickwick Publications
An Imprint of Wipf and Stock Publishers
199 W. 8th Ave., Suite 3
Eugene, OR 97401

www.wipfandstock.com

PAPERBACK ISBN: 978-1-5326-4170-1
HARDCOVER ISBN: 978-1-5326-4171-8
EBOOK ISBN: 978-1-5326-4172-5

Cataloguing-in-Publication data:

Names: Butner, Jr., D. Glenn, author.

Title: The Son who learned obedience : a theological case against the eternal submission of the Son / D. Glenn Butner Jr.

Description: Eugene, OR: Pickwick Publications, 2018 | Includes bibliographical references and index.

Identifiers: ISBN 978-1-5326-4170-1 (paperback) | ISBN 978-1-5326-4171-8 (hardcover) | ISBN 978-1-5326-4172-5 (ebook)

Subjects: LCSH: Jesus Christ—History of doctrines | Trinity—History of doctrines | Jesus Christ—Divinity—Biblical teaching | Monotheism

Classification: BT216.3 B875 2018 (print) | BT216.3 (ebook)

Manufactured in the U.S.A.   08/13/19

Unless otherwise indicated, scripture quotations are from the ESV® Bible (The Holy Bible, English Standard Version®), copyright © 2001 by Crossway, a publishing ministry of Good News Publishers. Used by permission. All rights reserved."

Scripture quotations marked NRSV are from the New Revised Standard Version Bible, copyright © 1989 National Council of the Churches of Christ in the United States of America. Used by permission. All rights reserved.

Scripture quotations marked CSB®, are taken from the Christian Standard Bible®, Copyright © 2017 by Holman Bible Publishers. Used by permission. Christian Standard Bible®, and CSB® are federally registered trademarks of Holman Bible Publishers.

For Lydia

Contents

Acknowledgements | ix

Introduction | 1

Chapter 1   The Father's Will Set Forth in Christ: The Evangelical Trinitarian Debate | 13

Excursus 1   *Common Objections to Inseparable Operations* | 49

Chapter 2   The Obedience of One Man: Christology and the Son's Obedience | 62

Chapter 3   Obedient to the Point of Death: Christ's Obedience and the Doctrine of Salvation | 95

Chapter 4   God's Good, Pleasing, and Perfect Will: The Doctrine of God and the Divine Will | 122

Excursus 2   *EFS and Theological Anthropology* | 150

Chapter 5   His Counsel Revealed to the Prophets: The Missing Scriptural Case for Eternal Submission | 160

Conclusion   The Son Who Learned Obedience | 193

Bibliography | 199
Scripture Index | 213
Index of Modern Authors | 221
Index of Historical Authors | 223

Acknowledgements

WRITING THIS WORK DEPENDED upon the input, encouragement, and generosity of many people for whom I am deeply thankful. I initially encountered the debate surrounding the eternal submission of the Son due to a generous invitation from Dan Allen to attend an event on the subject. My first publication on the question appeared in the *Journal of the Evangelical Theological Society* in 2015. I am grateful to Andreas Köstenberger for the chance to enter the debate publicly by publishing my ideas and for permission to reprint an excerpt from that article as part of chapter 1 of this book. An invitation by Jamin Hübner to present a related paper building on my *JETS* article at the Annual Meeting of the Evangelical Theological Society in 2016 prompted additional reflection on eternal submission. A subsequent invitation to publish my conference presentation in *Priscilla Papers* provided an excellent opportunity for feedback from Mimi Hadad, Jeff Miller, and Tim Krueger. This book is in large part the fruit of reflections stemming from these invitations. I am also grateful for direct feedback that I received on various portions of this book from Tom Bronleewe, Tim Gabrielson, Kirsten Guidero, and Roy Millhouse. Above all others, Kevin Giles and particularly Matt Estel invested significant time in offering constructive feedback to extensive portions of this work. Without their help, this book would lack much in terms of clarity, content, and precision. Laurel Watney, Mikki Millhouse, Anna Adamyk, and Sierra Gant retrieved well over a hundred texts through interlibrary loan to facilitate my research. Without their help it would have been quite literally impossible to write this text. I am thankful for all of the members of Pickwick Publications (an imprint of Wipf & Stock) for taking on an unknown author and for my editor Robin Parry. The Wipf & Stock 'family' is filling an important need in theological publishing. I am thankful to those veteran scholars willing to endorse this book, and to any who are willing to take the time to engage it seriously, either in agreement or disagreement. Finally, I am thankful for the support and encouragement of my wife Lydia, who listened to my ideas (which occasionally became rants), who supported me in the extra workload this project required, and who never pointed out the hypocrisy of the fact that my marriage proposal compared husband and wife to the Trinity. With her by my side, I have learned and grown considerably as she supported doctoral studies in theology and as I at times empirically proved that marriage is no image of the majesty of the Trinity. I dedicate this book to her.

Introduction

IN THE SUMMER OF 2016, Liam Goligher's two guest posts on the blog for Mortification of Spin, a Reformed podcast and website, fostered an evangelical civil war on the Trinity. They were the blog posts that launched a thousand trinitarian tweets. Goligher accused many complementarian theologians of "constructing a new deity," moving "to the verge of idolatry" and "beyond Scripture and Christian Orthodoxy as historically understood."[1] What concerned Goligher and prompted these harsh words was the fact that many evangelical theologians had been teaching that the Son eternally submits to the Father within the inner life of the Trinity. Shortly thereafter, Carl Trueman, who cohosts Mortification of Spin, wrote his own condemnation, calling the idea of eternal submission "a likely staging post to Arianism."[2] Trueman and Goligher were certainly not the first to raise such accusations, but these posts were the first to bring widespread online attention to the question of whether the Son eternally submits to the Father. Soon Wayne Grudem and Bruce Ware, leading figures who affirm eternal submission, defended their position as historic orthodoxy, and certainly not Arianism, prompting rejoinders ad infinitum. I am aware of at least fifty scholars who posted formal online responses, and there are hundreds of popular-level responses. Few have likely read all of the material available online.

The online evangelical debate about the doctrine of the Trinity brought public attention to a conflict that has been ongoing for decades. Prior to 2016, the debate was largely, though certainly not entirely,[3] waged between

1. Goligher, "Complementarianism Based on Eternal Subordination?"
2. Trueman, "Fahrenheit 318."
3. Notable exceptions include Paul Maxwell, a complementarian who opposed eternal submission prior to 2016, and Craig Keener, an egalitarian who sees an eternal

complementarians and egalitarians. On the one side, some complementarian theologians argued that the Father and Son, though equal in nature and essence, were distinct in role and function, so that the Son was eternally obedient and submissive to the Father. (Other complementarians simply ignored the question of submission altogether.) On the other side, a number of evangelical egalitarians rejected any language of eternal submission, subordination, or obedience as a deviation from historic Christian orthodoxy, an idea that divides the unity of the Trinity. Specifics of these two positions will be discussed in chapter 1, but for now it is sufficient to note that this particular debate was old, but often couched in terms that were not easily accessible to Christians outside of the academy. The debates of 2016 brought a deep evangelical rift to light, drew many complementarians into the debate for the first time, and prompted many lay evangelicals to seek to understand the doctrine of the Trinity in depth for the first time. Rarely had evangelical google searches so frequently featured terms like "Rahner's rule" and "*homoousios.*" Despite this peak in interest, much work remains to be done to outline what is at stake in this debate to a wider audience. One objective of this volume is to fill this knowledge gap.

In some sense, the debates of 2016 signaled a change in momentum. For the first time, complementarian scholars as notable as Carl Trueman spoke out against the idea of eternal submission/subordination. For the first time, nonevangelical scholars weighed in on the debate in a social media setting, with patristics heavyweights Lewis Ayres and Michel Barnes both dismissing the eternal submission of the Son. What began as an academic debate had spilled over into the pew and pulpit. Where many defended notable supporters of eternal submission like Wayne Grudem and Bruce Ware, others began to distance themselves from these figures. Even the Council for Biblical Manhood and Womanhood distanced itself from arguments that emphasized the Son's eternal submission, and eternal submission advocates like Grudem, Ware, and Denny Burk all made some limited concessions to their opponents' cause. Kevin Giles narrates the events of 2016 in a book entitled *The Rise and Fall of the Complementarian Doctrine of the Trinity*. In some respects, the debate was a vindication of Giles's position in a decades-long feud with those teaching eternal submission or subordination. However, the conflict is only partially resolved.

There are three reasons why I am not convinced that the debate surrounding the eternal obedience of the Son in the Trinity is as resolved as Giles's title to his book suggests. The first reason is the matter of existing

---

voluntary submission of the Son taught in several passages of Scripture. Maxwell, "Authority Analogy?" 541–70; Keener, "Subordination within the Trinity," 39–58.

publications. Whatever impact the online debate may have had on the larger church community, I doubt that the impact is as substantive as that fostered by the numerous major works of systematic theology that affirm eternal submission or subordination. Notable here is Wayne Grudem's *Systematic Theology*, which has sold over four hundred thousand copies, and which teaches that "the idea of eternal equality in being but subordination in role has been essential to the church's doctrine of the Trinity since it was first affirmed in the Nicene Creed."[4] Other evangelical systematic theology textbooks include eternal submission or subordination in their descriptions of the Trinity, including books by Norman Geisler and John Frame,[5] among others. The ESV study Bible is also characterized by language of the Father's authority and the Son's eternal submission.[6] Simply put, a significant percentage of evangelical pastors and laity have been trained in systematic theology using textbooks that affirm the eternal submission of the Son. Of course, in addition to the impact of these textbooks, we must reckon with the large number of books and chapters dedicated to defending the position that the Son eternally submits, published by noted evangelical scholars like Bruce Ware, Thomas Schreiner, Michael Ovey, Robert Letham, and others. In comparison, printed materials opposing this view are relatively sparse, with full works treating the subject only authored by Millard Erickson and Kevin Giles. Introductions to Systematic Theology that explicitly reject this position are unknown. As long as the balance of printed evangelical works on the Trinity heavily favors eternal submission or subordination, evangelical support for the eternal submission of the Son will be increasing, though perhaps at a slower pace as a result of the online civil war.

A second reason why it may be premature to declare complete victory over the eternal-obedience perspective can be illustrated by one response to Giles's most recent work on the demise of complementarian trinitarianism. When Wipf and Stock announced the release of Giles's volume on social media, someone commented that he had requested a review copy to help prepare his thesis and promised a scathing review in short order. The response is indicative of the theses and dissertations that continue to be written in defense of eternal submission—a new generation of eternal submission advocates is rising through the ranks of evangelicalism today. More significant, though, is the fact that the main arguments surrounding

---

4. Grudem, *Systematic Theology*, 251.

5. Geisler, *Systematic Theology: Volume Two*, 290–91; Frame, *Systematic Theology*, 501–2.

6. I first discovered this overlap through a post by Rachel Miller. While I will attempt to avoid citing much online material, this contribution certainly deserves notice. Miller, "Eternal Subordination of the Son and the ESV Study Bible."

eternal submission have been debated for so many years (decades even!) that scholars can reasonably predict the main arguments that each side will deploy. If someone has not been convinced by these arguments in the past, there is little reason to believe that a new presentation of the same material will convince them. While it may be uncharitable, unfair even, to plan a scathing review of a work you have not yet finished reading, I have no doubt that this individual could predict most of the material in Giles's work and could therefore reasonably infer the response that he would hold against Giles's position. Many remain unconvinced by the best arguments in print against eternal submission.

A third reason to write on the subject of eternal submission is that the evangelical world has largely gone silent on the question of eternal submission and subordination.[7] At the time that I write this, I am unaware of any retractions in print. In time the online debate will fade from memory, so it is important to ensure that more permanent resources like printed books ensure that eternal submission and subordination remain challenged by serious scholarship.

Though I find claims of eternal submission untenable myself, I have some sympathy for those who affirm the eternal obedience of the Son because I am convinced that one of the central arguments deployed against eternal submission does not actually work. The anti-submission argument usually accuses theologians who accept eternal submission of Arianism for denying the claim that Father and Son share the same essence or being *(ousia)*. The argument usually asserts that claiming that the Son submits but the Father does not submit results in Father and Son having different properties, which logically entails a difference in being, or so the argument goes. As I will explain in chapter 1, the form of the argument put forward usually fails, and the argument itself, even if rightly presented, would only hold if pro-submission theologians used the same meaning for the word *ousia* as many fourth-century theologians, but those who favor eternal submission do not. Given this fact, it is no surprise that many adamantly defend their positions and deny the charge of Arianism. A stronger and more durable rejection of eternal submission will require a new set of arguments, and long-entrenched positions will likely only change as a result of an entirely new dialogue, not through continued debate of the question of Arianism.

This book will recenter the debate surrounding the eternal submission of the Son on the issue of the single divine will of God. Whereas traditional versions of the doctrines of the Trinity, Christology, and the atonement treat the will as a faculty of the divine nature or being, a trinitarian theology

---

7. I am thankful to Kevin Giles for sharing this insight.

of eternal submission usually treats will as a property of the three divine persons, though some explain submission as a mode of willing proper to the persons who share a single will. Either formulation creates a number of significant problems for classical versions of the Trinity, Christology, and the atonement, problems that have not yet as a general rule been identified but which are vital to any thorough analysis of claims of eternal submission. It is also exceedingly difficult to explain how God's will might submit or obey, given what we know about the divine nature and attributes as revealed in Scripture. I will demonstrate that most eternal submission advocates adopt a trinitarian theology that is largely incompatible with their own views of Christology, the atonement, and the divine attributes, while others take problematic moves not only in terms of the Trinity but also in these other theological loci. I intend to demonstrate that while the direct biblical support for eternal subordination or submission is flimsy at best, the systematic case against eternal submission is nearly insurmountable precisely because language of eternal obedience and submission runs contrary to the long-held theological notion that will is proper to nature, not a personal property.

Scope, Method, and Trajectory of the Argument

I want to be precise from the start concerning the scope of my argument. I am evaluating claims that the Son eternally submits to the Father, or that he eternally obeys the commands of the Father. Evangelicals have used a number of other terms for the same concept, including "difference in roles" and "functional subordination," that I find problematic. These other terms, however, are not problematic for the same reasons or in the same magnitude, and they appear to be less universally accepted. Most evangelical trinitarian theologians I read use the language of obedience or submission, but some disagree on terms like subordination.[8] The scope of my argument is therefore limited to the use of terms like obedience and submission to describe the eternal relationship between Father and Son because they pertain to the divine will, which is one of the more central concepts of systematic theology. I may briefly treat other terms and concepts as necessary, but my opinion on such concepts lies outside of the scope of this work. I will also limit the scope of my argument in terms of sources consulted. While I use the online debates surrounding the Trinity that occurred in 2016 as a starting point for this work, I will restrict substantive analysis to those sources published as journal articles, chapters, or books. Because online content is

---

8. For example, Robert Letham rejects any language of subordination. See Letham and Giles, "Is the Son Eternally Submissive to the Father?" 10–21.

not peer reviewed and is rarely subject to a robust editorial process, the quality of content in print resources is higher. The rapidly changing landscape of the online debate makes it complicated to represent authors' content in the context of the ongoing dialogue, and no online posts are likely to be as influential as published works like Grudem's *Systematic Theology* or Ware's *Father, Son, & Holy Spirit*. Therefore, I consider the arguments in such print resources as more significant in precision, impact, and academic quality and therefore a more appropriate subject for analysis when engaging ideas of eternal submission.

I will develop a number of arguments that are proper to the discipline of systematic theology, so I must pause to note how systematic theology relates to the Bible. All theology must be biblical, but we must distinguish three ways that a theologian might use the Bible. Exegesis attempts to determine the intended meaning of a given text, attending to literary form, lexical meaning, textual variants, and historical and cultural context. Biblical theology is a type of hermeneutics, a theological interpretation of the Bible as a whole that considers key themes and ideas within their canonical context. The biblical theologian builds on exegesis, offering a first-order reflection on the information contained through exegesis by considering canonical narrative, intertextuality, and significance within the context of Christian community.[9] Therefore, biblical theology moves beyond the intended meaning of a given passage, but still develops scripturally informed theological insights. In chapter 5, I will argue that we cannot appeal to exegesis or biblical theology to resolve the debate on eternal submission or subordination. In the entire Bible, only 1 Corinthians 15:28 refers to the Son submitting outside the context of his incarnate ministry, but close exegesis reveals that Paul does not intend to explore the eternal relation between Father and Son in this passage. Even biblical theology cannot resolve the trinitarian debate because the doctrine of the Trinity requires more than just exegesis situated in the canonical context of redemption history for the benefit of the Christian community. This is because the doctrine of the Trinity is rightly the domain of systematic theology.

---

9. For example, G. K. Beale remarks of his own project, "A biblical-theological approach to a particular text seeks to give its interpretation first with regard to its own literary context and primarily in relation to its own redemptive-historical epoch, and then to the epoch or epochs preceding and following it." Beale, *A New Testament Biblical Theology*, 9. Similarly, when comparing New Testament theology to systematic theology, I. Howard Marshall remarks that in biblical theology "The New Testament must be understood first of all and as far as possible on its own terms, as an expression of through within the ways that were possible in the first century." Marshall, *New Testament Theology*, 44.

While the doctrine of the Trinity is profoundly biblical and a necessary inference from the Bible, the doctrine of the Trinity extends far beyond exegesis and biblical theology. No human author of the Bible has written anything intentionally designed to explain God's triune nature in any detail, and a robust doctrine of the Trinity requires vocabulary, concepts, and arguments that are rooted in and consistent with Scripture, but that exceed what is explicit in the biblical text. For example, the Bible does not provide philosophical explanations as to how God's oneness relates to the three names Father, Son, and Holy Spirit, or any technical guidance concerning how these persons eternally relate to one another. The classical terminology of eternal generation of the Son and procession of the Spirit are certainly rooted in the Bible, drawing on vocabulary found in Psalm 2:7 (and as interpreted in Acts 4:25, 13:33; Heb 1:5), for example, but any theory of how such generation occurs reaches beyond the explicit teaching of the Bible. Since the human biblical authors do not intend to teach us about the eternal relation between the Father and the Son or about the single or threefold will of God, evaluating claims of eternal submission cannot be an exercise in biblical exegesis. The doctrine of the Trinity claims that God is one being eternally subsisting as three persons, but this fundamental grammar is based in philosophical concepts that move beyond the limits of biblical theology. Therefore, what follows is necessarily a debate in the field of systematic theology.

Systematic theology stands one step further removed from the Bible than does biblical theology. Biblical theology attempts to explain synthetically the meaning of the biblical text in continuity with the meaning intended for its original audience, but it extends this meaning through redemptive historical analysis. Systematic theology draws on the Bible directly and on the conclusions of biblical theology to explain questions that are often foreign to the biblical authors and even the canon as a whole, questions which can nonetheless be answered with confidence given the scope of the Bible. Systematics treats the Bible in terms of the "comprehensive whole,"[10] the "overarching story"[11] in which we are called to participate. It seeks not only to explore the logical connection between the explicit or intended meaning

---

10. Henry, *God, Revelation, and Authority*. Vol. I, 239. Perhaps over ambitiously, Henry envisions systematic theology arranging the entire content of the Bible into a "system of axioms and theorems" (240).

11. Vanhoozer, "A Drama-of-Redemption Model," 158. Vanhoozer argues that the Bible is a script, that Christians are to live into the world of the script, and that each individual has some space for improvisation in new contexts and in light of new challenges. Where Henry sees the need for a set of axioms that summarizes the entire biblical narrative, Vanhoozer seeks a narrative within which individuals can perform. Both theologians see systematic theology extending beyond the scope of exegeting particular passages.

of various passages of Scripture, but also to uncover implicit meanings evident in the broad biblical witness but never elaborated in any detail in a single passage.[12] So far there is continuity with biblical theology, but for a doctrine to properly be an example of systematic theology, more is required. A systematic approach to the Trinity not only answers the question, "what does the Bible teach us about the Father, Son, and Spirit?" It must also answer the question, "who is the God who speaks to us in revelation, telling us of the work of redemption accomplished in Christ?"[13] Theology must therefore be "second-order reflection on first-order speech."[14] Reflection on the God speaking through the content of the Bible necessarily stands one step removed from reflection on the content of the Bible itself. The systematician must step back from the words of the text to consider the One who is present in the entirety of the text.

Systematic theology differs from biblical theology in the tools it deploys to make sense of the Bible. While it relies on the historical critical, literary, and linguistic insights of biblical interpretation, these insights are synthesized in an effort to provide conceptual clarity. The Bible speaks of the Son as "the radiance of the glory of God and the exact imprint of his nature" (Heb 1:3), the one who was "in the form of God" (Phil 2:6), and "the image of the invisible God" (Col 1:15). Biblical theology provides insight into the meaning of these phrases in historical and canonical context. Systematic theology draws on reason, tradition, and experience to provide the term *homoousios*. When we say that the Son is *homoousios*—of the same essence—with the Father, we are summarizing the broad testimony of Scripture as elucidated by biblical theology using terminology drawn from Greek philosophy and transformed for Christian purposes. The term is faithful to the biblical witness, though not explicitly taught there and beyond what the historical authors would have intended. It provides conceptual clarity in a manner that no isolated biblical phrase is able. It is a second-order reflection on the broad testimony of Scripture informed by reason, experience, and

---

12. A theological system need not deviate from the biblical narrative and the flow of the biblical canon; indeed, ideally a theological system unfolds in a manner that follows the biblical pattern. Nevertheless, systematic theology differs from biblical theology in its treatment of the whole, if not in the order in which the whole is treated. Allen, "Knowledge of God," 26.

13. As T. F. Torrance points out, the doctrine of the Trinity is not merely an inference. We can ask "who must God be in order to save us?" Asking this question leads us to the Trinity by inference, but if the Trinity was only this, then it would be something other than the self-disclosure of God. Against mere inference, we must affirm that "God's active self-revealing and the content of his self-revealing are one and the same." Torrance, *The Christian Doctrine of God*, 32.

14. Allen, "Knowledge of God," 29.

tradition and designed to facilitate a clearer understanding of the triune God with whom Christians experience communion as a result of the events described in the Bible, and in the very action of reading the Bible.[15] We can now fully define systematic theology as *a second-order reflection on biblical themes that draws on philosophy to provide conceptual clarity concerning who God must be or what God must have done, given scriptural teaching.*

If the Bible directly explained the doctrine of the Trinity in detail, or if it explicitly explored the question of whether God has one will or three, then this book would have to proceed in a very different manner than I intend to follow. We might begin by exploring certain key passages, move to consider historical context, pausing for several word studies, and conclude with a reflection on how key passages are normed by canonical context. The question of the eternal submission of the Son would be an exegetical question combined with the biblical theological question of how the text is prescriptive for Christian belief and practice today. The situation Christians actually face is that the Bible does not explicitly explore the question of eternal submission. The question of whether the Son eternally submits to the Father remains biblical, though it is not a matter of pure exegesis. The issue of eternal submission is a question of how best to make sense of the broad testimony of Scripture, a question of which terminology provides conceptual clarity for Scripture's broad testimony, and a question of whether the terminology considered is compatible with faith seeking understanding through reason and tradition. When theologians who speak of eternal obedience or submission offer a trinitarian theology, they are offering a second-order reflection on the Bible, an attempt to clarify the broad pattern of the Bible by offering terminology informed by reason and tradition that yields conceptual clarity. My contention is that the terminology of eternal submission is not the best way to make sense of the big picture of the Bible because it creates a number of conceptual problems with other parts of that biblical story, thereby failing to be coherent and consequently suffering from a number of insurmountable doctrinal problems. The case against eternal submission is therefore a systematic case, a dispute about the best second-order system of language to be used when speaking of the Trinity.

I begin to make my case in chapter 1 by exploring pro-Nicene accounts of the doctrine of the Trinity. While many object to eternal submission on the grounds that it violates the Council of Nicaea's claim that the Father and Son share the same essence and so are *homoousios*, I will show that this objection fails. The deeper problem with claims of eternal obedience are that

---

15. As Fred Sanders explains, "The hearing of the voice of God in Scripture is a single, concerted, trinitarian event." Sanders, *The Deep Things of God*, 208.

they entail that Father and Son have different wills and different operations, a claim that runs contrary to pro-Nicene thought. Pro-Nicene theologians, fourth-century theologians who supported Nicaea and who were vindicated at the First Council of Constantinople, unanimously taught that all of God's operations in the created world were joint operations, such that Father, Son, and Spirit worked inseparably in acts ranging from creation to sanctification. Pro-Nicene theologians believed that this argument followed from key passages like John 5:17–30 as well as common biblical accounts of Father, Son, and Spirit acting indivisibly. The doctrine of inseparable operations provided conceptual clarity, explaining precisely what was meant by terms like nature or being—such terms refer in part to that aspect of a thing that serves as the source or principle of operations. Those who speak of eternal submission treat operations and will (a particular subset of operations) as properties of the persons, an alternative doctrine that fails to fit the scriptural narrative and that provides less conceptual clarity than the traditional pro-Nicene theology. Excursus 1 follows chapter 1 and addresses common objections to inseparable operations.

Chapter 2 explores debates surrounding the number of wills found in the incarnate Christ. The Third Council of Constantinople affirmed that Christ has two wills—one proper to his human nature, and another proper to his divine nature. This conclusion, named dyothelite Christology, followed logically from the full counsel of God as presented in the Bible, for Jesus is depicted willing and doing both human and divine things. It follows from tradition, for the Council of Chalcedon had taught that Jesus had two natures (one human and divine) but only one person. If Jesus had a human will, it must be proper to his nature. Finally, it follows from reason. In pro-Nicene thought and subsequent theology, will and operation are a property of nature. If Jesus possessed a full human nature, he possessed a full human will. Dyothelite Christology raises questions concerning how Jesus still can act as a single person. Traditionally, the doctrine of the communication of idioms helps answer this question. After exploring Christ's theandric action through the communication of idioms, I explore the Christology of those who teach the eternal submission of the Son. Advocates of eternal submission treat will as a property of the divine persons, so there can be no human will in Christ since there is no human person. I show how this runs contrary to many christological statements made by those who advocate eternal submission, and how the best efforts to reconcile eternal submission with dyothelitism fail to provide a coherent synthesis. There is a rift between the theology of eternal submission and dyothelite Christology, even as certain theologians continue to affirm both.

Chapter 3 explores the implication of language of eternal obedience for soteriology, the doctrine of salvation. Anselm's satisfaction theory draws on the broad canonical depiction of Christ paying our debt, and explains this payment in terms of the Son offering a voluntary and nonobligatory payment to the Father on behalf of humanity, dying a death to the honor of God when he had already lived a life of perfect obedience and so need not die. I demonstrate that Reformed accounts of penal substitutionary atonement incorporate Anselm's basic account of satisfaction. This theology of satisfaction causes tremendous problems for the doctrine of eternal obedience. If will is a personal property, it is difficult to see how the divine person of Christ could offer a human obedience to the Father. If the Son was eternally commanded to carry out his mediatorial office, then he was obligated to do so—God's commands are morally binding. However, if the Son offered an obligatory payment for his own sake, he did not offer a voluntary payment above what was required for our sakes. The logic of satisfaction falls apart given eternal submission. I conclude the chapter by exploring the ethical implications of a shift in theological imagination arising from a theology of an eternally submissive Son—it becomes all too easy to misunderstand Christ's death on the cross as an example of divine child abuse, something that puts Christian women and children at risk.

Chapter 4 considers the claim that the Son eternally submits to the Father in light of the doctrine of God. Theologians throughout the centuries have distilled the Bible's depiction of God into specific claims about the divine attributes that God possesses. I begin the chapter by exploring how theologians like Thomas Aquinas and Francis Turretin explain the eternal generation of the Son by the Father in such a manner that this generation does not logically contradict the divine attributes. Aquinas and Turretin use an analogical understanding of procession to make sense of eternal generation in a manner that is compatible with the divine attributes. Theologians who speak of eternal submission, by contrast, rarely provide any specific meaning when they speak of submission, though they admit that it is analogous to human submission. I therefore explore how the language of eternal submission or obedience might fit with the divine attributes and find numerous serious flaws. "Eternal submission" is categorized as imprecise theological language. A brief excursus follows this chapter, explaining why the debate about eternal submission of the Son has little to do with theological anthropology.

In chapter 5 I finally turn to treat explicit New Testament teachings about the submission of the Son, arguing that these passages are ambiguous in meaning and that, in light of the broad testimony of Scripture explored in chapters 1–4, it is best to interpret the New Testament only speaking of temporary submission. I demonstrate that 1 Corinthians 15:28, the only passage in the Bible that uses the Greek word for submission of the Son outside of his life and ministry, clearly refers to the Son in an assumed *human* role as second Adam. Second Adam imagery also makes sense of the incarnate submission of the Son—this submission was proper to his human nature as the Son reversed the disobedience of the first Adam. I demonstrate that language of "sending," ordering of the trinitarian persons in the New Testament, and the name "Son" itself do not require eternal submission. I also treat 1 Corinthians 11:3, arguing that this passage may best be understood in terms Christ's humanity. Chapter 5 is where I reveal that the question of eternal submission cannot be decided by exegesis alone. I have decided to include this portion of my argument at the end of the work so that the reader can compare the scriptural case for eternal submission with the scriptural case against it that is manifest in second-order systematic summaries of the Bible presented in chapters 1–4. I am convinced that the systematic case against eternal submission is strong enough to persuade the reader of my position in chapter 5. However, if you are reading this book and are convinced that the Bible directly teaches the eternal submission of the Son, you should consider reading chapter 5 before you read the previous four chapters in the book. After all, a direct biblical teaching carries more weight than any second-order systematic synthesis of the Bible possibly could.

This work attempts to redirect the conversation surrounding eternal submission, but I do not expect to end the discussion. No doubt the able reader will see underdeveloped portions of my argument, lapses in logic, relevant portions of Scripture that I ignore, and sources that I neglect to consult. I beg the reader's patience; redirecting a debate in this manner is no easy task. Many come to this debate with rigid and preconceived notions about eternal submission. I invite you now to turn to the main content of the work, and ask that you set your existing ideas about eternal submission to the side, at least while you consider a fresh perspective. The time for another evangelical civil war, online or otherwise, may one day come. For now it is time to make my case as best as I am able to the glory of God and for the benefit of his people, hopefully with charity, accuracy, and humility.

1

The Father's Will Set Forth in Christ
The Evangelical Trinitarian Debate

"In him we have redemption through his blood, the forgiveness of our trespasses, according to the riches of his grace, which he lavished upon us, in all wisdom and insight, making known to us the mystery of his will, according to his purpose, which he set forth in Christ."
(Eph 1:7–9)

"The will of the Father and the Son is one, and their operation is inseparable."[1]

—Augustine of Hippo

DESCRIPTIONS OF THE INTIMATE relation between the Father and the Son fill the New Testament, particularly in depictions of the will and actions of God that contribute to trinitarian thought about God. This is clear in the Gospel of John when Jesus debates with a group of Jews over Sabbath observance. John 5:19–30 serves as an immediate response to what may have initially represented a juridical controversy over Sabbath observance (John 5:3–16),[2] something common in Jewish theological debates of the first several centuries AD as various Jewish groups sought clarity on how much

---

1. Augustine of Hippo, *On the Trinity*, II.5.9.
2. Asiedu-Peprah, *Johannine Sabbath Conflicts*, 77. See also the discussion in Witherington, *John's Wisdom*, 135–36.

work if any could be done on the Sabbath.³ The exchange quickly escalated when Jesus defends his actions by identifying his work with the work of the Father (5:17), something his accusers view as "making himself equal with God" (5:18). Here, Jesus could have easily corrected the misconception if he did not intend to equate himself with God; instead, he reinforces his equality with God by claiming for himself two actions that are shared with his Father.

Jesus's response to his Jewish opponents is to claim, "The Son can do nothing of his own accord, but only what he sees the Father doing. For whatever the Father does, the Son does likewise" (John 5:19). Jesus explains his equality with the Father by pointing to two paradigmatic divine actions: judgment and giving life. In 5:21 Jesus claims for himself the authority to give life (zōopoiei), a word often used of God in the Septuagint.⁴ Similar terminology is used to describe God in other Jewish texts preserved in Greek,⁵ so when Jesus claims the authority to give life, he is clearly accepting the charge of his opponents that he is equal to God. God is the one who breathed life into Adam and Eve, who created the world and everything in it, and likewise "the Son gives life to whom he will." Jesus also claims for himself the right to judge on the last day (5:27). Here again, we encounter a paradigmatic divine action. Claims that God will raise the dead to execute judgment are found throughout the Old Testament and Apocrypha (Isa 26:19, Dan 12:2, 2 Macc 7, 1 En. 22, 2 Esd 7, Bar 42:7, 15:2).⁶ The implications of Jesus's words is that his acts are the acts of the Father.

Initially, Jesus's response defends his healing on the Sabbath by appealing to a common Jewish notion that God still does the work of bringing life and death on the Sabbath.⁷ Christ does this same work of the Father

---

3. See for example *t.shab.* 15:16, *m.yom.* 8:6-7. A good survey of these rabbinic disputes can be found in Instone-Brewer, *Feasts and Sabbaths*.

4. In four of six canonical LXX occurrences of ζωοποιέω, this term is applied directly to God: 2 Kings 5:7, Nehemiah 9:6, Job 36:6, and Psalm 70:20. The fifth occurrence claims that wisdom will bring to life (ζωοποίησει) he who possesses it (Eccl 7:13). Given Second Temple Judaism's tendency to personify and sometimes even hypostasize wisdom, this example could have been interpreted by Second Temple readers as referring to either the divine nature or to a divinely sanctioned mediator. The sixth occurrence in Judges 21:14 speaks of the Israelites giving to the tribe of Benjamin the women they had kept alive (εζωοποίησαν) from their conquest of Jabesh Gilead. This reference clearly does not refer to God, but context suggests that the word was used with a different intended meaning: Benjamin gave life by withholding death, whereas God makes life from nothing.

5. For example in the Letter of Aristeas 16, and in 2 Esdras 9:8 and 19:6.

6. Schnackenburg, *The Gospel According to St. John*, 106.

7. We see this as a common claim in rabbinic thought. In *Genesis Rabbah* 11:10 Rabbi Phinehas says that God rested from creating the world, but not "from the work

because he does what the Father does. Besides serving as a response to his accusers, Jesus's words in John 5:20 also serve as something of a thesis for the festival cycle, that portion of John's gospel that focuses on Christ's actions and teachings during various Jewish festivals (John 5–11). The initially discussed acts of judging and giving life only begin to illustrate the fact that Jesus and his Father do the same works. Jesus clearly states that the Father "shows [the Son] all that he himself is doing" (5:20). The present active indicative (*deiknusin*) has an undefined aspect, suggesting the possibility that the Father is continuously showing the Son all that he does, such that the Father will do nothing new that the Son will not be aware of; there is a temporal exhaustiveness to the Son's knowledge. Moreover, the Father shows all (*panta*) that he is doing, leaving nothing hidden; there is a missional exhaustiveness to the Son's knowledge. In short, whatever the Father is doing or will do to elect, save, preserve, or sanctify his people is shown to the Son, and "whatever the Father does, that the Son does likewise" (John 5:19).

Throughout the festival cycle Jesus performs miracles and makes claims that identify his works with the work of the Father. Passover primarily commemorates the deliverance of Israel from Egypt (Deut 16:1–8).[8] During Passover in the festival cycle, Jesus feeds the 5,000 (6:1–15) and walks on water (6:16–24), recreating the two miraculous works of God by which he preserved Israel between Egypt and Canaan: miraculously providing means of crossing the Red Sea,[9] and miraculously providing manna from heaven. Jesus explicitly claims to be the "bread of life" (6:35) and the "bread that came down from heaven" (6:41), connecting his person with the Father's life-sustaining works of provision in the Exodus account. Similarly, Jesus is the one like the paschal lamb whose flesh must be eaten (6:53). In this teaching, Jesus claims that the festivals are pointing to the Son as much as they point to the works of the Father seen in salvation history, thereby identifying himself with the work of the Father. The Feast of Tabernacles emphasizes the light of God's glory.[10] A water libation pointing to an escha-

---

of the wicked and the work of the righteous" in punishing and bestowing reward. Similarly, *Exodus Rabbah* 30:9 talks about a "sectarian" who challenged the rabbis by pointing out that God does not rest on the Sabbath, to which they reply that since God is omnipresent, he does not move more than 1,000 cubits and violate the Sabbath. Likewise, the rabbis argue that since the earth is God's courtyard, he does not violate Sabbath by staying in it.

8. For present purposes, any connection between Passover or Tabernacles and agricultural cycles can be tabled. John appears to focus on the cultic significance of the festivals.

9. For a further discussion of this point, see Yee, *Jewish Feasts and the Gospel of John*, 65.

10. Light relates to the candles that were lit in the court of women during tabernacles

tological hope for God to renew the world is the feast's signature ritual.[11] During this festival, Jesus claims to be the "light of the world" (8:12), an allusion to divine glory.[12] When in John 7:37 Jesus stands up on the last day of Tabernacles and tells the thirsty to come to him for living water, he is identifying himself with the Father's historic provision of water to the Israelites in the wilderness (Exod 17:1–7). In each of these festivals, Jesus is associating himself with the redemptive historical work of the Father, continuing to illustrate the point made in John 5:19–20: the Son works as his Father works in history, even on the Sabbath.

This Johannine pattern of shared works between the Father and Son during the Sabbath debate and festival cycle is one of many scriptural patterns that can serve as a starting point for introducing the doctrine of the Trinity, which develops such scriptural tropes through use of philosophy to establish doctrinal statements that offer conceptual clarity. I choose this location to introduce the doctrine of the Trinity because it raises an important set of questions. Does Jesus do the same works as his Father because he shares in the actions of his Father inseparably? Or is there a division in this shared work such that the Son does the same works as the Father as one who obediently submits to the authority of the Father? Of course, similar questions are prompted elsewhere in the Bible. For example, Paul can confidently claim that the mystery of the Father's will and purpose is set forth or revealed in Christ (Eph 1:8–9), and Paul talks of "God's will for you in Christ Jesus" (1 Thess 5:18). Paul's comments raise similar questions. Is the Father's will revealed in Christ because the Son and Father work as one with one will? Or is the Father's will revealed in Christ because Christ is the one who perfectly and eternally obeys the Father's will?

In evangelical circles, these questions are the subject of a decades-long debate concerning the eternal relationship between the Father and Son, a debate that has gradually drawn comment from many noted evangelical theologians and that culminated in the fierce online debates of 2016. Simply put, one side argues that the Son eternally submits to the Father in the Godhead, and the other side rejects this proposition. These positions are clearly drawn, but the main battle lines have not focused on the question that John

---

such that "there was not a courtyard in Jerusalem that did not reflect the light" (*m. Sukkah* 5:3). This light is reminiscent of the glory of the Lord that dwelt among the Israelites during the time in the wilderness.

11. Köstenberger, *A Theology of John's Gospel and Letters*, 421. This offering may also refer to God's historic provision of water from the rock at Horeb (Exod 17:1–7).

12. Craig Keener notes that only God or the Torah would openly claim to be the light of the world during this time period among observant Jews. Keener, *The Gospel of John*, 739–40.

5 raises—do the Father and Son possess a single will and action or diverse wills and actions? The way one envisions the Trinity reverberates across theological doctrines. As we will see, theologians traditionally answered the question that John 5 raises by arguing that God had a single will and action. Those who affirm eternal submission offer a different set of answers, with deeply problematic consequences. This chapter will introduce these consequences, which only become more apparent in subsequent chapters, by first introducing the current evangelical trinitarian debate and then examining the historical tradition of the single will of God and the inseparable divine works in the economy of redemption in pro-Nicene thought.

The Submission of the Son: An Evangelical Debate

John 5 provides a helpful starting point for introducing the evangelical theology that claims the Son eternally submits to the Father. For many evangelical authors, this passage is one among numerous biblical texts that indicates, in Wayne Grudem's words, the Son's "obedience to the Father's will and submission to the Father's authority."[13] Commenting on John 5, Michael J. Ovey writes, "Jesus is not an independent operator, but one who has been sent by another, and, if that other has a will that Jesus does, then that other has a will which is distinguishable from Jesus's and which Jesus performs."[14] There are two basic ways to interpret this claim of distinguishable wills. First, we can grant that Jesus has a distinct human will that submits to the Father because he has assumed flesh in the incarnation, thereby offering a temporary human submission to God. (Of course we can debate whether or not such submission is in view in John 5). The second option is to argue that the Son must always submit to the Father's will in the eternal life of the Triune Godhead, and that because of such eternal submission the Son continues to do so in the incarnation as evident in various places in the Gospel of John. The second position is known as eternal functional subordination, hereafter EFS for short.

Reduced to its most basic form, the doctrine of the Trinity is the affirmation that there is both diversity and unity in the Godhead: God is both one essence or being and three persons or *hypostases*. Put another way, the Father, Son, and Spirit share perfectly in the single divine nature, but each is eternally distinct from the others without dividing the nature. The Niceano-Constantinopolitan Creed, long treated as the standard of

---

13. Grudem, "Biblical Evidence," 229; cf. Cowan, "The Father and the Son in the Gospel of John," 50–51, 62–63; Dahms, "Subordination," 360.

14. Ovey, *Your Will Be Done*, 82.

trinitarian orthodoxy in both the East and West, speaks of the unity in terms of identity of being: the Father and Son are *homoousios,* consubstantial, of one essence. The creed grounds the diversity of God in the Son being "begotten of the Father before all worlds," and the Spirit proceeding from the Father.[15] The creed was originally developed at the Council of Nicaea in 325 AD, but it did not resolve all trinitarian disputes. Instead, it prompted nearly a century of debate concerning how the Father, Son, and Spirit can be one God yet distinct persons. A group of theologians today known as pro-Nicene developed several key insights that built upon the initial creed at Nicaea to clarify trinitarian doctrine. The most important for present purposes is a distinction between the words *ousia* (being or essence) and *hypostasis* (subsistence). The former came to refer to what is one in God, such as the shared attributes of goodness and eternality. The latter word began to be associated with what is three in God: the Father, the Son, and the Holy Spirit each with distinct personal properties or *idiomata*. In the fourth century many Latin theologians following the practice of Tertullian used the word "person" instead of the word *hypostasis,* though with a roughly comparable meaning. Despite gradually developing trajectories in trinitarian thinking, for all trinitarian thought the distinction between *ousia* and *hypostasis,* between essence and persons, became foundational for all subsequent reflection on the Trinity. Notably for present purposes, a second ecumenical council held in Constantinople in 381 developed the insights of the Council of Nicaea by producing a revised creed, the Nicaeano-Constantinopolitan Creed cited above.

Many evangelicals argue that the Son eternally submits to the Father, a claim they believe builds upon the Nicene tradition. These theologians tie obedience and submission to a distinction in "roles,"[16] "subordination in role" or "function,"[17] or to a hierarchical "order" or *taxis* of the persons where the Father commands and the Son obeys[18]—there is little consensus on terminology, and the terminology used often lacks sufficient clarity, as we shall see in chapter 4. Early authors tended to use the language of "eternal relational subordination,"[19] while later authors developed more complex acronyms like "eternal relational authority-submission" (ERAS).[20] Opponents

15. "The Nicaeno-Constantinopolitan Creed," 58–59. Western Christians eventually claimed that the Spirit proceeded from the Father and Son, a later addition to the creed.

16. Ware, *Father, Son, and Holy Spirit,* 45.
17. Grudem, *Systematic Theology,* 251.
18. Letham, *The Holy Trinity,* 399.
19. House, "Eternal Relational Subordination." Cf., Dahms, "Subordination."
20. Ware, "A Denial of *Homoousios*?"

of the idea of eternal submission label this perspective "gradationist,"[21] or "the complementarian doctrine of the Trinity."[22] The latter term is accepted by some who affirm the eternal submission of the Son.[23] Though it is not accepted by all who speak of eternal submission, I have opted to use the terminology of eternal functional subordination (hereafter EFS). As far I can tell, language of subordination in function is older than other options, so when I use the acronym EFS I will intend to target early claims of eternal submission along with any subsequent variation. I will avoid using language of complementarian trinitarianism because there is no real connection between gender roles and the Trinity. There is no "egalitarian Trinity" or "complementarian Trinity," only the doctrine of the Trinity expressed in a better or worse manner.[24] I will not accuse those who I classify as EFS advocates of ontological subordinationism, and beg the patience of those who would prefer other titles for fear of such accusations under this title. Though I cannot use a name that all would accept for themselves, I will do my best to represent each scholar's thoughts accurately. Accurate interpretation is more important (and more obtainable) than a universally accepted label.

EFS theologians, as I shall call them, are adamant that claiming the Son eternally submits to the Father guarantees the unity and diversity which is basic to the doctrine of the Trinity.[25] Using various conceptual frameworks, EFS theologians agree that eternal submission pertains to the diversity or threeness of the Godhead. Wayne Grudem has argued that the eternal subordination of the Son, which he explains in terms of submission, is the sole basis for an eternal distinction between the divine persons, rather than more traditional language of the Son being eternally begotten and the Spirit eternally proceeding or being eternally breathed or spirated.[26] Others,

21. Erickson, *Who's Tampering?* 21.
22. Giles, *Rise and Fall*.
23. Horrell, "Complementarian Trinitarianism."
24. In any event, many complementarians, though slow to critique what I call EFS, never accepted this theology. Several egalitarians have endorsed EFS. When the eternal submission debate is considered in light of certain complementarian groups' theology and teaching the term may be appropriate, but in the context of this work it would only serve to confuse.
25. This affirmation is so widespread that I do not know a single scholar who affirms EFS that would deny it. At times, however, precision of language has broken down in a manner that those who write about EFS may use terminology in an inappropriate manner that implies a distinction in essence, being, or nature. However, I will treat such instances as a mistake, and not as evidence of the beliefs of EFS advocates. For a survey of such mistakes, see Giles, *Trinity and Subordinationism*, 75–80. Giles seems more convinced than I am that there is intentional language of difference in being.
26. "If we do not have ontological equality, not all the persons are fully God. But

such as Robert Letham, maintain the traditional language of eternal generation as the means of distinguishing the persons and simply articulate eternal submission as a logical consequence of the ordering resulting from such eternal generation and procession.[27] I will address issues of eternal generation in chapter 4 and issues surrounding eternal submission throughout the work. Analyzing the significance of the language of subordination lies outside of the scope of this work.

Despite their differences, there is widespread agreement on two points among EFS advocates: first, anything said of the eternal submission of the Son is said of the divine persons, as I will address more fully below, and second, this eternal submission has some implications for our understanding of human gender roles. I will begin by explaining the widespread, but not universal, connection drawn between EFS and the relationship between human men and women. Sometimes EFS serves as the foundation for a constructive argument for complementarianism, as when Wayne Grudem writes, "Just as God the Father has authority over the Son, though the two are equal in deity, so in a marriage, the husband has authority over the wife, though they are equal in personhood."[28] At other times, EFS is used as one of a number of weapons against egalitarianism. For instance, Letham can claim, "The feminist movement within the church is incompatible with the historical Christian doctrines of God and man."[29] What is interesting here, and something that I will discuss at greater length in excursus 2, is that to be classified as a feminist in Letham's usage of the term, one must merely be egalitarian.[30] In even sharper wording, Bruce Ware writes that egalitarianism has "chafed at . . . the very nature of God himself."[31] Of course, there are occasional scholars who affirm eternal submission but not complementarianism, but these are a rare exception.[32] As a general rule, the eternal submission of the Son is seen as a pattern for human gender roles.

Though its origins are disputed, the doctrine of EFS has been circulating with increasing popularity among evangelicals for decades. Those who

---

if we do not have economic subordination, then there is no inherent difference in the way the three persons relate to one another, and consequently we do not have the three distinct persons existing as Father, Son, and Holy Spirit for all eternity." Grudem, *Systematic Theology*, 251.

27. Letham, *The Holy Trinity*, 383–89, 399–400.
28. Grudem, *Systematic Theology*, 459.
29. Letham, "Man-Woman Debate," 66.
30. Ibid. Cf., Grudem, "Doctrinal Deviations;" Kovack and Schemm, "A Defense," 475–76.
31. Ware, *Father, Son, and Holy Spirit*, 73.
32. The most noted example is Keener, "Subordination within the Trinity," 39–58.

accept EFS claim that it is in continuity with the basic beliefs of Christians since the origins of the faith—they claim the doctrine is both biblical and accepted by numerous early Christians.[33] Those who reject EFS reject the purported biblical foundations of the doctrine, as I will in chapter 5. More significant for present purposes, they also often treat the doctrine as a violation of the Nicene Creed, particularly concerning the claim that the Father and Son are *homoousios*—consubstantial or one in nature and essence. Thus, EFS theologians are accused of admitting that God is three persons, but undermining the claim that God is only one being. Given that the Nicene Creed has served as a standard of trinitarian orthodoxy since the fourth century, this is a grave charge indeed. This critique has been so central to the online debate in the summer of 2016 that it warrants further consideration.

Thomas McCall puts forward the flawed standard *homoousios* objection to EFS in the clear syllogistic form typical to analytic theologians like McCall:

1. If Hard EFS[34] is true, then the Son has the property *being functionally subordinate in all time segments in all possible worlds*.
2. If the Son has this property in every possible world, then the Son has this property necessarily. Furthermore, the Son has this property with *de re* rather than *de dicto* necessity.
3. If the Son has this property necessarily (*de re*), then the Son has it essentially.
4. If Hard EFS is true, then the Son has this property essentially while the Father does not.
5. If the Son has this property essentially and the Father does not, then the Son is of a different essence than the Father. Thus the Son is *heteroousios* rather than *homoousios*.[35]

The problem with this argument lies in premises 3 and 5, where McCall equivocates regarding the word "essentially" and "essence." McCall cites Alvin Plantinga in a footnote to argue that a property is held essentially "if and only if [a thing] has [that property] and could not possibly

---

33. I will address claims of biblical support in chapter 5; key sources presenting historical evidence will be treated in this chapter. Important treatments of historical acceptance of the doctrine of EFS that claim fundamental continuity with the tradition include: Ovey, *Your Will Be Done*; Kovack and Schemm, "A Defense," 461–76; House, "Eternal Relational Subordination," 133–81.

34. McCall uses this term to denote submission in reference to the eternal life of the Trinity.

35. McCall, *Which Trinity? Whose Monotheism?* 179–80. Emphasis in original.

have lacked it."³⁶ However, pro-Nicene trinitarian theology did not use the word "essence" in this manner (as McCall assumes when he equates "essentially" and "essence" in premise 5). As just noted, there are two aspects of the divine reality that are necessary to the Trinity, something that the Trinity has and could not possibly have lacked. The first is the shared divine essence, being, or nature, including the divine attributes like omniscience, goodness, or simplicity that are constitutive of what it means to be God. On Plantinga's definition, these attributes are held essentially. However, the second aspect of the divine reality affirmed within trinitarian doctrine is the three divine persons, Father, Son, and Holy Spirit, with their corresponding personal properties. Trinitarian doctrine also describes who God is as three persons with distinctive personal properties that are unique and defined relationally. For God to be God, there must be unbegotten Father, eternally begotten Son, and eternally spirated Spirit—this could not be otherwise. At the very least this commits us to claim that the Son is the Son and not the Father and could not possibly have been otherwise, and the Father is not the Son and could not possibly have been otherwise.³⁷ Nevertheless, this is not to say that talking about the Son, or the Son's eternal generation, is making a claim about the divine essence that would entail that the Son was somehow *heteroousios* from the Father. Rather, the claims made are about the divine *hypostases* or persons, claims that are necessary (or "essential" in McCall and Plantinga's terminology), but nevertheless not claims about the essence. McCall's syllogism fails because he wrongly conflates Plantinga's term "essential" with the pro-Nicene word "essence." In pro-Nicene thought, it is quite possible for Father and Son to be *homoousios* and for the Son to have the personal property "submits to the Father," while the Father lacks this property.

Millard Erickson makes a similar anti-EFS argument rooted in the *homoousios*, one worth addressing to again illustrate the problems with this line of argumentation. Erickson argues:

> If authority over the Son is an essential, not an accidental, attribute of the Father, and subordination to the Father is an essential, not an accidental, attribute of the Son, then something significant follows. Authority is part of the Father's essence, and subordination is part of the Son's essence, and each attribute is not part of the essence of the other person. That means that the essence of the Son is different from the essence of the Father. The Father's essence includes omnipresence, omniscience, love,

---

36. Ibid., 179n15.
37. McCall assumes as much throughout his analysis of trinitarian theology.

etc., and authority over the Son. The Son's essence includes omnipresence, omniscience, love, etc., and submission to the Father. But that is equivalent to saying that they are not *homoousios* with one another.[38]

Erickson makes a similar move to McCall when he assumes that anything predicated of God that is not accidental, that is to say anything eternally true of God, is something that is said of the essence. This is not true of pro-Nicene theology. The distinction between eternal essence and eternal persons is fundamental to the doctrine of the Trinity. The Son is not Son accidentally. His generation is not accidental but eternal. Nevertheless, the title of "Son" and the property of "eternally generated" does not apply to the divine essence, but only to the person of the Son. The Father is not the Son, nor is the Father eternally generated. When speaking of the Trinity, we must distinguish between substantial predication, where what is said refers to the essence, and relational predication, where what is said refers to a single divine person in its unique subsistence. Many other authors make similar arguments against EFS,[39] but it simply is not true that claiming the Son eternally submits to the Father entails a denial of *homoousios*, provided that whatever is said of the Son submitting is said of the *person* of the Son through relational predication and not the shared *divine nature* or essence through substantial predication.[40]

The standard *homoousios* objection has led to increasing clarity among EFS advocates concerning what they mean by eternal submission. Bruce Ware, for example, initially and frequently wrote of the Son having a "yielding will" and the Father an "exigent will," always citing P. T. Forsyth's usage of these terms favorably.[41] This language implies that submission is predicated

---

38. Erickson, *Who's Tampering?* 172.

39. Yandell, "How Many Times?" 160; Carnley, *Reflections in Glass*, 234; Bilezikian, "Hermeneutical Bungee-Jumping," 64; Giles, "Trinity without Tiers," 267.

40. In a recent article, Millard Erickson has doubled down on his position, acknowledging the common defense of Ware, Gons, Naselli, and others that submission refers to the persons or relations, but denying that relations can be properties while insisting that properties are either necessary and essential or else contingent and accidental. Erickson apparently rejects the person/nature distinction altogether. This flies in the face of the entire history of trinitarian thought from the time of the Cappadocian discussion of personal *idiomata* through Thomas Aquinas's notion of subsistent relations even up to modern Barthian discussion of the Revealer, Revelation, and Revealedness. Without granting such a distinction, it is unclear how Erickson could remain trinitarian. See Erickson, "Language, Logic, and Trinity," 9–10.

41. Ware, *Father, Son, and Spirit*, 81; Ware, "Equal in Essence," 36; Ware, "How Shall We Think," 274.

of a will proper to the persons and not the divine nature, but this early language is not as clear as Ware's later language, when he states:

> The property of the "eternal functional subordination" of the Son, or of his eternal submission to the Father, surely is a property *exclusively* of the Son and one that the Father does not possess. But is not this property *strictly and only a personal property*? That is, this is a property of the person of the Son, and it is a property that could exist only in relation to another person. The Son could not possess this property were he a monad or a Unitarian deity. But as the person of the Son, he is under the authority of the Father, and as such his property of eternally submitting to the Father is a property of his personhood in relation (and only in relation) to the Father; hence *it is nothing other than a "personal property."*[42] [Emphasis added]

Ware could not be more clear as to his meaning: submission or eternal functional subordination is "a property exclusively of the Son," "strictly and only a personal property," and "a property of his personhood in relation (and only in relation) to the Father." This increased clarity has been accompanied by a change in terminology: Ware now speaks of "eternal relational authority-submission," or ERAS for short.[43] This defense works well against the standard *homoousios* objection: Ware is not saying anything at all about the divine nature or essence, so he cannot possibly be jeopardizing the *homoousion*.

A similar increase in clarity is found among many EFS theologians and philosophers. Philip Gons and Andrew Naselli argue that eternal submission "inheres in what it means for the Son to be Son, not in what it means for the Son to be God." Therefore, eternal submission is not a property of the divine essence, "but unique incommunicable properties of the persons that define their intratrinitarian relationship."[44] Tom Smail describes the eternal subordination of the Son as a "willing responsiveness" of eternal submission, which is the "*proprium*, the defining hypostatic characteristic" of the Son.[45] J. Scott Horrell insists that the Son's eternal submission is an "active expression" of the Son's "distinguishing personal characteristic."[46] John Frame teaches, "There is no subordination within the divine nature ... [but] there is subordination of role among the persons, which constitutes

42. Ware, "A Denial of *Homoousios*?" 244.
43. Ibid., 237.
44. Gons and Naselli, "Arguments against Hierarchy," 204–5.
45. Smail, *Like Father, Like Son*, 169.
46. Horrell, "Complementarian Trinitarianism," 352.

part of the distinctiveness of each."[47] Examples could be multiplied, but the point is clear: whatever advocates of EFS mean when they speak of eternal submission, eternal functional subordination, the eternal obedience of the Son, or ERAS, they are speaking about the divine *persons* and not the divine *nature*. Therefore, the claim that EFS necessarily violates the consubstantiality of the Father and the Son, dividing their shared essence and nature, is a flawed claim.

In noting that EFS does not fall to the standard *homoousios* objection, I do not mean to indicate that advocates of EFS are no longer facing theological difficulties in their position. On the contrary, by positing submission as a personal property, they have created a number of substantial theological problems originating within trinitarian theology and echoing across the doctrines of Christ, salvation, and the divine attributes. By claiming that submission is a personal property, these theologians are committing to making will a personal property, because submission is an operation of will. Most classical theology, however, has treated will as a property of essence or nature. A shift from will as a property of the shared divine essence to a property of the divine persons has tremendous consequences across systematic theology, as I will argue throughout this work. Before I can explain the problems behind this shift, I must first demonstrate that I am rightly characterizing the theology of eternal submission.[48]

Many advocates of EFS treat will as a divine property quite explicitly. I have already noted Ware's adoption of P. T. Forsyth's language of the Father possessing an "exigent will" and the Son possessing a "yielding will." Michael Ovey is unequivocal when he writes,

> Submission and obedience seems necessarily to involve the will or desire *of another* which one prefers to one's own. One has conformed one's will to the will of another—someone who is not oneself. For that to happen, there must be a will that is not one's own but belongs to another.[49] [emphasis in original]

Wayne Grudem describes submission as a "disposition to yield." A wife does not face "an absolute surrender of her will" because the wife may have to take a stand against the husband's "sinful will." Though not "absolute," Grudem certainly considers submission a *qualified* yielding of one will to

---

47. Frame, *Systematic Theology*, 501.

48. Significant portions of the paragraphs following this paragraph until the end of the section are taken directly from D. Glenn Butner Jr., "Eternal Functional Subordination" and are used with the permission of Andreas Köstenberger, the editor of the *Journal of the Evangelical Theological Society*.

49. Ovey, *Your Will Be Done*, 110.

another.⁵⁰ Here are three theologians whose understanding of submission compels them to explicitly affirm will as a personal property.

Other theologians who affirm EFS recognize that will was historically treated as a shared property of the divine nature, and so struggle in their efforts to affirm the traditional view alongside of EFS. Robert Letham's early writings are a notable example here.⁵¹ Letham is clear in his position: "To speak of three wills is heterodox, implying tritheism."⁵² Despite this clarity, Letham struggles to explain how submission is possible with a single will. In the same article in which he rejects three divine wills, Letham defines submission as "free action *chosen willingly* by the one who submits [emphasis added]."⁵³ How the Son can willingly chose *qua* hypostasis⁵⁴ to submit to the Father without suggesting that the Son has a distinct will from the Father's will is not explained. J. Scott Horrell also struggles to affirm both the tradition and EFS. He writes, "We may say that there are both one mind and three minds, one will and three wills, as each [person] indwells the other,"⁵⁵ a solution quite distinct from the tradition, as we shall see, and one that simply muddies the waters. Kyle Claunch openly admits that the single divine will precludes speaking of eternal submission because it entails, "A commitment to three distinct wills in the immanent Trinity. In order for the Son to submit *willingly* to the *will* of the Father, the two must possess distinct wills."⁵⁶ Nevertheless, Claunch strives to maintain the second key tenant of EFS when he posits that complementarian gender roles are still rooted in the Trinity in an "indirect" manner.⁵⁷ Each of these author's ideas will be treated at greater length later in this work. For now, it is simply important to establish the clear connection between positing submission as a personal property and being forced to admit that will is a personal property.

---

50. Grudem and Piper, "Central Concerns," 61. I do not include John Piper, coauthor of this article, in my critique because I do not know whether or not Piper agrees with EFS. Regardless of Piper's position, the article does reveal Grudem's understanding of submission.

51. In personal correspondence Kevin Giles suggested to me that Letham's current position is not so far from his own, though I am unaware of evidence of this change in writing.

52. Letham, "Reply to Kevin Giles," 340.

53. Ibid., 344.

54. If the free choice is made "by" the one submitting, it would seem to be an operation of the hypostasis.

55. Horrell, "Complementarian Trinitarianism," 355.

56. Kyle Claunch, "God is the Head of Christ," 88.

57. Ibid., 93.

Given the meaning of words like "submit" and "obey," it is no surprise that theologians who recognize the traditional doctrine struggle to affirm EFS and a singular will of God. The Greek word most commonly used for "to submit" is the word *hypotassō*, a word that in both biblical and patristic times meant "to obey" in the passive voice but "to bring someone to subjection" in the active voice.[58] Discussing *hypotassō* Delling notes, "the general rule" for understanding the meaning of submission "demands readiness to renounce one's own will for the sake of others."[59] The notion of "obedience" clearly implies one person yielding their will to follow the directives of another person's will. In the Greek, the word *hypotassō* is typically paraenetic, meaning it is deployed in an attempt to persuade a change of will, suggesting again that submission is an act of will.[60] Ceslas Spicq repeatedly emphasizes that submission is a matter of "accepting" what God has ordained,[61] where Merriam Webster defines "to accept" as "to receive *willingly*" [emphasis added].[62] Clearly, the connotation of *hypotassō* suggests a distinct will from the one who submits to the one with authority. Interestingly, the active of *hypotassō* may mean "to place under,"[63] a term that would not require distinct wills for Father and Son, insofar as one could be "placed under" another in a nonvolitional way. However, the English word "submit" does not retain this meaning, and rather signifies, to cite *Merriam-Webster* again, "to yield oneself to the authority or will of another."[64] The *Oxford Dictionary* defines "submit" as "to accept or yield to a superior force or to the authority or will of another person."[65] Therefore, any rendering of *hypotassō* that intends to merely point to an ordering is best translated by something other than the English word "submit." Otherwise, both the Greek *hypotassō* and the English "submit" and "obey" strongly suggest a distinct will belonging to the one who submits. In the face of this connection, EFS theologians continue to see the New Testament's language of the Son submitting to the Father as an eternal action. Because the only distinction or diversity in the eternal Godhead is found in the three persons, clearly theologians embracing EFS

---

58. BDAG, 1042; *PGL*, 1462; *LSJ*, 1897.
59. *Theological Dictionary of the New Testament*, Vol. VIII, 45.
60. *EDNT*, 408. This is especially true in the household codes.
61. Spicq, *Theological Lexicon of the New Testament*, 425–26.
62. *Merriam-Webster's Collegiate Dictionary*, 7.
63. Lidell, Scott, 1897; *EDNT*, 408; *Theological Dictionary of the New Testament*, vol. VIII, 39.
64. This is the preferred definition of the verb when used in an intransitive sense, as it is used by advocates of EFS (*Merriam-Webster*, 1244).
65. *Oxford Dictionary of English*, 1760.

must be speaking of the persons and therefore immune to the standard *homoousios* objection.

Pro-Nicene Theology and Eternal Functional Subordination

We turn now to the question of whether a theology of eternal submission can fit with pro-Nicene trinitarian theology. When I use the term pro-Nicene theology (in continuity especially with Lewis Ayres), I intend to designate those related yet distinct systematic theologies of the fourth and early fifth centuries that affirm and develop the theology of the Nicene Creed. Pro-Nicene theologies were accepted as orthodox at the ecumenical First Council of Constantinople in 381 and have been received by the universal church in its various forms, Orthodox, Catholic, and Protestant.[66] The most significant theologians associated with pro-Nicene theology are Athanasius of Alexandria, the trio of Basil of Caesarea, Gregory of Nyssa, and Gregory Nazianzus, collectively designated as the Cappadocians, Hilary of Poitiers, and Augustine of Hippo, though there were many other figures involved. It is important to recognize that simple affirmation that the Father and Son are *homoousios,* sharing the same being, is not enough to guarantee that a trinitarian theology is pro-Nicene. That fact is often overlooked by figures in the EFS debate.[67] For example, Marcellus of Ancyra affirmed that the Father and Son are *homoousios,* but understood this term to indicate that there is no eternal difference between the Father and Son. His theology was rightly rejected as contrary to the scriptural testimony and the intentions of Nicaea.

In point of fact, the term *homoousios* was only important in the fourth-century trinitarian debates for certain figures at certain times, and it should not be treated as the solitary standard of trinitarian orthodoxy. It is not clear that the Council of Nicaea intended this word to be the focal point of the creed, but likely considered it a clarification of the creed's claim that the Son was "from the *ousia* of the Father."[68] Athanasius initially emphasized the phrase "from the *ousia* of the Father" more than *homoousios,* and only came to prioritize this phrase several decades after Nicaea convened in 325.[69] As R. P. C. Hanson notes, Basil of Caesarea did not "treat *homoousios* as an

---

66. Ayres, *Nicaea and Its Legacy*, 236–40.

67. Noted exceptions include Kevin Giles and Robert Letham. See Giles, *Jesus and the Father*, 140; Letham, *The Holy Trinity*, 123–24.

68. Ayres, *Nicaea and Its Legacy*, 93, 96.

69. Ibid., 140.

indispensable watchword."[70] Hanson suggests all the Cappadocians defended the term "on occasion," but not while treating it as "indispensable."[71] The Cappadocians tended to emphasize other ideas as central to right trinitarian thought. Judging whether EFS is in continuity with pro-Nicene theology based on the *homoousios* alone is simply insufficient.

Another inadequate approach would seek isolated statements within which pro-Nicene theologians appeared to affirm or reject eternal submission or obedience within the Godhead. Such is the approach of H. Wayne House,[72] or Steven Kovack and Peter Schemm.[73] A right treatment of pro-Nicene theology cannot be limited to isolated quotations taken out of context for several reasons. First, theologians themselves developed across time: Athanasius, for example, was not able to affirm the terminology of three *hypostases* to distinguish Father, Son, and Spirit until near the end of his career, in the *Antiochene Tome* of 362.[74] Basil of Caesarea began his career treating the Son as only *like* in nature to the Father before gradually moving to affirm the *homoousios*.[75] Second, some pro-Nicene theologians never grasped the entirety of the pro-Nicene program. Hilary of Poitiers, for example, never developed an adequate and consistent way to distinguish between what is one and what is three in God.[76] Basil of Caesarea is infamous for avoiding using the term *homoousios* of the Holy Spirit. Finally, pro-Nicene theology does not entail a complete unity among theologians in this group.[77] Each pro-Nicene theologian retained idiosyncrasies and theological claims that other pro-Nicenes might reject. In any event, many of the favorite proof texts of EFS theologians do not clearly indicate submission as is often claimed.[78] To rightly describe pro-Nicene theology, proof texting will not do.

70. Hanson, *Christian Doctrine of God*, 693.

71. Ibid., 678.

72. House, "Eternal Relational Subordination," 133–82.

73. Kovack and Schemm, "A Defense."

74. Ayres, *Nicaea and Its Legacy*, 174. Even here, Athanasius notes that while those who spoke of three *hypostases* meant something similar to those who, like Athanasius, had previously spoken of one *hypostasis*, both sides still agreed "that the faith confessed by the Fathers at Nicaea is better than such phrases, and that for the future they would prefer to be content to use its language." Athanasius, *Tomus ad Antioches*, §7.

75. Ayres, *Nicaea and Its Legacy*, 190–91.

76. Hanson, *Christian Doctrine of God*, 486–88.

77. In fact, some have even objected to the term "pro-Nicene" as altogether too homogenizing. While we ought not neglect genuine diversity, I do not see the term itself as unduly problematic. See Behr, "Response to Ayres," 145–52.

78. House, for example, provides a curious list of patristic citations that include quotes discussing eternal generation, appeals to language of order in the Trinity, and

If pro-Nicene theology is irreducible to an affirmation of the *homoousios*, and if it cannot be determined through uncritical selective citations of major pro-Nicene figures, how can we determine pro-Nicene theology? Several things are necessary to delineate the contours of pro-Nicene thought. First, anything identified as a component of pro-Nicene theology must be present in a proportionately high number of pro-Nicene theologians.[79] Second, an element identified as pro-Nicene thought ought to have a central role in those theologians' understanding of the Trinity. Third, the significance of a central element of pro-Nicene thought must be demonstrated by noting the role that this element played in establishing the validity of the Nicene tradition in the context of fourth and early fifth-century trinitarian debates.[80] Lewis Ayres surveys pro-Nicene theology and demonstrates that there are three widely shared claims central to trinitarian thought that played a major role in debates of the era. He writes,

> I take three central principles to identify a theology as fully pro-Nicene:
>
> 1. A clear vision of the person and nature distinction, entailing the principle that whatever is predicated of the divine nature is predicated of the three persons equally and understood to be one (this distinction may or may not be articulated via a consistent technical terminology);
>
> 2. Clear expression that the eternal generation of the Son occurs within the unitary and incomprehensible divine being;
>
> 3. Clear expression of the doctrine that the persons work inseparably.[81]

---

a citation from the Council of Serdica, from which pro-Nicenes eventually distanced themselves. Each of these citations could be challenged in terms of their applicability.

79. While universal affirmation is ideal, my cursory introduction has shown that even key aspects of the trinitarian consensus emerging from Constantinople in 381 were not universally held.

80. While certain theological claims affirmed at Nicaea might be acceptable to pro-Nicene, anti-Nicene, and non-Nicene thought, only those ideas affirmed against anti-Nicene claims demonstrate what makes a theology truly *pro*-Nicene. If a claim is acceptable to a wider audience, it may well be true, but it is not a distinguishing characteristic of anything identifiably favorable toward Nicaea relative to other theologies on offer.

81. Ayres, *Nicaea and Its Legacy*, 236.

While there are many smaller theological features of pro-Nicene theology (many of which Ayres addresses in his work), he rightly identifies these three as the most important dimensions of pro-Nicene thought.

The track record for EFS theologians on the first central principle of pro-Nicene thought is fairly strong. To my knowledge, all theologians who speak of eternal submission affirm the basic distinction between the divine persons and the divine nature or essence, though they may explain this distinction in a non-Nicene manner. EFS advocates have less consistently affirmed the second central pro-Nicene principle. Both pro-Nicene and anti-Nicene theologians tended to speak of the Son as begotten by the Father, here offering differing interpretations of the earlier theological claims of Origen of Alexandria. For anti-Nicenes eternal generation entailed that the Father was of a different essence than the Son, but for pro-Nicenes eternal generation ensured that the Son received the same indivisible essence of the Father. Eternal generation also unambiguously posited a distinction between the Father and the Son—the Son is begotten God, but the Father is unbegotten God. Eventually, ideas of the eternal procession of the Spirit played a similar role. As noted above, several theologians associated with EFS at one time rejected the notion of eternal generation as the means of distinguishing between the Father and the Son. However, excellent work by theologians on both sides of the functional subordination debate[82] have convinced both Wayne Grudem and Bruce Ware to accept eternal generation.[83] Many of their writings, however, remain anti-Nicene in rejecting this key tenet of pro-Nicene thought and in instead differentiating the persons through language of eternal submission.

The third key aspect of pro-Nicene theology is an emphasis on the undivided work of the divine persons. In modern theology this pro-Nicene insight has been preserved in the dictum *opera trinitatis ad extra indivisa sunt*, a slight variation of pro-Nicene language. The operations of God *ad extra*—that is in the creation, governance, and redemption of the created order, as opposed to *ad intra* in the immanent divine life of the Trinity—are the joint work of Father, Son, and Spirit in an inseparable manner. In the introduction to this chapter, I considered how John 5:19 and the text surrounding it illustrate the divinity of the Son insofar as he completes paradigmatically divine works such as judging and creating. When I introduced the theology of eternal functional subordination, I returned to John 5:19 and the surrounding passage to introduce EFS. Theologians who accept EFS

---

82. See especially: Giles, *Eternal Generation*; Letham, *Holy Trinity*, 383–89; Letham, "Eternal Generation."

83. Grudem and Ware both acknowledged the need for language of eternal generation at the 2016 annual conference of the Evangelical Theological Society.

tend to treat John 5 as demonstrating that the Son is divine in doing things that the Father does, but he is restricted in authority in that he can only do what he sees the Father doing. Therefore, the Son eternally submits and obeys, while the Father eternally commands. Now that we consider the undivided divine works of the Godhead in pro-Nicene theology, I again return to John 5:19, for as Lewis Ayres remarks, "John 5:19 appears to have become an increasingly important battleground in the 360s probably both because of its utility to Homoians and because of increasingly clear pro-Nicene articulation of the common nature of the three."[84]

Hilary of Poitiers offered a thorough interpretation of John 5:19 that illustrates the pro-Nicene commitment to the Father, Son, and Spirit completing the same operation inseparably. Commenting on the fact that "whatever the Father does, the Son does likewise," Hilary wrote that the words "whatever" and "likewise" make it "impossible that there should be any actions of His that are different from, or outside, the actions of the Father." Hilary deduced two points from this fact. First, because the Son has the "same power" as the Father, he must have the same nature as the Father.[85] Here, Hilary is drawing on the common philosophical meaning of nature during his time. A power is something intrinsic to a nature, a capacity within that nature that allows for a certain operation. Even the distinct term *energeia*, which I will translate as "operation" throughout this work, should not be taken to simply refer to what a nature does in and through a hypostasis. An operation is fundamentally indicative of what a nature is.[86] To put the matter in simple form: agents that undertake only the same kinds of operations possess the same kind of nature, but agents who only undertake identical operations, like the Father, Son, and Spirit possess identical natures. So, my wife and I complete the same kind of actions, such as eating, breathing, sleeping, communicating, and so forth. These actions are indicative of the fact that we possess the same kind of nature—human nature. The Father and the Son, however, complete exhaustively identical operations and so possess identical natures. As Hilary remarked, the Son's "liberty of action coincides in its range with his knowledge of the powers of the nature of God the Father; a nature inseparable from himself."[87] This was an important polemical point in the context of debate with anti- and non-Nicene theologians, who frequently saw the Father and Son as having either similar or different natures, but certainly not identical natures. These

---

84. Ayres, *Nicaea and Its Legacy*, 183.
85. Hilary of Poitiers, *On the Trinity*, VII.18.
86. Bradshaw, "The Concept of Divine Energies," 182.
87. Hilary of Poitiers, *On the Trinity*, VII.17.

theologies asserted that the Father and Son completed either the same kind of or identical operations, but only through a unity of will.[88] Hilary and other pro-Nicene theologians insisted that if the Son does all the works of the Father, the Son must possess the same nature as the Father.

Pro-Nicene theology's insistence on the unity of nature and operation between Father and Son certainly caused some concern among non- and anti-Nicenes, who feared that such a strong concept of unity might reduce the Father and Son to modes of the same single divine person. In other words, they feared that there might be no real distinction between Father and Son. Hilary treated the claim that the Son works "likewise" in John 5:19 as evidence against this concern, for "the fact that the works are like those of another is fatal to the supposition that He who does them works in isolation."[89] Though there is a single operation and nature, the Father, Son, and Spirit are still eternally distinct. Hilary does not come to a point where he adopts sufficient terminology to account for this unity and distinction; as noted above he never adequately adopted the persons/being distinction of many other pro-Nicene theologians. Perhaps this is why he could speak of a unity of operations and also a diversity of wills in the Godhead, even though willing is an operation. Here Hilary is different than many pro-Nicene theologians. Chapter 2 will explore how later theologians treat any diversity of wills between Father and Son as a result of the incarnation, but Hilary never considered whether this distinction is eternal or merely incarnational.[90] For Hilary it is sufficient to note in John 5 that "two truths are combined in one proposition; that his works are done likewise proves his birth; that they are the same works proves his nature."[91] We must continue to explore the significance of this claim for the divine will throughout the course of this book.

Whereas Hilary did not fully develop his theology of undivided divine actions drawn from John 5 when he spoke of a diversity of wills, other

---

88. Anatolios. *Retrieving Nicaea*, 41–78. Anatolios convincingly demonstrates that Arius, Asterius, Eusebius of Caesarea, and Eunomius of Cyzicus try to posit some unity between Father and Son based on the Father working through the Son whom he wills into existence.

89. Hilary of Poitiers, *On the Trinity*, VII.18.

90. See Hilary of Poitiers, *On the Trinity* IX.40–50. R. P. C. Hanson notes: "As far as the distinction of the will of the Son and that of the Father goes, Hilary is more realistic than Athanasius. He insists that the Son's activity is the Father's, but he allows that the Son has an independent will of his own, which he voluntarily aligns with the Father's will. He never raises the interesting question, whether this will of the Son is a human or divine will." Hanson, *Christian Doctrine of God*, 478. Perhaps this is why EFS theologians appeal so frequently to Hilary's theology. See for example Ovey, *Your Will Be Done*, 50–62.

91. Hilary of Poitiers, *On the Trinity*, VII.18.

pro-Nicenes wrote more clearly in treating the passage. When exegeting John 5, pro-Nicene theologians generally admitted no division in divine actions (for example between an act of commanding and obeying). Thus, Ambrose of Milan insisted that the fact that the Son does the same works, doing whatever the Father does, reveals that "in the Son there is unity in the Father's works, not imitation of them."[92] Athanasius of Alexandria was adamant that John 5:19 reveals more than a conformity of will, instead positing a unity of essence from which all operations (presumably including willing) originate. After all, Athanasius wrote, originate things do not create, but the Son creates, so the Son must share the identical unoriginated nature as the Father.[93] Pro-Nicene theologians consistently saw this passage as a proof text of the Son's consubstantiality with the Father due to identical operation, but they did not construe it as evidence of a relationship of eternal submission. Basil of Caesarea, for example, interpreted the claim that the Son can do nothing by himself in the following way: "To me this saying too seems distinctly declaratory of the Son's being of the same nature as the Father." In the same paragraph he affirms, "The Son does what He wills in heaven and in earth. Therefore the Son is not a creature." Clearly, the Son has the same nature, but he is not constrained in will by eternal obedience.[94] Other pro-Nicene theologians saw a similar freedom of will unconstrained by divine command.[95] This does not imply lack of differentiation, though. As Athanasius explained, the Son's act of creating, as revealed in John 5:19, shows his divine nature, but we can still claim that "the Father creates all things through the Word in the Spirit."[96] Many pro-Nicene theologians used such a phrase to illustrate how a single operation could still distinctly manifest three persons, an important qualification to the idea of inseparable operations and one drawn from language of Scripture.[97] Many pro-Nicenes cited

---

92. Ambrose of Milan, *Of the Christian Faith*, IV.4.
93. Athanasius of Alexandria, *Ad Afros Epistola Synodica*, §8.
94. Basil the Great, "Letter VIII," §9.
95. For example Augustine of Hippo: "The Son is almighty, in doing all things that he willeth to do. For if the Father doeth some things which the Son doeth not, the Son said falsely, 'Whatsoever things the Father doeth, these also the Son doeth likewise." Augustine of Hippo, "On the Creed," §5.
96. Athanasius of Alexandria, *Letters to Serapion*, 2.14.1.
97. See Gregory of Nyssa, "An Answer to Ablabius," 262; Hilary of Poitiers, *On the Trinity*, VIII.38–39; Augustine of Hippo, *Tractates*, XX.9. In his *On the Trinity*, Augustine of Hippo appeals to Romans 11:36 but does not clearly link Father, Son, and Spirit with "from," "through," and "in" respectively. Augustine of Hippo, *On the Trinity*, V.9.

Romans 11:36, "from him and through him and to him are all things," to develop this threefold language for inseparable operations.[98]

The doctrine of inseparable operations follows logically from the common understanding of *ousia* shared by pro-Nicene theologians. In philosophical thought of the time, power (*dunamis*) refers to "the capacity of an existent to affect," to use the definition of Michel Barnes.[99] A power in turn produces certain operations. In the fourth-century trinitarian debates, there were three different perspectives on how the single power of God related to the Son.[100] The anti-Nicene position held by Arius, Eunomius, Asterius, and others insisted that the one power of God is proper to the Father, while the Son is only an image of that power, where image is treated as a copy. Hence, the Son was different in essence from the Father. Two pro-Nicene options existed. Drawing on 1 Corinthians 1:24, Athanasius of Alexandria notably treated the Son as the one power of God, so he must be proper to the Father's essence lest the Father once be powerless.[101] A full theology of the faculty of the will was not developed until the later theology of Maximus the Confessor, but will was commonly treated as either a power or operation. Athanasius appears to make such an identification when he also wrote that the Son is the Father's will. When God created through the Son (John 1:3), for example, Athanasius clarified that it was "not that, as in the case of men, some under-worker might hear, and learning the will of him who spoke might go away and do it; for this is what is proper to creatures, but it is unseemly so to think or speak of the word." Rather, since the Word "is the Father's will," there "is no questioning and answer." A simple act of divine willing results in the Word carrying out the act of creation.[102] On this account operations of the Father are inseparable from operations of the Son because the Son is the power and will through whom the Father acts.

The third historical understanding, found in thinkers like Hilary, Gregory of Nyssa, Augustine, and Ambrose, argued that power is a property of the divine essence, such that the *homoousios* demands a single divine power. On this pro-Nicene interpretation, since the essence is the persons, the persons are also identical to the one power.[103] Because will is frequently treated as a power or operation, such theologians saw will as a property of

---

98. Pace. Basil of Caesarea, *On the Holy Spirit*, §7.
99. Barnes, "One Nature, One Power," 206.
100. Ibid., 205–6.
101. See discussion in Anatolios, *Retrieving Nicaea*, 116.
102. Athanasius of Alexandria, *Orationes contra Arianos IV*, II.18.31.
103. Barnes, *Power of God*, 269.

the divine essence.[104] On this account, operations of the Father are inseparable from operations of the Son and Spirit because all three possess the same power. All three trajectories drew on earlier Christian understandings of power,[105] but the pro-Nicene theology rejected the anti-Nicene notion that there were two powers in God: the Father's, and the Son's power as distinct image of the Father's. Eventually, the third trajectory became dominant, a central feature of pro-Nicene argumentation against their opponents. We can already see how this central feature runs contrary to typical EFS theology that treats will and submission as personal properties, thereby positing multiple wills in the Godhead, or at least multiple modes of willing.

Though discussion so far has focused on John 5:19 to illustrate pro-Nicene thought, it is important to recognize that a theology of undivided divine operations is not rooted in proof texting an isolated passage like John 5, or even the entirety of the Johannine festival cycle. Nor is such theology unduly captive to Greek philosophical categories, despite drawing on the best philosophy of the day. Rather, pro-Nicene theologians developed the theology of undivided divine actions as a second-order reflection on the entire canonical witness as to the works of the Father, Son, and Holy Spirit. Using the philosophical understanding of nature and *ousia* available to them at that time, they then offered an account of inseparable operations that provided conceptual clarity useful during fourth-century debates.

To illustrate the point, let us consider the account of Didymus the Blind, a pro-Nicene theologian influential in the debate surrounding the Spirit's consubstantiality with the Father and Son. Didymus's *On the Holy Spirit* demonstrated that the Father, Son, and Spirit work in unison by deploying a canonical and trinitarian hermeneutic. He began by noting that the Father and Son are said to give grace in Romans 1:7, but Hebrews 10:29 calls the Spirit "the Spirit of grace" and indicates that the grace of sanctification occurs in the Spirit. So Didymus concluded, there is a "single grace" that is a shared operation of the Father, Son, and Spirit.[106] Jesus teaches that the Spirit will guide disciples called before authorities to give an answer (Luke 12:11-12), but he also says that he is the one who will provide the disciples with a mouth and wisdom beyond refutation (Luke 21:14-15).

---

104. Augustine of Hippo, *On the Trinity*, II.5.9; Gregory of Nazianzus, *Theological Orations*, IV.12; Didymus the Blind, *On the Holy Spirit*, §85; Gregory of Nyssa, "Answer to Ablabius," 262.

105. Barnes, "One Nature, One Power," 210-11. Barnes notes the usage of Tertullian, Clement, and Hippolytus as precursors to the pro-Nicene position in this respect, and Origen of Alexandria as a precursor of "two powers" theology found in anti-Nicene thinkers.

106. Didymus the Blind, *On the Holy Spirit*, §75-76.

Didymus reasoned from this shared operation that "the partnership which the Spirit has with the Son is one in both nature and will."[107] Didymus went on to argue that the Father, Son, and Spirit have a single power: the Spirit is the "finger of God" by which Jesus casts out demons (Luke 11:19–20; cf. Matt 12:28). This same "finger of God" wrote the law of Moses on the tablets (Exod 31:18), though we can speak of the Father giving the law. Exorcisms and lawgiving are the joint work of Father, Son, and Spirit.[108] So, too, the Father is the "only-wise" (Rom 16:27), which Didymus took to illustrate that the Father "generates wisdom and makes others wise." The Son is "the Wisdom of God" (1 Cor 1:24), and the Holy Spirit is the "Spirit of Wisdom," the one who bestows wisdom (Deut 34:9). In this way, Didymus demonstrated that all three persons bestow wisdom.[109] Didymus read 1 Corinthians 12:4–7 to indicate that the Father, Son, and Spirit work together in distributing spiritual gifts.[110] The call to ministry is both being set apart by the Holy Spirit (Acts 13:2), being worked in by the Father (Gal 2:8), and being made "ministers of the Word" (Acts 6:4).[111] Likewise, the Father, Son, and Spirit all indwell (2 Cor 6:16; Lev 26:12; Ezek 37:27; Eph 3:16–17; 1 Cor 3:16).[112] Didymus provided additional examples and offered a more thorough exegesis of each set of the passages that I provided here. The present point is simply to note that Didymus developed the doctrine of undivided divine actions as a second-order reflection on the broad canonical pattern of Scripture. He wrote, "On the basis of *all these passages* it is proved that the activity of the Father and the Son and the Holy Spirit is the same. But those who have a single activity also have a single substance."[113] Similar surveys of the Bible are found in Gregory of Nyssa,[114] Basil of Caesarea,[115] Ambrose of Milan,[116] and others.

---

107. Ibid., §84–85.
108. Ibid., §88–90.
109. Ibid., §91–92.
110. Ibid., §96.
111. Ibid., §98–99.
112. Ibid., 106–7.
113. Ibid., §81. Emphasis added.
114. Nyssa points to Scriptures suggesting the shared operations of creating, ruling, giving life, and manifesting the glory of God. Gregory of Nyssa, *On the Holy Spirit*, 319–24.
115. Basil attends to biblical testimony of the shared operations of creating, saving, and judging. Basil of Caesarea, *On the Holy Spirit* 16.37–40.
116. Besides the fairly common analysis of the shared role of judging, Ambrose offers a fascinating argument that focuses on the Spirit as the "finger of God" and the Son as the "hand," as well as analysis of the joint work of Father, Son, and Spirit in rebuking

Pro-Nicene authors certainly recognized a biblical pattern when they claimed that the Father, Son, and Spirit worked inseparably. An obvious example is the act of creation: the Father speaks and the universe is created (Gen 1), and the Spirit is present hovering over the waters (Gen 1:2). Of course, the New Testament is clear that nothing was made apart from Christ's operation (John 1:3), for all things were made through him (Col 1:16). Or consider Acts 28:25–26, which attributes a prophecy to the Holy Spirit that Isaiah 6:8–11 attributes to the "word of the Lord," which pro-Nicene thinkers saw as a reference to the Word of God (John 1:1), the eternal Son.[117] More generally speaking, we see a pattern of all three persons being involved in the divine act of revelation. It was the Father who spoke through the prophets (Heb 1:2), but these same prophets were inspired by the Holy Spirit (2 Pet 1:21). The Son is treated as a prophet in the New Testament (Acts 3:17–23; Luke 3:23), bearing a message from the Father (John 8:26–28), so that his message and life are often seen by the gospel writers as the fulfillment of Old Testament prophecy. His life and ministry is the culmination of the triune act of divine self-revelation. We might even turn to something so paradigmatic to standard accounts of the distinctive work of the Spirit as sanctification. True, the Holy Spirit sanctifies (1 Pet 1:2, etc.), but we also see Paul pray that "the God of peace" (i.e., the Father) may "sanctify you completely" (1 Thess 5:23).[118] Paul even claims that we are "sanctified in Christ Jesus" (1 Cor 1:2), who is himself our sanctification (1 Cor 1:30). The New Testament never provides a fully developed theology of undivided divine works *ad extra* (John 5 perhaps comes close), but it is nevertheless clear that this doctrine is a valid second-order reflection on the broad narrative of the Bible where the three persons are repeatedly shown to perform the same acts. Based on this narrative, pro-Nicenes used the standard philosophical understanding of nature coupled with Nicaea's commitment to the *homoousion* to articulate the doctrine of inseparable operations as a means of providing conceptual clarity to scriptural patterns.

Contemporary theologians who reject EFS have done well to point out that claims of eternal submission and obedience do not fit with the pro-Nicene theology of undivided divine operations, an argument much stronger than accusations of violating the *homoousios*. This argument is particularly clear in Keith Johnson, Kevin Giles, Nancy Hedberg, and Millard Erickson. Johnson considers Augustine of Hippo as exemplary of what I

---

the sinner. Ambrose of Milan, *Of the Holy Spirit*, III.2–7.

117. Didymus the Blind, *On the Holy Spirit*, §125.

118. Typically the title "God" must be taken to refer to the Father in New Testament passages, but particularly here, where Jesus is identified distinctively in the verse.

have called pro-Nicene theology. He demonstrates that the undivided divine operations of God *ad extra* entailed for Augustine that God possessed a single power and will, so that any "sending" language in the Bible was interpreted by Augustine as the joint work of Father, Son, and Spirit, not as evidence of eternal submission.[119] Giles notes that the inseparable operations do not entail that there is no distinction between the divine persons, but neither does it entail that we can speak of a functional subordination.[120] Hedberg considers the doctrine of inseparable operations in light of the distinction between the economic and immanent Trinity (i.e., God's work in the world and his inward life). She notes that even in the economy the Father, Son, and Spirit work inseparably in numerous acts like creating, so any functional subordination of the Son must only be a result of the incarnation and not proper to the economic Trinity as a whole.[121] Millard Erickson provides scriptural warrant for the claim that the divine persons work inseparably. Besides covering much of the evidence I have noted above, Erickson identifies the sending of the Spirit (John 14:26; 15:26), the giving of gifts (Matt 7:11; John 6:33; 5:21; Rom 15:5; 1 Cor 12:11; 2 Cor 3:6), and receiving prayer (Acts 7:59–60; 2 Cor 12:8–9; Rev 22:20) as evidence of inseparable operations. Their arguments in this area have not become as central as they deserve in the EFS debate, so I will explain the problem in a manner that suits their objection in this chapter, then will explore how this problem has tremendous ramifications for systematic theology in future chapters.

While several EFS theologians were once anti-Nicene in their rejection of eternal generation (most have since verbally recanted that position), all EFS advocates present a non-Nicene theology at best, and anti-Nicene theology at worst when their ideas are considered in relation to the undivided divine operations. This is the case in two ways. First, EFS posits that all divine actions are divisible into an operation of commanding by the Father and an operation of obeying by the Son. The Son does not share in the distinct operation of commanding, and the Father does not share in the distinct operation of obeying.[122] Here we do not have a theology of a single

---

119. Johnson, "Trinitarian Agency," 108–32.

120. Giles, *Jesus and the Father*, 143–44, 163–64.

121. Hedberg, "One Essence, One Goodness, One Power," 8–9.

122. Here one might respond that the indivisibility of divine operations only applies to *ad extra* activities, and obeying and commanding are *ad intra* activities. However, this prompts two questions that make this possibility fail. First, what, precisely, was God commanding Christ to do before any *ad extra* acts occurred? And second, do EFS theologians truly intend to only apply obedience and commanding to this *ad intra* relationship, not to the *ad extra* acts of creating, redeeming, providentially guiding, and so forth? Any cursory survey of EFS literature reveals that the language of "submission" and "obedience" is not limited to the *ad intra* life of God, though many treat such

operation carried out in a threefold manner, from the Father, through the Son, in the Spirit. Rather, we have claims of coordinated-yet-distinct operations of the Father and Son. In fact, as Kevin Giles notes, the very language of "roles" and "functions" is commonly understood to refer to what someone does, so referring to an eternal distinction in role or function implies a division in operation.[123] Second, positing eternal submission as a property of the persons requires that each person have a distinct will, as demonstrated above. Will is but one example of a divine operation and/or power, so pro-Nicene theology entails that will is a faculty of the divine essence, not a property of the persons. Some pro-Nicene theologians recognized this implication, but others did not make this connection. However, as time passed and pro-Nicene theology influenced the development of Christology, soteriology, and the doctrine of God, we will see that the claim that will was a property of the divine essence became increasingly important.[124]

The way that EFS undermines the indivisibility of the divine actions and the claim that will is a property of the divine essence may seem an obscure theological point, perhaps akin to the legendary (yet as far as I can tell entirely fictional) medieval debates concerning how many angels can dance on the head of a pin. Nevertheless, a theology of inseparable divine operations was both central to pro-Nicene theology and axiomatic to later theological developments in other doctrinal areas, as we will see in subsequent chapters. I have demonstrated that a theology of undivided divine actions was shared by the major pro-Nicene figures: Athanasius, Hillary, the Cappadocians, Didymus the Blind, Ambrose of Milan, and Augustine of Hippo. The theology of divine operations is not something mentioned in passing, but rather is crucial to the pro-Nicene understanding of what it means to affirm a Trinity: at a minimum the doctrine of the Trinity teaches that God is three *hypostases* or persons in one *ousia* or essence—again, terminology varied during this time period and after. What the doctrine of undivided divine activities reveals is what, precisely, pro-Nicene theologians meant when they referred to God's oneness, under the name *ousia* or otherwise. God's oneness included both the capacity or power to act, and

---

submission as determinative of the immanent Trinity.

123. Giles, *Jesus and the Father*, 52. One popularized presentation of EFS explicitly identifies function with "activities." See Credo House's *The Theology Program: Trinitarianism*, 70.

124. I have documented elsewhere that after Nicaea there was broad theological consensus that the divine will was a property of the divine nature. I cited John of Damascus, Gregory Palamas, Anselm of Canterbury, Hugh of St. Victor, Richard of St. Victor, Heinrich Bullinger, John Owen, and William Ames as illustrative. The duration of this work will provide opportunity for even further examples of theologians in agreement with this basic point. Butner, "Eternal Functional Subordination," 139–42.

the actions or operations themselves. EFS theologians affirming the *homoousios* apparently do not mean the same thing by the word *ousia*. Finally, the idea of undivided operations was central to many of the late-stage debates as pro-Nicene theology headed toward eventual endorsement at the Council of Constantinople. Many of the texts cited deal with debates that played a crucial role in the development of a mature pro-Nicene theology, such as debates over the divinity of the Holy Spirit or with Eunomius of Cyzicus.[125] The fact that EFS violates the principles of the unity of divine action and the corollary claim that will is a property of essence must be seen as a much deeper problem than any accusation of violating the *homoousios* given the at times more peripheral nature of this term.[126] Nor is a simple affirmation of the *homoousios* sufficient to warrant calling EFS compatible with pro-Nicene thought. This problem also should bear much more weight than any proof-texts to the contrary, where isolated pro-Nicene figures may speak of a divisible will between Father and Son in contexts central neither to the development of pro-Nicene trinitarian doctrine nor arguments against their interlocutors. In light of these problems, EFS theologians have responded in different ways.

Some EFS theologians mistakenly see the claim of undivided operations as fully compatible with the teaching that the Father commands and the Son obeys. Thus, John Starke writes, "The unity in which the persons operate is one of *harmony*, not *unison*, since . . . each person is irreducibly distinct." As he sees it, "The Father initiates, and the Son obediently responds, since the Son does only what he sees the Father doing, and the power to do it comes from his Father (John 5:19)."[127] Starke moves quickly and indiscriminately between a series of terms in his discussion of inseparable operations. He claims that Augustine of Hippo (the specific pro-Nicene theologian he is considering) "is not interested in disposing of the trinitar-

125. Anatolios, *Retrieving Nicaea*, 77–8, 138–40. Anatolios demonstrates that appeal to undivided operations was a central feature of pro-Nicene argumentation against the *tropikoi*/Macedonians and against the Eunomians.

126. As G. L. Prestige notes, the idea of inseparable operations was likely more widely accepted than the idea of the *homoousios*, for the pro-Nicene argument generally runs from unity of operation to unity of essence, rather than from unity of essence to unity of operation. Prestige, *God in Patristic Thought*, 260.

127. Starke, "Augustine," 168–69. Starke cites Ayres, *Nicaea and Its Legacy*, 372 and following in his support. I confess that I cannot see where Ayres explaining the indivisibility of operations in this passage fits Starke's claim at all. Ayres references the incarnation as an event where only the Son was incarnate, but both Father and Son were responsible for the birth and suffering of the Son. Here there is a single divine operation that is the work of all three persons, but that affects or terminates on a single person. Starke posits two distinguishable operations: the Father initiates/commands, and the Son obeys/responds.

ian order." This is certainly true—pro-Nicene theologians attempted to retain the differentiation between the divine persons, as we have seen. Starke then grants that the Son is sent into the world by the joint work of Father, Son, and Spirit, yet "the Son is not the sender *in the same way* the Father is the sender." Here again, Starke is correct, for most pro-Nicene theologians speak of divine action as from the Father and through the Son. Presumably this is where Starke gets the claim that "the Son does not initiate; the Father does," though this terminology is not quite the same as the common patristic language. So far, so good.

At this point in his argument Starke introduces new terminology: "The Father initiates by way of his Word, and the Son obeys."[128] Suddenly and without consideration, Starke has moved from discussing a single work from the Father through the Son in the Spirit to distinctive works of initiating and obeying (with the Spirit entirely absent). Claiming that an undivided work is from the Father through the Son is simply not the same thing as claiming that a work begins with the Father initiating, or in the common language of EFS "commanding," and the Son responding or obeying. Commanding and obeying are different acts, and they imply a difference in will. Insofar as will is a power, Starke is positing a difference in power between Father and Son because submission and obeying require a distinction in wills. As demonstrated earlier in the chapter, many EFS theologians are very clear on this fact. Insofar as commanding and obeying are distinct operations, Starke is positing a difference in *ad extra* operations between Father and Son: the Son does not command the Father, and the Father does not obey the Son. However, unless we attribute this difference in operation to Christ's humanity, the distinction between commanding and obeying undermines the basic pro-Nicene principle—persons with an identical nature complete identical actions with the same power. By dividing the power and operation of the Father and Son, Starke is both misunderstanding the pro-Nicene position and claiming something contrary to the idea of the shared essence and nature of the Father and Son, at least given what pro-Nicene theologians meant when discussing such terms as essence and nature. Starke claims the operations are in harmony, but pro-Nicene theology sees the operations as a matter of unison, or to use Gregory of Nazianzus' language, "identity of motion."[129]

Other EFS theologians recognize the inherent contradiction between claims of eternal submission and pro-Nicene claims regarding the unity of divine operations. Where Starke misreads the doctrine of indivisible

---

128. Starke, "Augustine," 169.

129. Gregory of Nazianzus, *The Theological Orations*, III.6; cf. Augustine of Hippo, *Tractates*, XX.9.

operations, Kyle Claunch is much more accurate in his presentation. In a 2013 article in the *Journal of the Evangelical Theological Society*, Claunch adeptly introduces the doctrine and defends it against recent evangelical objections.[130] Claunch recognizes what I have argued above: "In order for the Son to submit *willingly* to the *will* of the Father, the two must possess distinct wills." Claunch openly acknowledges that "this way of understanding the immanent Trinity does run counter to the pro-Nicene tradition, as well as the medieval, Reformation, and post-Reformation Reformed traditions that grew from it."[131] As a result, he rejects language of eternal submission and obedience, instead preferring to speak of the "one eternal will of God" being ordered in such a way that it "finds analogical expression in a created relationship of authority and submission."[132] So the Father wills "first," which Claunch defines "as the one sending the Son," the Son wills "second . . . as the one sent by the Father."[133] This is manifest in the incarnation as a relationship of authority and obedience due to Christ's humanity, a relationship that in turn serves to illuminate male/female relationships. At this point Claunch has abandoned the central language of EFS, and with it apparently the majority of scriptural passages typically (and mistakenly) put forward in defense of eternal submission. It is not at all clear that willing first and second is a fitting analogy for authority and submission—after all a factory worker may will to get a drink of water, expressing that will to his supervisor who then secondarily wills that the employee take a break. The simple fact that the employee desired water before the supervisor desired that he take a break to get it does not entail that the employee somehow possessed authority over his supervisor. Any analogy requires similarity and dissimilarity, and many possible similarities may exist. It is not at all clear why Claunch retains an emphasis on similarity between willing as one begotten and obedience instead of another analogical similarity. Nor is it clear that his emaciated version of EFS actually illustrates a real connection between the immanent Trinity and gender roles such that "gender relationships reflect something about the very being of God."[134] Here we see

---

130. Claunch, "What God Hath Done Together," 781–800.
131. Claunch, "God is the Head of Christ," 88.
132. Ibid., 91.
133. Ibid., 91–92.
134. Ibid., 93. Claunch roots his claim in an interpretation of 1 Cor 11:3, which will be treated at length in chapter 6. However, it is also worth noting that Claunch's argument has come under heavy criticism for misunderstanding the extent to which 1 Cor 11:3 can apply to the immanent life of the Trinity. He makes an assertion about the economy, and then from this deduces principles concerning the immanent life of God without any stated argument defending these deductions. See the technical treatment

full acceptance of inseparable operations *ad extra* mixed with a very flimsy version of EFS.

Some theologians who are aware of the fact that a division in wills would run contrary to pro-Nicene trinitarian thought instead suggest that the persons do not have their own wills, but rather something like their own distinctive modes of willing. So, for example, J. Scott Horrell seeks to affirm "distinct functions among the members of the Godhead."[135] At times, he uses terminology similar to the classical language: "Biblical theology depicts an order within the Godhead of creation *ex nihilo* which initiates with the Father's will, the Son as the means, and the Spirit as the enlivening power."[136] Typically, though, Horrell provides nontraditional language that blurs the difference between person and essence. He defines functions as "*an activity natural to a person* or thing" but also insists that "the *function* of each member of the Godhead is the active expression of each persons [sic] of the Trinity's distinguishing personal characteristics" [emphasis in original].[137] I admit I do not entirely understand this definition, but it appears as if a function is both proper to nature (i.e., what is shared by the persons) and to the persons (i.e., what is unique to Father, Son, and Spirit). As a result of this blurring, Horrell can affirm that there is "one will and three wills."[138] Horrell does affirm equality of authority but suggests that each chooses to use that authority to "do what each does within the relations and activities of the Godhead."[139]

The most favorable interpretation I can make of Horrell's position runs something like this: the divine persons share a single nature and hence a single will and authority, but they also are distinct persons who therefore manifest that single will and authority in distinctive ways such that, in another sense, we can speak of three wills and distinct functions. Perhaps will and authority are essential attributes (attributes of the one *ousia*), but willing and functioning are properties of the persons. Translating this into pro-Nicene language, Horrell could be admitting a single power proper to the shared divine essence but distinctions in operation between Father, Son, and Spirit. Perhaps, to use terminology developed by Maximus the Confessor, Horrell may be advocating something like a distinction in modes of willing. On this reading of Horrell, he is admittedly able to evade some

---

in Maxwell, "Authority Analogy?" 555–57.

135. Horrell, "Complementarian Trinitairanism," 339.
136. Ibid., 349.
137. Ibid., 352.
138. Ibid., 355.
139. Ibid., 357.

objections raised throughout the course of this book. However, insofar as functions are explicitly identified with operations ("activities"), this is an overt rejection of the pro-Nicene principle of inseparable operations, one that will still foster substantial problems across systematic theology.

While some theologians have attempted to conjoin language of eternal submission and inseparable operations or unity of will, others openly reject a pro-Nicene theology of inseparable operations. Wayne Grudem writes, "When one person of the Trinity is acting, it is also true, in some sense that we only understand very faintly, that the entire being of God is acting."[140] In another sense, however, Grudem rejects the claim that "the actions of any one person of the Trinity are the actions, *not just of the whole being of God*, but *of every person in the Trinity*" [emphasis original].[141] He sees this version of inseparable operations as "carelessly close" to rejecting the scriptural testimony that the divine persons act individually. "Some activities are done by more than one person," but not all, he insists. Grudem fears that making all operations inseparable is "very close" to patripassianism, a "heresy that said that the Father also suffered for our sins on the cross."[142] He also claims that the doctrine of inseparable operations comes "very close to obliterating the distinctions among the members of the Trinity" and thus to "the ancient heresy of modalism," which claimed that Father, Son, and Spirit were not three eternally distinct realities, but only temporary manifestations of God.[143] I will treat these objections in an excursus following this chapter. For now it is sufficient to note Grudem's position and his heated polemic against pro-Nicene theology.

Grudem's version of inseparable operations is certainly non-Nicene, and arguably anti-Nicene. As we have seen, because all divine operations are proper to the single divine essence, according to pro-Nicene use of the terminology of essence, operation, and power, all divine works are works of all three persons, except those unique works performed by the Son in and through his humanity. Pro-Nicene theologians believed that this followed from Jesus's claim that "*whatever* the Father does, that the Son does likewise" (John 5:19). Even if we grant that only some divine actions are inseparable, many of Grudem's writings treat eternal submission as the basis for distinguishing the divine persons, such that *any* divine action involves

---

140. Grudem, "Biblical Evidence," 256. Grudem attributes the inseparability of operations to the shared divine *ousia* manifest in the three divine persons through perichoresis, not quite following the logic of pro-Nicene theology.

141. Ibid.

142. Ibid., 257.

143. Ibid., 258.

the command of the Father and the obedience of the Son.[144] Yet this divides even those inseparable operations that Grudem allows into distinctive acts of commanding and obeying. It is difficult to see how Grudem preserves anything of inseparable operations. Furthermore, the divine essence simply *is* the three persons—we cannot envisage the essence working somehow apart from the three persons, as Grudem appears to in his explanation. So Grudem calls pro-Nicene theology here non-scriptural and bordering on two ancient heresies. At this stage of my argument, I would simply note that in order to defend EFS, Grudem puts forward a version of inseparable operations quite distinct from that found in pro-Nicene theology and one facing a number of significant flaws. It is therefore simply incorrect to assert, as he does, that EFS is "clearly . . . part of the church's doctrine of the Trinity (in Catholic, Protestant, and Orthodox expressions), at least since Nicea."[145] EFS requires a distinction in God's wills and operations, but the pro-Nicene theology emerging from the Council of Nicaea and endorsed at the First Council of Constantinople understood God to have one will, and saw Father, Son, and Spirit working indivisibly.

Conclusion: Evangelical and Pro-Nicene Trinitarianism

In this chapter, I have argued that EFS is contrary to one of three important assumptions of pro-Nicene theology. To say God has a single essence, or that the Father is *homoousios* with the Son and Holy Spirit, is to admit, according to the fourth-century pro-Nicene definition of *ousia*, that Father, Son, and Holy Spirit have a single power and indivisible operations. Since the First Council of Constantinople affirmed pro-Nicene theology, including the single power and the indivisible operations of Father, Son, and Spirit, EFS thus runs contrary to the impulse of this ecumenical council, if not its actual creedal statement.[146] This is the first major problem with EFS that this work will explore.

The issue of inseparable operations may seem too abstract to adequately serve as a starting point for a sustained critique of EFS. I grant that human claims about the Trinity must be taken with a grain of salt given

---

144. Grudem, *Systematic Theology,* 248–49.

145. Ibid., 251.

146. The creedal statement itself is not explicit about inseparable operations and powers, though given the meaning of *ousia* at the time this would be understood by the educated reader. Lewis Ayres points to a letter from the council preserved in Theodoret's *Ecclesiastical History* that affirms one power of God. The emperor Theodosius also decreed in his *Episcopis tradi* of 382 that all churches be handed over to bishops who would affirm the one power of God. Ayres, *Retrieving Nicaea,* 252, 258.

that we are reflecting on something that exceeds our full comprehension such that we must rely on partial and analogical knowledge. Some may be suspicious of any second-order of language attempting to speak of the Trinity in nonscriptural terms, believing (mistakenly as I will show) that EFS is drawn directly from the Bible. Others may simply prefer non- or anti-Nicene language here. Thus, I expect that many who began reading this work already sympathetic to EFS will not yet be convinced by my position. Even if pro-Nicene claims about indivisible operations serve to explain patterns in Scripture that seem to point to shared works of the Father, Son, and Spirit, both extended passages like John 5 and the subsequent festival cycle, and shorter cross-canonical references found in pro-Nicene thinkers (and modern authors like Millard Erickson), other readers may believe that the immanent Trinity is too opaque to human understanding to decide on the matter of EFS one way or another. Such readers undoubtedly view any discussion of inseparable operations, or of the relation between power, operation, and essence as too abstract to provide any clarity. I recognize and am sympathetic to those who are not yet on board with my argument, even if I have a somewhat higher view both of pro-Nicene thought and human ability to know the Trinity, albeit in a limited manner.

While a pure trinitarian theology focusing on indivisible operations of the Father, Son, and Spirit may seem abstract, it functioned in a very practical way to set a standard for orthodoxy that would be upheld by Catholic, Orthodox, and Protestant theologians for centuries. From the beginning, pro-Nicene thinkers integrated their thought about the Trinity with their theological reflections on the atonement, their practical and dogmatic analysis of the transformation of Christians through union with Christ, their ideas about who Jesus of Nazareth was, and their understanding of the attributes of God. From the fourth century onward, when Christians used such terms as operation, power, essence, person, or will, they were conditioned by pro-Nicene thought in important ways. Subsequent theology either was an intentional expansion of certain pro-Nicene principles, or a self-conscious redirecting of the theological trajectories established in the fourth century. In either circumstance, this means that the claim that the operations of God in the economy are undivided affected subsequent developments in Christology, soteriology, and the doctrine of God.

Since EFS stands in contradiction to pro-Nicene thought in positing will as a personal property rather than a faculty of the divine essence, and because EFS divides the operations of the Father and Son into distinct operations of commanding and obeying, we can expect and indeed will find a growing chasm between EFS views on the Trinity and important historical developments in systematic theology. Indeed, insofar as many

EFS theologians retain classical and fully orthodox accounts of Christology, soteriology, and the doctrine of God, we will see a divide between the trinitarian thought of key EFS thinkers and the rest of their theological affirmations. As later theological conflicts occasioned the development of second-order language that provided conceptual clarity and allowed theologians to make sense of broad scriptural patterns, they developed an increasingly sophisticated trinitarian hermeneutic that incorporated ever larger portions of Scripture, treating passages as if will were a property of nature or essence, and as if Father, Son, and Holy Spirit work inseparably in all things. This is in large part why the rejection of inseparable operations by positing will as a property of the divine persons is a far more problematic challenge for EFS theologians, and a far more important debate to be had, than usual disputes about the *homoousion*. To prove my point, and hopefully to convince readers who remain suspicious, I now turn to consider the reception of pro-Nicene thought in Christology. But first, I must attend to some common objections to inseparable operations in a brief excursus.

Excursus

Common Objections to Inseparable Operations

I HAVE ARGUED THAT the doctrine of inseparable operations emerges from scriptural patterns and key texts like John 5:19 while using extra-biblical terminology and philosophical concepts to make sense of these passages in a manner that offers conceptual clarity. I have also argued that this doctrine is pro-Nicene. However, I recognize that the idea that the divine persons work indivisibly *ad extra* has faced considerable objections from modern theologians. EFS advocates often deploy such objections in their response to their critics, so I must now briefly attend to three basic objections.

Inseparable Operations and Indistinguishable Persons

Wayne Grudem argues, "If we are to maintain the doctrine of the Trinity, we may not erase the distinctions between the persons or preclude that one person in the Trinity does something the others do not." He claims that eliminating the eternal distinctions or divisible operations is modalism, the ancient heresy that denied that the Father, Son, and Spirit were eternally distinct subsistences.[1] Grudem does not explain his argument with sufficient detail to allow a thorough response, so I will try to fill in the gaps. Grudem seems to be following a common modern trinitarian argument exemplified by Catherine Mowry LaCugna. LaCugna argues that Augustine's treatment[2] of the indivisibility of divine works "tends to blur any real

---

1. Grudem, "Doctrinal Deviations," 25.
2. LaCugna fails to recognize the extent to which this strategy is found among

distinctions among the divine persons." The divine works in the redemptive economy thus become severed from who God is in eternity to the result that we no longer possess real knowledge of God.[3] The ultimate consequence of Augustine's principle as maintained through Catholic, Orthodox, and Protestant Scholasticism is a "metaphysical chasm" between the three persons and what occurs in salvation, a series of acts that can no longer be properly attributed to the persons themselves.[4] To fix the problem, LaCugna argues that we need to recognize the "essential identity" between what God does in redemption and who God is in eternity.[5] I take LaCugna to be a close approximation to what Grudem means here: rejecting modalism requires not only that Father, Son, and Holy Spirit are eternal names of God referencing distinct persons, but also that the economy of redemption reveals to us truths about the eternal Father, Son, and Spirit.[6]

As a first step in responding to this objection, we ought to note that the connection between God's work in redemption and God's eternal life as Father, Son, and Spirit must include both similarity and difference. God is revealed as Father, Son, and Spirit in the historical actions taken toward the redemption of humanity, and it is indispensable that we acknowledge that God is eternally Father, Son, and Spirit. If we deny this, then we do not know the God who has redeemed us, nor do we know the shape of our redeemed life if it is not a life in Christ that draws us into the eternal Father/Son relationship through adoption. However, we certainly do not want to posit an exhaustive degree of identity between God's economic acts in redemption and God's eternal life as Father, Son, and Spirit. For example, Grudem sees one key part of atonement in the Father "inflict[ing] . . . pain on his own deeply loved Son," but he is very clear that "Jesus did not suffer eternally."[7] Here is an example of something revealed in the economy of redemption that we do *not* want to posit in eternity. After all, theologians on both sides of the EFS debate would drastically have to change their views of the Trinity

---

pro-Nicene theologians. Instead, she defends a now-disproven theory where Western trinitarianism overemphasizes the unity of the divine being against Eastern person-centered approaches. On problems with this approach, see: Butner, "De Régnon."

3. LaCugna, *God for Us*, 99.
4. Ibid., 144.
5. Ibid., 210.
6. Grudem may also have in mind concerns about the eternal distinctions within the Godhead. At the time that he wrote this argument, he did not accept eternal generation or spiration, so on the assumption that eternal processions are theologically invalid, without eternal submission there may indeed be no eternal differentiation and modalism. I have already explained why it is mistaken to deny the processions.
7. Grudem, *Systematic Theology*, 577.

EXCURSUS: COMMON OBJECTIONS TO INSEPARABLE OPERATIONS 51

if they considered the eternal relationship between Father and Son to be characterized by the Father eternally pouring out wrath upon the Son. So when we read EFS advocates like Robert Letham arguing in a manner close to Grudem that if the obedience of the Son to the Father on earth "does not reflect the eternal relation of Father and Son we are left with modalism," it is important to see that they are begging the question.[8] Certain aspects of the divine life are so central to who God is that they must be revealed or else what is revealed in Christ is something other than God as God truly is. However, if someone claims that we must accept EFS or risk modalism, this is only true on the assumption that God is eternally defined by eternal functional subordination, which is the very claim under dispute. Such charges of modalism cannot, therefore, serve as persuasive argumentation for accepting EFS because they assume precisely what they try to prove.

While it is clear that there must be a correlation between who God eternally is and how God is revealed in the economy of redemption, to my knowledge there are no clear and objective standards for determining how extensively details revealed in the economy of redemption must correspond to the eternal, tri-personal being of God.[9] The example of God's wrath directed to Christ on the cross illustrates the point well: we cannot even say that certain contrary claims of the relationships between the persons in the economy of redemption and in the eternal life of God are automatically false. In eternity, the Father does not pour out wrath on the Son, but in time the Father does pour out wrath on the Son. Admitting such a contradiction between God acting toward salvation and God eternal is not modalism provided a theologian can explain the continuity between God as revealed in redemptive history and God as eternally Father, Son, and Spirit. Likewise, it may well be, as I am arguing, that in the economy the Son *in his humanity* submits to the Father, but in eternity the Son does not submit to the Father. Such a claim need not entail modalism.

A minimum standard to avoid modalism (a necessary condition, but perhaps not a sufficient condition) requires that the names Father, Son, and Spirit pick out something distinct in the economy of redemption and in the eternal life of the Godhead, and that the persons identified through these names in the economy and immanent Trinity are the same persons. Grudem seems to think that the doctrine of inseparable operations means that the names Father, Son, and Spirit do not eternally distinguish the persons since all do the same works—inseparable operations comes "very close to

---

8. Letham, "Man-Woman Debate," 69.

9. There are numerous positions regarding the relationship between the immanent and economic Trinity. For a good survey, see LaCugna, *God For Us*, 214–22.

obliterating the distinctions among the members of the Trinity," he writes.[10] Close attention to theological tradition reveals that theologians affirming inseparable operations directly opposed Grudem's position by explaining the doctrine in a manner that guaranteed an eternal distinction between the divine persons. While all three persons work inseparably because they have the same essence and therefore the same power and operations, it is not the case that the three persons act indistinguishably. In pro-Nicene theology, for example, we have already seen the common claim that all operations *ad extra* are from the Father, through the Son, in the Spirit. This claim reflects the fact that each divine action is completed in a manner that corresponds with and preserves the eternal personal distinctions: the Father begets the Son and with (or through)[11] the Son breathes or spirates the Holy Spirit. Divine actions reflect this pattern as any given act proceeds from the Father through the Son to the Spirit such that personal distinctions are maintained. Different formulas emerged throughout history. Bonaventure, for example, draws on Aristotelian thought to distinguish the causal agency of the three persons in any operation *ad extra*: the Father is efficient cause, the Son is formal cause, and the Spirit is final cause, while the material cause is whatever created term upon which God works.[12] As Protestants inherited the Augustinian terminology for the inseparable operations—"the external works of God are indivisible"—Philip Melanchthon added an important clarification that became a commonplace among Protestants: the external works of God are indivisible "preserving, of course, the properties of each person."[13] In each case the doctrine of inseparable operations is articulated to explain a single operation arising from a single nature and power performed in a threefold manner that preserves personal distinctions.

Grudem's objection could also be interpreted as follows: inseparable operations, though granting a metaphysical distinction between Father, Son, and Spirit, prevent any genuine knowledge or experience of the difference between the persons due to their joint operation. Therefore, it is modalistic. Here again, this runs contrary to the historical development of the idea of inseparable operations, which allowed Christians to recognize the oneness of God through indivisible operations and the threeness of God through how these operations reflected the distinctive personal properties of Father, Son, and Spirit. In the medieval era, Hugh and Richard of St. Victor

---

10. Grudem, "Biblical Evidence," 258.

11. This variance in prepositions is the subject of a centuries-old debate between Orthodox Christians and their Roman Catholic and Protestant counterparts, a debate that goes well beyond the scope of this book.

12. Bonaventure, *Disputed Questions*, IV.2.

13. See the helpful discussion in Beckwith, *Holy Trinity*, 329–32.

developed a doctrine called appropriation that allowed certain divine attributes or actions to be particularly identified with one divine person based on a likeness between that attribute or action and the personal property of that person.[14] For example, Father, Son, and Spirit are all involved in creating (Gen 1:1-2; John 1:3; Ps 33:6, etc.), but we can rightly identify the Father as Creator because there is a likeness between creation and his eternal generation of the Son and eternal spiration of the Spirit. This identification can in turn shape our devotion toward the Father and our experience of the Father. The practice of appropriation continued among Protestant Scholastics.[15] The doctrine of inseparable operations is not modalistic in denying true knowledge of God as God eternally is, nor in preventing a distinction between Father, Son, and Spirit in the divine economy, nor in allowing for distinct knowledge and experience of each person. Grudem's accusation of modalism fails.

Of course some EFS theologians draw on the sorts of distinctions I have identified here in their defense of eternal submission. H. Wayne House, for example, notes that the single divine will is not expressed in an identical way, a claim fully in line with the tradition. He writes that:

> Apparently the will of the one *ousia* may be accessed in a different manner and for different purposes by each *hypostasis*, so that the Father wills to love the Son, to give the Son, to send the Son, to create through the Son, whereas the Son wills to love the Father, to be given by the Father, to be sent by the Father, and to have the Father create through him.[16]

So far, House is offering a nuanced and accurate theology of the divine will. However, it would be mistaken, having granted that any act of will is an act of Father, Son, and Spirit in distinctive ways, to therefore assume that eternal obedience and submission are acceptable. Language of the Father commanding and the Son obeying divides and separates a divine operation into two operations. Submission itself seems to require, in the words of some EFS advocates themselves, not just a distinction in mode of willing, but a distinction of wills. Further, claiming submission as a mode of willing is problematic in terms of the doctrine of God and the doctrine of salvation, as we shall see. For now, suffice it to say that inseparable operations does not fall to the charge of modalism, nor does my defense open the door for admitting EFS.

---

14. Hugh of St. Victor, *On the Sacraments*, I.3.27; Richard of St. Victor, *On the Trinity*, 4.22.

15. See Muller, *Reformed Dogmatics*, vol. 4, 267-74.

16. House, "Eternal Relational Subordination," 164.

Undivided Divine Actions and the Incarnation

Many astute readers no doubt have reservations about the previous section. These objections are probably centered around the incarnation of the Son. After all, at the very least the Bible demands that we say that the Son was crucified and not the Father. This necessity lies behind Grudem's argument that inseparable operations results in patripassianism, the heresy that Father and Son both suffered on the cross. Robert Letham puts forward a similar argument: "If there were no differentiations between the trinitarian persons in God's works, the result would be confusion akin to patripassianism, in which the Father is said to have died on the cross."[17] Letham is more restrained than Grudem, accepting the inseparability of operations but noting that "some attempts by egalitarians" at rejecting EFS in fact erase personal distinctions in a manner that risks patripassianism.[18] Of course Grudem and Letham are correct in a sense: inseparable operations must not be taken to deny that the Son and only the Son was crucified. However, Grudem in particular goes too far in suggesting that inseparable operations is therefore a problematic doctrine that must be rejected. This is because the incarnation is treated as part of a distinct category: it is the divine mission of the Son.

The divine mission of the Son is the incarnation, life, death, resurrection, and ascension of the Son. In all of these events, we must properly speak of the Son's unique operation. Only the Son was born of the virgin Mary, only the Son died on the cross, and only the Son was raised on the third day. These claims are in no way contrary to the doctrine of inseparable operations, as expressed in historical and contemporary theology. I will explain drawing on the theology of Robert Doran, who is in agreement with pro-Nicene precedent but offers clearer in terminology.[19] Doran explains that a divine mission is best understood as a divine procession plus a created term, where this created term allows for contingent predication of any incarnational operation of the Son.[20] Let me break down this definition in terms of the incarnation. The Father eternally generates the Son—this is the procession of the Son, which allows for a distinctive relationship to the

---

17. Letham, "Eternal Generation," 125.

18. Ibid., 123.

19 Gregory of Nyssa, *Against Eunomius*, I.27. For example Gregory of Nyssa notes that the same operation can result in different contingent effects due to different terms upon which the operation works. So heat from fire melts bronze, hardens mud, causes wax to vanish, and destroys animal life. What is critical here is the term of the action. This principle, when applied to the doctrine of the hypostatic union and clarified conceptually results in Doran's explanation.

20. See the discussion in Doran, *Trinity in History*, 40–57.

Father (filiation) and a unique personal property (the Son is generated). When we speak of the procession of the Son, we speak of what is unique to the Son. The divine mission of the Son is rooted in the procession of the Son—it is a continuation of the eternal Father/Son relationship into the created temporal order. For this relationship to continue into the created order, a created term is required. By the word "term" Doran simply means a created reality that serves as a condition for the mission occurring. A term is a condition for a divine mission because the mission is contingent, but God is necessary, so for Son taking on any contingent state requires a created term as a condition for this state. In this case, the incarnation of Jesus Christ involves the acceptance of a full human nature (a doctrine called the hypostatic union and discussed in detail next chapter). The assumed human nature of Christ is brought into the Father/Son relationship through union with what is unique to the Son. As a result of the procession joined to a created term, we can practice contingent predication, meaning that we can say things of the Son that could be otherwise by pointing to the contingent nature of the created term. The Son's death is conditional and contingent, requiring a created term. It is the death of the Son and not the Father because the mission is the continuation of the Son's unique procession into history and because of the created term, the assumed human nature of Christ—it is the human nature of the Son that actually suffers on the cross. Thus we can say that the Son alone was crucified, and this is true because of the Son's unique procession, because only the Son assumed flesh, and because the act of suffering is actually proper to the human nature, not the divine. (A full theology of how the human and divine natures co-operate is also developed next chapter. For now a brief explanation must suffice.)

It is important to recognize that though we only say that the Son suffered and was crucified, not the Father, because only the humanity of the Son assumed in the incarnation was nailed to a cross, the divine nature works with the assumed humanity of Christ in such a way that the doctrine of inseparable operations still applies. As Christology developed, key scriptural phrases about the Son suffering "in the flesh," (1 Pet 4:1) were taken to point to the fact that the human nature of Christ suffered (recall that operations are proper to natures), but it was taken as a rule that the divine nature worked in harmony, strengthening the human nature so that it could bear the wrath of God, work miracles, and so forth. Like most doctrines discussed in this book, we do not see a clear scriptural explanation of these principles, but we do see a clear scriptural pattern of the Father and Holy Spirit working with the Son to empower him in his mission. The claim that the Father, Son, and Spirit work inseparably through the divine nature that works in coordination with the human nature is thus a claim attempting to make sense of the broad pattern of Scripture in a way that provides conceptual clarity. The Synoptic Gospels, for example, depict the Holy Spirit as vitally involved with every stage of the Son's early ministry. The Spirit comes upon Mary that she may conceive Christ (Luke 1:35; Matt 1:20). The Spirit descends upon the Jesus at the baptism (Matt 3:16 and pars.), which many early Christians took as a sign of the Spirit's empowerment. The Spirit leads Jesus into the desert to be tempted (Matt 4:1 and pars.) and works through him in his healings and exorcisms (Matt 12:28). Indeed, Jesus announces his ministry in Luke by citing a passage from Isaiah beginning with the phrase, "the Spirit of the Lord is upon me" (Luke 4:18, citing Isa 61:1–2) suggesting that Jesus's ministry is empowered by the Spirit in a manner that mirrors the eventual Spirit-empowered ministry of the disciples in Acts. When coupled with John 5:19's claim for that the Son does everything the Father does, we see strong scriptural pattern suggesting that even during the incarnation the works of the divine nature are indivisible, even as Christ's assumed humanity allows him to uniquely be born, walk, sleep, eat, experience pain, die, and be raised according to the flesh.

Historical treatments of the incarnation of the Son recognize the need for undivided operations coupled with actions unique to the Son as a result of his assumed humanity in the incarnation. This is expressed with varying degrees of clarity. Anselm of Canterbury notes that "only the person of the Son became flesh (although with the co-operation of the other two persons)."[21] Later in the Reformed tradition, Johannes Wollebius offers a more complex explanation: "The incarnation of Christ in its origin is the work of the entire Holy Trinity, but the event is an experience of the Son only." We see the typical pattern for differentiating the persons in inseparable operations: the Father formed a human nature through the power of the Spirit that was assumed by the Son in the hypostatic union.[22] When we come to the passion, Wollebius insists that only the Son suffered, not the Father or Spirit. Yet, "the principle efficient cause of this passion is the Holy Trinity." The entire Godhead worked inseparably to cause the passion, but only the Son died. We cannot say that "deity suffered," for the Son only suffered "in the flesh," that is, in the human nature.[23] We see through these contemporary and historical treatments that a sophisticated doctrinal theology of divine missions, coupled with a proper Christology where only the person of the Son is incarnate, allows both for the doctrine of inseparable operations according to the Son's divinity and unique acts such as dying and

---

21. Anselm of Canterbury, *On the Incarnation*, §3.
22. Wollebius, *Compendium*, 87.
23. Ibid., 100.

being born proper to the Son's assumed humanity. Therefore, the accusation that the doctrine of inseparable operations entails the heresy of patripassianism is wrong.

I must also briefly address one other common defense of EFS related to inseparable operations and the incarnation. Bruce Ware illustrates this common objection when he writes,

> The egalitarian denial of any eternal submission of the Son to the Father makes it impossible to answer the question why it was the "Son" and not the "Father" or "Spirit"' who was sent to become incarnate.[24]

It is certainly true that some theologians throughout history have suggested that any person in the Trinity could have become incarnate, but Ware makes too strong of an objection in claiming the impossibility of explaining the Son's incarnation. Certainly, inseparable operations would deny any unique *ad extra* operation such as submission that might explain why the Son and not the Father was incarnate. However, the fact that a divine mission is a procession with a created term suggests that only divine persons who proceed from the Father possess missions in the created order. The pro-Nicene dictum that all divine actions are from the Father, through the Son, and in the Spirit also provides warrant for claiming that redemption must be accomplished through the Son, whose ministry proceeded in the power of the Holy Spirit. I see no reason to conclude that the doctrine of inseparable operations stands in contradiction to Christian beliefs about the unique incarnation of the Son and only the Son.

Eternal Submission and the *Pactum Salutis*

A third common objection to any claim of a singular will and activity in the Godhead is particularly rooted in the Reformed tradition and its notion of a *pactum salutis*—the eternal covenant between the Father, Son, and Holy Spirit concerning the plan to redeem the elect. I have most often seen this objection raised in online discussions or in personal conversations, but Robert Letham does note in printed form the significance of the *pactum salutis* in a dialogue with Kevin Giles in the *Evangelical Quarterly*. Letham suggests that Giles neglects the historical precedent for EFS found in the *pactum*, insofar as "the Father makes certain stipulations, which the Son agrees to fulfill."[25] Interestingly, Letham himself rejects this notion of an

---

24. Ware, "How Shall We Think?" 275.
25. Letham, "Reply," 341.

eternal covenant between the Father and the Son, but some contemporary evangelicals who accept the *pactum* do describe it in terminology similar to EFS. So J. V. Fesko writes that while "there is one trinitarian will," it is also the case that "each member of the Godhead acts in a manner suited to his person and mission."[26] While Fesko treats obedience as only a feature of the divine economy, not constitutive of the eternal procession of the Son, he is willing to speak of "the Father's command" and "the Son's obedience" in the eternal *pactum salutis*.[27] One can see why many may see warrant for EFS in this doctrine.

During the 2016 online debates surrounding EFS, an article by Scott Swain and Michael Allen was widely circulated that seemed to offer a similar read of the *pactum*, without emphasizing this particular terminology. Swain and Allen argue that Karl Barth shifted the Son's obedience from a feature of the incarnate Christ to something intrinsic to the divine person of the Son. The authors note that many incorporate this claim into their theology through a massive revision of historical trinitarian thought (and they include common evangelical social trinitarianism speaking of "roles" here—citing Grudem, Ware, and Horrell).[28] Swain and Allen, however, seek to establish that such a claim of eternal obedience need not entail a massive revision of classical trinitarian metaphysics. In affirming that God has a single will,[29] that the divine persons work together indivisibly,[30] and that any talk of obedience must be rooted in the eternal generation of the Son,[31] Swain and Allen are clearly distinct from such noted EFS advocates like Ware, Ovey, and Grudem who deviate from pro-Nicene theology. Nevertheless, Swain and Allen go on to interpret John 5:19–30 to reach an analogous conclusion: the Son does nothing of his own initiative acting instead in obedience but also does everything that the Father does, sharing in the undivided work of the Trinity.[32] In short, "The manner in which the Son works in obedience" is not merely proper to his humanity, but is also "of his own proper filial relation to the Father."[33] Though the authors do not address the *pactum* directly, their account of an eternal obedience of the

---

26. Fesko, *Trinity and the Covenant*, 177–78.
27. Ibid., 192–93.
28. Swain and Allen, "Obedience of the Eternal Son," 115 n. 5.
29. Ibid., 122.
30. Ibid., 123.
31. Ibid., 119.
32. Ibid., 124.
33. Ibid., 125.

Son manifest only in relation to the drama of redemption is functionally analogous to the role of the *pactum salutis* in Reformed thought.

Before addressing the *pactum salutis* head on, I would first like to note several features of an appeal to the *pactum* that must be kept in mind. First it must be clear that any simple appeal to the *pactum salutis* does not resolve the dogmatic questions discussed in chapters 1–4 of this work. If the *pactum salutis* entails a plurality of divine wills, or an eternal obligation of the Son to act according to the command of the Father, or that will is not a property of nature but of the divine persons, then it is not only EFS but also the *pactum salutis* that must be revised or rejected in light of the same theological problems. Second, it is important to remember that the *pactum salutis* is a doctrine explaining the eternal counsel of God. While we are not without scriptural data that can be developed into a dogmatic statement of the eternal counsel of God serving as a second-order of language to make sense of the scriptural testimony, it is also the case that we possess far greater scriptural resources to analyze Christ's life, ministry, and redemptive work. If the seemingly clear dogmatic formulations of scriptural teaching on Christ's life, ministry, and redemptive work contradict with seemingly clear dogmatic formulations of scriptural teaching on the divine counsel, it is prudent to seek to reformulate our theology of the eternal decrees and counsel of God rather than the entirety of Christology and soteriology. In other words, if the *pactum salutis* does indeed agree with EFS, then this work must be read as an argument for abandoning the *pactum*. That being said, I do not see that a theology of the *pactum salutis* necessarily supports EFS.

Reformed theological accounts of the *pactum salutis* do not obviously fit with the language of eternal obedience and submission in the Godhead. Precursors to the full doctrine of the *pactum salutis* (often expressed in the theology of the divine decrees) occasionally spoke of a sort of subordination, but were nearly always at pains to clearly state that all three persons willed the mediatorial role of the Son, who by virtue of the shared divine will voluntarily assumed this role. Nevertheless the Son could be said to fulfill the role of mediator in both natures, as was fitting due to his eternal generation.[34] Richard Muller summarizes,

> The predestinarian antecedents of the *pactum* [*salutis*] indicate an intratrinitarian willing of salvation and offer an understanding of the common willing of the entire Godhead toward the accomplishment of a temporal work that involves the *ad extra* actions of the Son and Spirit, namely the *opera appropriata* or

---

34. Muller, "Toward the *Pactum Salutis*," 48–61.

common works of the Godhead that terminate in particular ways on particular persons.[35]

While there is indeed a differentiation of how the divine wills are possessed by the persons, and where this differentiation made it fitting for the Son to become incarnate—and here I agree with Swain and Allen's article—for reasons that will become clear in chapter 3 it was not generally acceptable in the Reformed tradition to speak of this differentiation in terms of eternal "submission" and "obedience." Nor does language of eternal submission easily fit the fully developed theology of the *pactum salutis*, which is why we see Herman Witsius and Johannes Cocceius, two of the first theologians to extensively explain the *pactum*, clearly teach that Father and Son have a single will. Witsius writes,

> The Son, as God, neither was, nor could be subject to any law, to any superior; that being contrary to the nature of the Godhead, which we now suppose the Son to have in common with the Father.... By undertaking to perform this obedience [the obedience serving as the foundation of our salvation], in the human nature, in its proper time, the Son, as God, did no more subject himself to the Father, than the Father with respect to the Son, to the owing that reward of debt, which he promised him a right to claim.[36]

Though full treatment of the historical picture lies beyond the bounds of this project—the citation of Witsius and his predecessors will have to suffice—it should be clear that there is an important conceptual distinction between eternal submission and an eternal covenant. The idea of a covenant can be explained in terms of agreement, and it is easy to explain agreement in the Godhead. The single divine will is expressed in a threefold fashion, each person willing the same object: the redemption of the church. The Father possesses this willing as one who is unbegotten and gives existence eternally to the Son, and the Son possesses this willing as one who is begotten and receives existence eternally from the Father. As argued above, it is therefore best to say that the threefold act of divine willing the *pactum* proceeds from the Father, through the Son, to the Spirit. This language could

---

35. Ibid., 61.

36. Witsius, *Economy*, II.3.6–7. Compare with a similar statement by Johannes Cocceius: "Indeed, the will of the Father and the Son is the same, not differing, because they are also one; but since the Father is not the Son nor the Son the Father the same will is appropriated distinctly and in its own manner on both sides, namely, the one as giving and sending and the other as being given and being sent." Cocceius, *Doctrine of the Covenant*, §92.

fittingly be called agreement, and thus it can fit within a theology of the *pactum salutis*. Such theology does not, however, indicate that it is appropriate to speak of distinct and cooperative acts of the Father commanding and the Son obeying and submitting, as EFS requires. EFS and the *pactum salutis* are distinctive dogmatic claims, and the latter is more defensible than the former because it avoids the theological problems discussed in subsequent chapters.

2

The Obedience of One Man
Christology and the Son's Obedience

"For as by the one man's disobedience the many were made sinners, so by the one man's obedience the many will be made righteous."
(Rom 5:19)

"The human will of Christ responds fully to his divine will, but through this the distinction between them is not suppressed. The divine will always remains as that which offers, calls, seeks a response, and imposes a responsibility. The human will remains that which responds."[1]

—Dumitru Staniloae

THE APOSTLE PAUL WRITES, "By the one man's obedience the many will be made righteous" (Rom 5:19). The author of Hebrews adds, "Although he was a son, he learned obedience" (Heb 5:8). What does it mean to say that Jesus offers the obedience of a man? How is it possible to say that the omniscient Son learned obedience? Here, the New Testament authors prompt theologians to connect their treatment of God's single will perfectly shared among Father, Son, and Spirit with the life, death, and resurrection of Jesus of Nazareth, God's Son incarnate. This is an important task but a task where no single passage of Scripture can fully answer all the theological questions. Instead, theologians find themselves once more with the need to develop a

---

1. Staniloae, *Orthodox Dogmatic Theology*, 169.

theological understanding of one doctrine—in this case Christology—by drawing on the broad pattern of Scripture and offering non-scriptural terminology under the guidance of philosophy.

Connecting the one will of God to Christology is one facet of a larger theological challenge. Christology must treat the question of the incarnation, exploring what it means to say that God the Son "became flesh" (John 1:14), how he "emptied himself, taking the form of a servant" (Phil 2:7), and how the Son was made like human beings "in every respect" (Heb 2:17). Broadly speaking, systematic theology must be able to make sense of two things: we must explain what Christ is as human and as God, and we must explain what Christ does as human and as God. The Bible affirms that he is "the image of the invisible God" (Col 1:15), "the radiance of the glory of God and the exact imprint of his nature" (Heb 1:3), but it also teaches that he is "the one man Jesus Christ" (Rom 5:15), the "last Adam" (1 Cor 15:45). Jesus is at once Lord[2] (a title used elsewhere in the Bible as a pious substitute for the divine name), our great high priest who serves as a human representative before God (Heb 3:1; 4:14; 8:1–6), and the Son of David, the descendent in the flesh of king David himself (Matt 1:1–16; Luke 3:23–38). Centrally important to the question of EFS is whether Jesus Christ has a human will and a divine will, just as he is said to be both human and God. As we will see, this question was answered in an ecumenical council following what is known as the monothelite controversy.

A theology exploring how the Son "became flesh" and human "in every respect" must make sense of the things Jesus said and did. Jesus did things that are only appropriate for God to do, such as forgiving sins (Luke 7:48), for example. Christ also did things that are appropriate for human beings to do but uncharacteristic of God, mundane things like sleeping (Mark 4:38 and pars.), crying (John 11:35), being hungry (Mark 11:12), and learning (Luke 2:52), as well as salvific things like dying. Particularly pertinent for any study of God's will is the issue of Christ's temptation. "God cannot be tempted with evil" (Jas 1:13), yet we read that Satan tempted Jesus in the desert (Matt 4:1–11 and pars.) and that Christ is a great high priest who "in every respect has been tempted as we are" (Heb 4:15). Theologians must explain how it is possible to affirm both that Jesus is God and also tempted like any other human being. In other words, they must address how he does things appropriate for God and for human beings. This is a question historically treated under the doctrine known as the communication of idioms, or by the Latin name *communicatio idiomatum*. The more we attend to the classical explanation of who Christ was and how Christ acted as the

---

2. Paul alone uses this title for Christ 230 times! O'Collins, *Christology*, 142.

God-man, the more clearly it is apparent that EFS does not easily fit with traditional accounts of Christology.

Historical Context: The Council of Chalcedon

The most important historical development in Christology occurred at the Council of Chalcedon in 451 AD. Christians had long wrestled with the relationship between the humanity and divinity of Christ. Some early Christians denied the Son's divinity altogether, or claimed that he was a human being who had been adopted by God through the work of the Holy Spirit at the beginning of his ministry.[3] Other Christians emphasized the divinity of Jesus, claiming that he was merely human in appearance, and actually was only fully divine.[4] Early theological debates quickly revealed that no imbalanced presentation of Christ's humanity and divinity would suffice. Only when Christians affirm the full humanity and full divinity of Jesus can they make sense of the scriptural narrative. Moreover, our salvation is only possible if Jesus is both fully human and fully God.

The biblical witness to Jesus's life and ministry compels Christians to affirm that Jesus is fully human and fully divine. Jesus's messianic role is rooted in the fact that he is descended from David, something highlighted in the genealogies found at the beginning of both Matthew and Luke (Matt 1:1–17; Luke 3:23–38). This Davidic lineage is only comprehensible if Jesus is human (Rom 1:3). Similarly, the title "Son of God," so commonly applied to Jesus, is a title that not only points to Jesus's messianic role and his universal lordship but also implies, to quote N. T. Wright, "that he is the one in whom the living God, Israel's God, has become personally present in the world." Wright notes that throughout Paul's writing we see a clear relational dynamic between Father and Son that occurs within the context of monotheistic claims in Old Testament passages Paul is interpreting (i.e., Phil 2:10f, citing Isa 45:23; 1 Cor 8:6, drawing on Deut 6:4; and 1 Cor 15:25–28, using Ps 110:1).[5] This relationship centers on the resurrection: God is precisely the God who has raised Jesus from the dead, while Jesus is most clearly revealed as the Son of God through the same event.[6] In Christ's

---

3. These are the approaches of the Ebionites and the Adoptionists, respectively.
4. This is roughly the approach of Docetism.
5. Wright, *Resurrection*, 731–32.
6. Ibid. Cf. Harris, *Raised Immortal*, 74. Harris writes, "The Resurrection was the vindication and confirmation of the sonship of Jesus. During his ministry Jesus laid claim to an intimate and unique relation to God (e.g., Matt 11:27) that was epitomized in the term 'Abba' ('Father,' 'my Father') by which he addressed or referred to God, and in the title 'Son (of God)' by which he sometimes referred to himself (e.g., Mark 12:6;

resurrection, he is vindicated as the Son of God, yet such a resurrection is only possible in the flesh of human nature, for the Son's resurrection is a resurrection of the body.[7] At the very core of the gospel, then, is a claim that Jesus is both God and human (and this claim can be supplemented with dozens of additional key texts and arguments to make the point). As Paul writes, Jesus is "descended from David according to the flesh" but also "declared to be the Son of God in power according to the Spirit of holiness by his resurrection from the dead" (Rom 1:3–4). Once Christians understood this claim, the task of determining how to speak of Jesus being both human and divine remained.

A second pivotal argument played a role in early christological debates. Following the Council of Nicea discussed in the previous chapter, Christians began to acknowledge that Jesus was *homoousios* with the Father, and therefore fully divine. Christians had by this time also long recognized that Jesus was also human, but it was not yet clear whether Jesus was fully human, one might say *homoousios* with us. Enter Gregory of Nazianzus, a theologian who would leave his mark on Christology through his claim that "that which [the Son] has not assumed he has not healed; but that which is united to his Godhead is also saved."[8] Gregory of Nazianzus would have originally explained this in terms of deification, which depended upon the full humanity of Christ. To avoid the lengthy digression needed to introduce patristic accounts of salvation, I will instead explain Nazianzus' within a robust theology of union with Christ unto sanctification. The rule functions in a similar fashion in either patristic or Protestant soteriological systems. Paul tells us that Christ became our sanctification (1 Cor 1:30; cf. John 11:25). Paul's claim makes sense when we recognize that both the process of sanctification and the eventual Christian state of resurrection and glorification do not happen apart from Christ. Sanctification is not a matter of developing certain moral qualities disconnected from Christ. Rather, as Paul likes to tell us, sanctification and glorification are fully "in Christ."[9]

13:32) or others sometimes referred to him (e.g., Matt 16:16, 27:54). What Jesus had always been, although in hidden form, the Resurrection openly declared him to be, viz. the Son of God."

7. Wright, *Resurrection*, 201–4. Wright demonstrates that resurrection in ancient Jewish writings referred either to a metaphorical event happening to the nation of Israel, or to a literal and bodily event expected to occur to all human beings at the future judgment. Christians retained the bodily nature of individual resurrection, but claimed that Jesus was the firstfruits of the resurrection.

8. Gregory of Nazianzus, "Letters on the Apollinarian Controversy," 218.

9. This phrase is used seventy-three times throughout Paul's epistles, and is accompanied by a number of other terms and metaphors for union. After surveying each instance of key union terms and metaphors, Constantine Campbell concludes that union

After all, when Christians are resurrected into perfected spiritual bodies, they are raised into the same kind of humanity that Christ shared after the resurrection (1 Cor 15:20–49). Marcus Peter Johnson helpfully clarifies how Paul can call Christ our sanctification: "Although it may at first be difficult to imagine how or why Jesus 'became' sanctification to us when he was already perfectly holy, we should remember that he took on our human nature in order to present us holy before the Father." Here Johnson cites John 17:19, which teaches that Jesus sanctifies himself that we may be sanctified. He continues, "Christ is uniquely our sanctification because in him alone the sanctification of our human nature has taken place by union with his divine life. What unholy humanity so desperately needs is union with the Sanctified One."[10] Christian sanctification is nothing short of our sharing in the perfected humanity of Jesus Christ through the power of the Holy Spirit.

Accepting this biblical conclusion, Gregory of Nazianzus insists that Christ must have been fully human in order to fully sanctify Christians who are in union with him. This follows from the fact that sin has infected the entirety of human nature, a doctrine Protestants often refer to as total depravity. Across the Bible, sin is depicted as a darkening of the understanding (Eph 4:18), a lack of self-control of the will and the possession of wrongly ordered desires (2 Tim 3:3–4), a lack of love (John 5:42), and captivity within sinful bodies (Rom 6:6). It is no surprise, then, that the Bible depicts sanctification as a transformation of all aspects of human nature. Sanctification calls for the renewal of our minds (Col 3:10; Rom 12:2), our emotions or desires (1 Pet 2:11), our wills (Phil 2:13), and our bodies (1 Cor 6:19–20). But if sanctification is only in Christ, a participation in the perfected humanity assumed by the Son in the incarnation, and if sanctification affects the heart, mind, body, and will, then Jesus must have assumed a full human nature, heart, mind, body, and will for us to have the hope of sanctification.

As debates concerning Christ's humanity and divinity grew, Christians influenced by the biblical need to affirm Jesus's full humanity and full divinity sought a second-order theological explanation that could make sense of the broad scriptural testimony concerning the Son while moving beyond this testimony to offer philosophical clarity. A solution must affirm the full

---

indicates for the Christian life that Christian activities such as obedience or worship and characteristics like love or godliness are both "conditioned by their union with Christ." Campbell concludes, "The status and identity that believers enjoy, which is so programmatic for Paul's ethical framework and instruction, are inextricably bound up with union with Christ. From there flow the activities and characteristics of believers, which again are entwined with union with Christ. The Christian life is so weaved of the fabric of union with Christ that the most appropriate moniker for believers is 'in Christ.'" Campbell, *Paul and Union*, 374–75.

10. Johnson, *One with Christ*, 119–20.

divinity and full humanity of Christ without dividing Jesus into two separate subjects, one divine and the other human. Amid intense debate, the Council of Chalcedon (AD 451) offered a solution that has become the standard of orthodoxy among Eastern Orthodox, Roman Catholic, and Protestant Christians. The definition of Chalcedon reads as follows:

> We, then, following the holy Fathers, all with one consent, teach men to confess one and the same Son, our Lord Jesus Christ, the same perfect in deity and also perfect in humanity; truly God and truly man, or a rational soul and body; consubstantial with the Father according to the deity, and consubstantial with us according to the humanity; in all things like unto us, without sin; begotten before all ages of the Father according to the deity, and in these latter days, for us and for our salvation, born of the virgin Mary, the mother of God, according to the humanity; one and the same Christ, Son, Lord, Only-begotten, to be acknowledged in two natures, inconfusedly, unchangeably, indivisibly, inseparably; the distinction of natures being by no means taken away by the union, but rather the property of each nature being preserved, and concurring in one Person and one Subsistence, not parted or divided into two persons, but one and the same Son, and only begotten, God the Word, the Lord Jesus Christ, as the prophets from the beginning have declared concerning him, and the Lord Jesus Christ himself has taught us, and the creed of the holy Fathers has handed down to us.[11]

The definition establishes two important theological truths.[12] First, the one who is Jesus of Nazareth is the same one who eternally is the Son of God. Second, this one who is both Jesus of Nazareth and the eternal Son of God is *two natures* united in *one person*, one full and perfect divine nature united with one full and perfect human nature in the person of the Son. When we speak of Christ's humanity, we speak of his sharing a human nature with human beings. This nature is not mixed with the divine nature to create some third thing. Christ subsists in two natures; he is not one nature from two natures.[13] When we seek the unity of these two natures, we look to the category of person, for the person who is eternally Son of God has assumed a full human nature inseparably.

---

11. "The Symbol of Chalcedon," 62–63.
12. Here I appreciate the insights of Fairbairn, *Life in the Trinity*, 144–45.
13. This claim was meant to ensure that Christ's humanity and divinity could not be mixed into a third thing that was neither God nor human. Nor could the divinity assume a human nature in such a way that it was annihilated. Kelly, *Early Christian Doctrines*, 330–34, 340–41.

The Chalcedonian definition provides a helpful hermeneutic for reading the Bible, but one that requires further philosophical clarification. Consider, for example, the mind of Christ. At times, Jesus seems omniscient, as for example when he knows the thoughts of others (i.e., Matt 9:4). At other times, he admits that "no one knows that day nor hour, not even the angels in heaven, nor the son" (Matt 24:36). If Jesus possesses a full human nature and a full divine nature, as Chalcedon affirms, and if actions arise out of natures, as was demonstrated in chapter 1, then Jesus's omniscient acts here arise from the divine nature and mind, but his limited knowledge arises from his human nature and mind. Both finite human knowledge and infinite divine knowledge are found in the person of the Son, and both passages are upheld. However, several major theological questions remain: in this case, how do we relate the divine and human minds of Christ? Furthermore, how do we adequately explain the unity of the Son as a single person? Exploring Christ's human and divine minds is a task beyond the scope of this work,[14] but it illustrates well the philosophical challenges that arise from Chalcedon. Insofar as the believer's sanctified human nature is a participation in Christ's humanity, and insofar as sanctification requires a transformation of the mind, we must affirm that Christ had a human mind. This also follows from the claim that Jesus is fully human. Yet it is also important to unify Christ in such a manner that these two minds are still coherently a single person. Christological developments after Chalcedon often wrestled with these sorts of questions, seeking to develop theology that is rationally consistent with the Bible and with the Chalcedonian definition (itself derived from scriptural patterns). For our present purposes, one such debate warrants particular attention: the monothelite controversy.

The Monothelite Controversy: Who Jesus Is and the Question of Christ's Will(s)

Although the Council of Chalcedon provided Christians with answers to fundamental questions concerning the relationship between Christ's humanity and his divinity, it also opened the door to a new set of questions regarding how Christians ought to think of the God-man who was two natures united into a single person. The main debate relating to our discussion of eternal functional subordination is the question of Christ's will(s).

---

14. For a helpful contemporary treatment of the two minds of Christ, I refer the reader to Morris, *The Logic of God Incarnate*. It should be noted that Morris's treatment of the unity of Christ as a whole is not clearly compatible with the theology described here.

If Chalcedon is correct that Jesus is two natures in one person, then two options lie before us. Either a will is proper to nature, in which case Jesus logically must have two wills (one human and one divine) if he indeed possesses a complete human nature and a complete divine nature, or else a will is a proper to a person, in which case Jesus would only have one divine will because he is only a single divine person. In the seventh century, theologians in the Byzantine Empire considered each of these options in a debate that eventually led up to the seventh ecumenical council, the Third Council of Constantinople.

By the seventh century, the Byzantine state (heir to the Roman Empire) had lost much of its territory to several hostile neighboring empires, but the emperor Heraclitus had begun to reclaim land once belonging to Byzantium. As he did so, he found a number of Christian groups in newly reconquered border territories that questioned the theology of the Council of Chalcedon.[15] These Christians preferred to emphasize the unity of Christ's divinity and humanity, and they worried that Chalcedon created an artificial division within Christ. Heraclitus needed these populations to stand in union with Byzantine Orthodoxy to ensure a united military front at the borders of the newly expanded Empire, so he sought a theological solution that might reconcile all parts of the church within the empire.[16] Patriarch Sergius of Constantinople provided Heraclitus with his potential source of union. Sergius developed a theological formula that affirmed two natures in Christ united in one person but that, in several different forms over the course of the debate, claimed there was either single energy/operation in Christ or a single will in Christ. The former theology is known as monoenergism and the latter was known as monothelitism. In their basic contours, each put forward a similar theological proposal: though there are two natures in Christ, there is only the single divine person of the Son who is the source of all Christ's actions and/or willing. For a time it seemed that Sergius' proposal was a viable theological solution to division within the church and empire, but as time went on resistance to this proposal grew, particularly with the writings of Maximus the Confessor. This resistance culminated with monothelitism's condemnation at the Third Council of Constantinople in 681 in favor of a view known as dyothelitism, which claimed that will and energy/operation were both properties of nature. Because Christ had a complete human and a complete divine nature, he must have two wills.

15. For a helpful analysis of the theological questions lingering after Chalcedon that led to the monothelite controversy, see Hussey, *The Orthodox Church*, 10–13.

16. For a thorough analysis of the historical events surrounding the monothelite controversy, see Davis, *Ecumenical Councils*, 13–24.

Maximus skillfully raised a number of objections against monothelitism, the claim that Christ only had a single will. At its most rudimentary level, monothelitism was wrong simply because it did not continue within the theological tradition that saw any operation, willing included, as originating in nature or substance. This was the assumed meaning of such terms as nature in earlier trinitarian debates, as we have seen in chapter 1, and Maximus intentionally placed himself within this tradition.[17] More important to Maximus's argument were three closely related theological claims. First, Maximus argued that if Jesus Christ was fully human, then he must have had a human will and a nature that made human operations possible. Second, if we are sanctified[18] by union to Christ's humanity, then Christ must have a human will. Corrupted and fallen humanity has a polluted will that must be redeemed through union with Christ's perfect humanity, so Christ must have a human will. Third, Maximus recognized that any christological claims about the nature and person of the Son in the incarnation would have ramifications in trinitarian theology. After all, as the Chalcedonian definition emphasized, the one who is Son of God is also the one who is incarnate in Christ. Maximus argued that monothelitism undermined the core of trinitarian theology by undermining the inseparable operations so essential to pro-Nicene thought.

Maximus inherited the argument that Christ's full humanity required him to possess a human will from previous theologians who had argued against monoenergism and monothelitism. Sophronius of Jerusalem argued that natures are distinguished by operations, so we must affirm distinct operations to affirm Chalcedon's claim that Christ's human and divine natures were combined without confusion.[19] Stephen of Dora also argued that Jesus must have had both a human will and a divine will in order to be fully human.[20] Leo Donald Davis summarizes the argument well:

> If the natures in Christ are really two, then the operations of those natures must also be two. For activity, operation is essential to an existent being. Only through operations can natures be discerned and distinguished. Natures and operations are thus necessarily and ineluctably connected. If there are two natures

---

17. Meyendorff, *Byzantine Theology*, 37. Operation as proper to nature was assumed by dyothelites throughout the debate. Hovorun, *Will, Action, and Freedom*, 154–55.

18. Here Maximus would use the terminology of deification. For present purposes I will treat deification as roughly a functional equivalent to Protestant views of sanctification as expressed above.

19. Davis, *Ecumenical Councils*, 265.

20. Dorner, *Doctrine of the Person of Christ*, Vol. 3, 182.

really existent in Christ, there must be as well two really existent operations.[21]

This conclusion followed clearly from the common definition of nature used by early theologians in conjunction with the Chalcedonian definition.

Jesus Christ's full humanity, clear from the Scriptures and affirmed in the Chalcedonian definition, also led Maximus to insist that Jesus had a human will. As Christopher Beeley remarks, "Various patristic figures are credited with defending Christ's full humanity; the one who did so most thoroughly was Maximus."[22] Maximus followed the traditional understanding of nature when he argued that if something has no will or operation, it does not exist.[23] Therefore, to claim that Jesus subsisted in a human nature and not just from a human nature (in other words to claim that nature exists throughout Jesus's life and was not simply a factor in Jesus's origin), it must have a natural operation and will. Here Maximus adds a degree of precision to his forbearers, granting that the divine and human nature may have the same objective willed. Christ's human and divine wills must have shared a common object to preserve the personal unity of Christ. However, claiming that God and man have the same will would be, in Demetrios Bathrellos's words, "tantamount to confusing divinity and humanity."[24] If Jesus did not assume a human will, he did not assume a human nature, so he must have a human will.[25] Here, Maximus appealed to Psalm 39, which he viewed as a prophetic foreshadowing of the temptations and suffering of Christ to affirm Jesus's human nature. We might make the same point with stronger exegetical footing by pointing to the temptation in the desert (Matt 4:1–11 and pars.). Jesus was tempted, but God cannot be tempted (Jas 1:13), so Jesus must have a human will. However, Jesus also has a "divine will, which is both his and the Father's,"[26] because it is "*by nature* the same as the Father's."[27] Maximus saw Jesus's divine will clearly revealed in Luke 13:34's claim that Jesus had often willed to gather Israel to him when they were persecuting the prophets.[28] Since his human nature did not yet exist at the time prior to the incarnation when prophets were being killed, the Son must have willed this in the divine nature shared with the Father.

21. Davis, *Ecumenical Councils*, 272.
22. Beeley, *The Unity of Christ*, 296.
23. Maximus the Confessor, "Dispute at Bizya," §3.
24. Demetrios Bathrellos, *Byzantine Christ*, 119.
25. Maximus the Confessor, *Opuscule 3*, 195.
26. Maximus the Confessor, *Opusculum 6*, 174.
27. Maximus the Confessor, *Opuscule 3*, 194. Emphasis added.
28. Bathrellos, *Byzantine Christ*, 139.

Maximus clearly connected his dyothelitism (the claim that Jesus had two wills) to his understanding of salvation. He saw clearly that human will was corrupted in the fall because Adam ate willingly, so he saw that the Son must have assumed a human will to heal it.[29] As John Meyendorff comments, the restoration "of human nature in Christ implies that the incarnate Word assumed human energy [i.e., operations] and restored it in conformity with the primitive divine plan."[30] Maximus argued that Christ submitted to human temptations and responded with obedience not for his own sake, but for ours. Adam deliberately succumbed to "hedonistic passions," to the end that human will "inclines toward wicked pleasure against his own self-interest."[31] Christ overcame temptation, learning an obedience (Heb 5:8–9) in his humanity that was not needed in his divinity so that in overcoming temptation he was "thereby healing the whole of human nature of the passion connected with pleasure."[32] Maximus recognized that sin entered the world through human will at the fall, and that, in accordance with Gregory of Nazianzus' formula, the Son must have assumed a human will in order to sanctify it.[33]

Maximus most clearly connected Jesus's human will in his human nature to the redemptive significance of overcoming temptation when he examines Jesus's prayer, "Father, if possible, let this cup pass from me" (Matt 26:39). Previous commentators who treated Christ's agony in the garden considered his request to let the cup pass to be hypothetical—the Son could not will something contrary to the divine plan. Perhaps this was merely an expression of human experience, but not genuine deliberation. Maximus, however, suggested that this was a deliberation of the human will that submitted to the divine will.[34] Maximus argued that this cannot be a request arising from Jesus's divine nature, for we know that God wills our salvation "by his very nature," and the Father and the Son share a "common will" according to their common nature.[35] Simply put, Jesus could never say "not what I will, but what you will" in his divinity because there is no distinction between what the Father and Son will, due to their shared nature and therefore shared will. Maximus therefore concluded:

---

29. Ibid., 131.
30. John Meyendorff, *Christ in Eastern Christian Thought*, 111.
31. Maximus the Confessor, *Ad Thalassium* 21, 112.
32. Ibid., 113.
33. Hovorun, *Will, Action, and Freedom*, 129–30.
34. See the discussion in Wilken, *Early Christian Thought*, 126–31.
35. Maximus the Confessor, *Opusculum* 6, 175.

> It follows, then, that having become like us for our sake, he was calling on his God and Father in a human manner when he said, *Let not what I will, but what you will prevail*, inasmuch as, being God by nature, he also in his humanity has, as his human volition, the fulfillment of the will of the Father. This is why, considering both of the nature from which, in which, and of which his person was, he is acknowledged as able both to will and to effect our salvation. As God, he approved that salvation along with the Father and the Holy Spirit; as man, he *became* for the sake of that salvation *obedient* to his Father *unto death, even death on a cross* (Phil 2:8). He accomplished this great feat of the economy of salvation for our sake through the mystery of his incarnation.[36]

Notice how clear Maximus is here: the Son learned obedience in his human nature through the incarnation that he might become obedient in his humanity to heal fallen human nature. He could not possibly have been obedient in his divinity because there could not be any negation, any yielding of his will to the Father's will, since all three divine persons share a single common will.[37] Moreover, if Christ had offered a divine obedience, he would not have healed the human will, and Christians' wills would not be healed when they participate in Christ's humanity through the work of the Spirit in sanctification. This is the opposite position of EFS, which sees the Son's obedience as a divine obedience manifest in the history of redemption as a reflection of what is necessarily and eternally true in God, not as a contingent result of the incarnation.

Maximus's first two arguments are rooted in the Chalcedonian definition. Jesus is a human and a divine nature united in the person of the eternal Son, so if Jesus must have a human will to be fully human, and if he must have a human will to ensure the transformation and sanctification of all aspects of the Christian, then will must be a property of nature, for there was no human person in Christ. Maximus reached a similar conclusion through the doctrine of the Trinity. As was demonstrated in chapter 1, the standard patristic understanding of the Trinity from the fourth century and onward recognized the indivisible work of the Father, Son, and Spirit as a necessary consequence of the claim that the three persons were of the same essence and nature. Persons with an identical essence and nature do identical operations because an operation arises from a nature. This theological position does not require that the three persons work indistinguishably, but it does

---

36. Ibid., 176.

37. Compare with Maximus' argument in Maximus the Confessor, *Disputation with Pyrrhus*, §73.

prohibit any claim that the three persons perform distinct acts, except in the specific cases of the divine missions. (I discussed this exception briefly in excursus 1, but we will return to the question of the unique acts of the incarnate Son below.) Maximus was well aware of this tradition, so he connected his Christology to his trinitarian theology. The problem, Maximus declared, is that monothelites posit a single will in Christ, which contradicts this traditional understanding of the Trinity.

Let us consider Maximus' argument in detail. Monothelites claim that there is only one will in Christ, which would follow only if will is a personal property. After all, if will is a property of nature, the dyothelite position would be correct, for the incarnate Son has two complete natures. Maximus noted that in attributing a will to the person of the Son, "We will be forced to attribute hypostatic activities both to the Father and the Spirit in the same way as to the Son." Given that trinitarian orthodoxy affirmed at the Constantinople in AD 381 also admits a single will and operation in the shared divine nature, this would force us to admit four wills in the Godhead, which would muddle the threefold nature of the deity—"we will be suffering from the sickness of a fourfold God." Maximus also recognized that patristic theologians "declare every activity to be natural, not hypostatic," and he knew that distinct operations or activities are the means by which natures are distinguished.[38] If we say that the Son has a will proper to his person, we must therefore admit the same of the Father and Spirit, which leads to the conclusion that the "blessed monad will also be a triad of natures." This follows from the claim that distinctive wills and operations allow us to identify distinctive natures. Or else we can preserve the unity of being by positing one will, but if will is a personal property, and "if there is one will of the triad beyond being, there will be a Godhead with three names and a single person."[39] The first option is tritheism and the second is modalism, and Maximus will accept neither option. Thus it is no surprise when Maximus asked his debate partner Pyrrhus, "Wilt thou say that . . . because there are three hypostases there are also three wills, and because of this, three natures as well, since the canons and definitions of the Fathers say that the distinction of wills implieth a distinction of natures? So said Arius!"[40]

Maximus connected any effort to attribute will to the divine persons to the arch-heretic Arius, a claim with dubious historical accuracy (the question of wills did not play a significant role in the Arian debate), but a claim that nevertheless illustrates how strongly he rejects associating will with

---

38. Maximus the Confessor, "Dispute at Bizya," §4.
39. Maximus the Confessor, *Opuscule 3*, 195–96.
40. Maximus, *Disputation*, §15.

person. Maximus was not alone in making such an argument for dyothelitism.[41] However, this is precisely the move that defenders of EFS are making. Bruce Ware writes clearly that the Son's eternal submission "is nothing other than a 'personal property.'"[42] Even if we read Ware charitably, and take him to mean that will is a property of nature, but submission is a personal property, we still have considerable problems when we keep Maximus' dyothelitism in mind. First, Maximus understood fallen humans to possess what he called a gnomic or deliberative will, which referred to a human being's ability to choose whether or not to act according to the intended purpose of human nature reflected in the natural will. However, Maximus explicitly denied this to the Godhead and to the incarnate Christ, because Christ is not imperfect and therefore does not need to deliberate as to what must be done in a given situation.[43] Thus, even this charitable reading of Ware is inconsistent with Maximus' theology.[44] Second, as noted above, Maximus insists that the Son assume a human will so that he can transform what Adam damaged through his life of sinless obedience. Assuming Ware means that will is a property of nature but submission is a personal property, it is unclear how the Son might offer a human submission thereby healing human nature, for there was no human person. At least Ware offers no adequate explanation, and as we will see no explanation could fit with traditional understandings of how the incarnate Son undertakes any operation, including submission.

41. Consider the argument made by Pope Agatho, which was read to the delegates at the third Council of Constantinople: "For if anybody should mean a personal will, when in the holy Trinity there are said to be three Persons, it would be necessary that there should be asserted three personal wills, and three personal operations (which is absurd and truly profane). Since, as the truth of the Christian faith holds, the will is natural, where the one nature of the holy and inseparable Trinity is spoken of, it must be consistently understood that there is one natural will, and one natural operation. But when in truth we confess that in the one person of our Lord Jesus Christ the mediator between God and men, there are two natures (that is to say the divine and the human), even after his admirable union, just as we canonically confess the two natures of one and the same person, so we confess his two natural wills and two natural operations." Agatho of Rome, "The Letter of Pope Agatho," 332–23. Agatho also put forward similar arguments to Maximus concerning the full humanity of Christ and the need for a human will in Christ for sanctification.

42. Ware, "A Denial of *Homoousios?*" 244.

43. Hovorun, *Will, Action, and Freedom*, 134.

44. "Maximus made repeated reference to the long-held connection between nature and will that had been established in trinitarian theology. If a will introduced a person, and vice versa, there would be either one person in the Trinity, because of the one will, or three wills because of the three persons. If these wills were natural, we would have three Gods, whereas if they were 'gnomic', there would be an internal opposition in the Trinity, which, for Maximus, was unacceptable." Bathrellos, *Byzantine Christ*, 130.

So EFS, at least as Ware explains it, seems quite incompatible with dyothelite Christology. If Ware actually does mean that both the will and the act of submitting are proper to the person only, Maximus' entire theological argument collapses. As I. A. Dorner summarizes,

> Part of [Christ's] work, [Maximus] says, was to exercise obedience, and to fulfill the will and law of His Father.... Now if the rational soul of Christ had no will at all, in accordance with, or by means of, what will, did He keep the Father's commands? According to the will of the Divine Logos? But the will of the Logos is a will that commands and rules; and the will of the Father is one and the same with the will of the Son. By means of what will, then? For the will that commands is one thing, and the will that obeys, another. We are thus reduced to an alternative, either of saying that the will of obedience was the will of the Logos, or of granting that there was a true human will in Christ. The former alternative makes the divine nature of the Logos a subject and servant, after the manner of Arius;—an error which needs no refutation.[45]

No refutation was needed, at least, until the time of modern evangelical debates on the eternal submission of the Son.

The *Communicatio Idiomatum*: What Christ Does as Perfect Human and Perfect God

Maximus provided a clear set of theological arguments for why Jesus must have possessed a human will and a divine will in the incarnation. Through his theology we have an idea of what we must think about the Son's wills in the incarnation when we affirm that Jesus was fully God and fully human—Jesus has two wills, one proper to his human nature and one proper to his divine nature that he shares in common with the Father and the Holy Spirit. His basic theological insight was declared orthodox at a council at the Lateran palace (AD 649) for the Roman Catholic Church, and then again at the Third Council of Constantinople (AD 680/1), the sixth ecumenical council. Despite clarifying what it must mean for Christ to be the God-man, the councils leave a second theological question only partially answered: how do we make sense of what Christ does as perfect God and perfect man?

Maximus's theology provides a limited starting point in answering the question of how Christ's humanity and divinity work together, but

---

45. Dorner, *The Person of Christ*, 192.

unfortunately his views are not entirely clear on the subject. As Bathrellos explains, there is a longstanding dispute among scholars concerning how Maximus relates the human and divine wills in Christ. One school of interpretation claims that Maximus entirely subsumed the human to the divine will, which has complete "hegemony" over it. The other dominant interpretation thinks Maximus granted significant autonomy to the human will to ensure its independence.[46] Bathrellos puts forward his own novel interpretation of Maximus's theology, arguing that a willer moves his will, and so the willer of the enfleshed Logos moves both the human and the divine will.[47] There are two important things to note here. First, there is not enough scholarly consensus on Maximus's theology to use it as a foundation for understanding the divine and human acts of the incarnate Son. Second, it is clear that one key element of a solution found in both the decrees of the Council of Chalcedon and at the Third Council of Constantinople is missing from Maximus's theology. As Bathrellos notes, "Nowhere does Maximus say that each nature wills and works in communion with the other."[48] However, this is a key element of the solution eventually adopted at the councils and widely accepted among Roman Catholic, Orthodox, and Protestant theologians, as we will see below. Despite this shortcoming, we can still note one feature of Maximus's theology that serves as a starting point for a discussion of how the divine and human wills result in a unified act of the eternal Son that does not divine the person of the Son. Maximus clearly explained that "to will is always rooted in the willing nature," but willing belongs to the person.[49] In other words, persons act according to their nature, but it is always a person who acts, not a nature in the abstract. As Maximus explains elsewhere,

> Nobody as a person acts hypostatically [i.e., in a way proper to their specific personhood], but as something acts naturally. For example, Peter and Paul act, but not in a Peter-like and Paul-like manner, but in a human manner: they are both human beings by nature and according to the common and definitive principle of nature, but not hypostatically according to what each does personally.[50]

This point deserves some clarification. We must certainly grant that there are some acts or operations that are typical of certain persons, whether it

46. Demetrios Bathrellos, *Byzantine Christ*, 164.
47. Ibid., 168.
48. Ibid., 182.
49. Maximus the Confessor, *Opuscule 3*, 193.
50. Maximus the Confessor, "Dispute at Bizya," §7.

be a particularly Michael Jordan-like dunk, or a novel that is so typically Jane Austin. To say that actions are rooted in nature, and that humans act in a human manner is not to deny that individual persons may complete specific patterns of acts that become associated with them. Michael Jordan is associated with athletic success in a way that I never will be. Maximus was after a more fundamental point: the reason why Jordan is known for dunking a basketball, or why Austin is known for writing a certain style of novel, is because both possess a human nature that bears within it the possibility of writing or performing athletic feats in a way that the nature of a plant, for example, would lack. We will return later to the chapter to the question of how distinctively different persons may utilize operations common to all human beings, but for now the more basic point is our starting point: persons act in a manner appropriate to their nature.

Once we recognize that persons act according to their nature, but individual persons are the ones who act, we begin to clearly see a potential problem with dyothelite Christology. Dyothelitism affirms two wills and two operations in the incarnate Son, one proper to each nature, but a human nature has certain operations proper to it, and a divine nature has certain operations proper to it. How do we affirm that these natures and operations are joined hypostatically in the person of the Son without either confusing the natures by conflating the operations or dividing the natures by rendering the operations entirely unrelated to one another? To answer this question, we must begin with the traditional claim that the two natures work in communion with one another.

From the time that the Council of Chalcedon codified the doctrine of the hypostatic union until the Third Council of Constantinople rejected monothelitism, Christology consistently affirmed the claim that the Son's human and divine natures cooperated with one another as a result of the incarnation. The Council of Chalcedon canonized a document known as the *Tome* of Pope Leo the Great, establishing it as a standard for determining orthodox Christology.[51] Leo's *Tome* played a tremendous role in subsequent christological developments, including the monothelite controversy. In the *Tome*, Leo writes that each nature "does the acts which belong to it, in communion with the other." As he goes on to explain, this is by "the Word, that is, performing what belongs to the Word, and the flesh carrying out what belongs to the flesh. The one of these shines out in miracles; the other succumbs to injuries."[52] Many theologians defending dyothelitism (but notably

---

51. Kelly, *Doctrines*, 339. Two letters from Cyril of Alexandria were also canonized.

52. Leo the Great, *The Tome of Leo*, 365. Leo used the word "form" instead of nature, since he wrote before the Chalcedonian definition had established agreed upon terminology for what is human and what is divine in Christ. However, subsequent appeal to

not Maximus) incorporated Leo's claim of natures working in communion into their works. Anastasius, for example, argued that the two wills in Christ were "united together according to their natures . . . and as we may say, like the Fathers, each of those had 'communion with the other.'"[53] Though there is no mention of "communion" specifically, the same idea was incorporated into a council at the Lateran palace (AD 649) where the Catholic Church condemned monothelitism under the leadership of Martin I.[54] This same theology was passed on from Pope Agatho and a Roman Synod of 125 bishops by letter to the delegates at Constantinople III.[55] Thus, it is no surprise that the third Council of Constantinople incorporated this idea into its statement. After affirming "two natural willings or wills in [Christ] and two natural operations," the council clarifies that there are "two natural wills not contrary [to each other], God forbid, as the impious heretics have said [they would be], but his human will following, and not resisting or opposing, but rather subject to his divine and all powerful will." Here, the council cites John 6:38—"For I have come down from heaven, not to do my own will but the will of him who sent me," interpreting this verse to demonstrate that the Son calls the "will of the flesh his own" through the incarnation.[56] The statement from Constantinople III goes on to cite the *Tome* of Leo before concluding, "Each nature wills and works what is proper to it, in communion with the other."[57]

The claim that each of Christ's natures works out what is proper to it gradually developed over time into a doctrine known as the communication of idioms, or *communicatio idiomatum*, a doctrine which establishes rules for speaking of Christ in an orthodox manner. The doctrine attempts to discern between properties and operations that are proper to the divine nature (i.e., omniscience as a property and the act of foreknowing as an operation) and properties and operations that are proper to the human nature (i.e., the property of being finite and the operation of dying) without losing the

---

this formula uses the terminology of "nature" established at Chalcedon.

53. Anastasius, "Letter of Anastasius," §4.

54. Davis, *Ecumenical Councils*, 276. This particular emphasis is especially found in the tenth canon from the Lateran meeting held under Martin I.

55. Agatho and the bishops used the same language as Leo, emphasizing a particularly Roman version of the doctrine, affirming "each form acting in communion with the other what is proper to itself . . . so also the rule of piety instructs us that he has two natural wills and two natural operations, as perfect God and perfect man, one and the same our Lord Jesus Christ." Agatho of Rome, "The Letter of Agatho and of the Roman Synod of 125 Bishops," 341.

56. "The Statement of Faith of the Third Council of Constantinople," 383.

57. Ibid., 384.

hypostatic or personal unity of the two natures. Often disregarded in evangelical systematic theology textbooks today because of its pedantic flavor, the doctrine of the communication of idioms is actually essential to clearly expressing both the unity of Christ and the unconfused-yet-indivisible operations of the human and divine natures.

Martin Chemnitz offered one of the most thorough and clear explanations of the communication of idioms developed during the Protestant scholastic era, and little has surpassed his clarity since. His work serves as a fruitful summary of the historical development of the communication of idioms. For that reason I will explain Chemnitz's theology to clarify precisely how Jesus's humanity and divinity worked together during the incarnation. Recall that I argued above (in agreement with Gregory of Nazianzus and Maximus the Confessor) that the sanctification of a Christian entails participating in the sort of humanity that the Son assumed in the incarnation and healed through his obedient life. Chemnitz accepted this notion of sanctification and argued that the communication (*koinonia*) of attributes involves the same sort of relation between Christ's human nature and divine nature that is seen in a Christian's fellowship (*koinonia*) with the Spirit (2 Cor 13:14) or in a Christian's partaking (*koinonia*) of the divine nature (2 Pet 1:4). Of course, Christians are not hypostatically united to the divine nature the way that Christ's human nature was hypostatically united to divinity, but the Scriptures do speak of one aspect of the incarnation as Christ partaking (*kekoinoneken*) in flesh (Heb 2:14).[58] This insight requires Chemnitz to explain how Jesus's two natures work in harmony, as is the case with a Christian led by the Spirit, while also explaining how these natures are united into a single person, a degree of concurrence between the wills never present between a Christian and God.

The first aspect of the doctrine of the communication of idioms is to lay a foundation that ensures that whatever is said of Christ concerning his humanity and divinity neither confuses the two natures nor divides them. This is rooted in the Chalcedonian definition's claim that the natures are united without confusion or separation.[59] Monothelitism, wrote Chemnitz, "taught that all the attributes which are attributed to the person apply indiscriminately and equally to both natures."[60] This is one form of confusing the natures. For example, if we say that Jesus died and consider this an operation of the person of Christ, we do not sufficiently distinguish between the immortal divine nature and the mortal human nature. A second aspect of

---

58. Chemnitz, *The Two Natures of Christ*, 160.
59. "The Symbol of Chalcedon," 62–63.
60. Chemnitz, *The Two Natures in Christ*, 174.

the doctrine requires that we nevertheless insist that it is the same Jesus who was omniscient in his divinity and limited in knowledge in his humanity. From these two requirements emerges the doctrine of the communication of idioms, a doctrine with several parts.

Chemnitz distinguished between speaking in the concrete and speaking in the abstract. The communication of idioms allows us to attribute both divine and human properties and acts to the person of the Son in whom these natures are concrete, or in whom they subsist. When we speak in this manner, the words spoken indicate the person of the Son in whom the action is concrete, which is to say the person who does the actions. Chemnitz gave examples of where Scripture speaks in this manner. So we read that "the second man is from heaven" (1 Cor 5:17), though the Son's human nature was technically assumed during the virgin conception, and the Son who came down from heaven was not yet a man but only possessed the divine nature. Similarly, it is written that "God has redeemed the church with his own blood" (Acts 20:28), even though the divine nature is neither material nor in possession of blood that could be shed. In each of these instances, Chemnitz explained that speaking in this manner allows the natures to remain distinct while preserving their hypostatic unity in the person of the Son.[61] So when the Bible teaches that "You have killed the author of life" (Acts 3:15), the human nature that was killed is referenced as is the divine nature that authored life, but both can refer to the same subject or person in the concrete, communicating idioms from both natures to the same person. What is not allowed, Chemnitz insisted, is communicating attributes from one abstract nature to another without reference to the person in whom these attributes or actions subsist. So it is not permissible to claim in the abstract that "humanity is divinity," even though we can affirm that the Son is human and divine.[62] "Whatever things regarding human nature

---

61. Ibid., 174-76.

62. Treating the communication of idioms in the abstract is a challenging task that lies beyond the scope of this work. Chemnitz was cautious concerning speaking in the abstract, but Francis Turretin serves as one example of a theologian engaged in extensive Reformed/Lutheran debate concerning whether it is ever possible to communicate idioms in the abstract. Both sides of the debate affirmed communication in the concrete. Contemporary philosophical problems arise from the communication of idioms with respect to natures in the abstract as well, except in a different sense. The account I am offering here treats both natures as concrete in the person of the Son, but some accounts treat natures not as specific concrete realities, but rather as abstract sets of properties conjoined in the single person of the Son. In this case it is not immediately clear that communication of idioms *in concreto* is actually possible in a manner classically envisioned, where a nature is a concrete particular subsisting in the Son in such a manner that properties of that nature can be attributed to the Son, though they are distinct from properties of the other concrete particular nature. An abstract view of nature

are said to be taken only in the abstract, these are not predicated essentially (*uparxtixos*) of the hypostasis."[63]

Though speaking in the concrete provides a general rule here, there are still some things that, for reason of heresy, are not predicated of the Son in the concrete. So, for example, we would not say, "The Son of God did not exist from eternity," even though the human nature did not exist from eternity, and despite the fact that usually we can communicate any idiom spoken of the human nature to the person of the Son in which it concretely subsists. When a property of one nature cannot apply to the other, it is best to clarify our statement with a "distinguishing expression," whereby we clearly identify one nature. The Bible does this in numerous places, claiming that "Christ suffered *in the flesh*" (1 Pet 4:1), that "He was put to death *in the flesh*" (1 Pet 3:18), and was "descended from David *according to the flesh*" (Rom 1:3). Chemnitz saw each of these passages clarifying which particular nature was the one who completed an action appropriate to it.[64] While it is doubtful that the biblical authors had anything like a full-fledged doctrine of the communication of idioms in mind here, it is clear that this doctrine emerged, as most doctrines do, in an effort to synthesize broad patterns of language in Scripture and distill these patterns through second-order philosophical reflection using non-biblical terminology.

At this point, we can return to our example of Michael Jordan and Jane Austin. Recall that Maximus would claim that Jordan could shoot a three pointer or Austin write a novel based on their human nature and not their persons. The doctrine of the communication of idioms assumes something similar: natures are the sources of particular actions. However, all concrete natures subsist within a particular hypostasis or person that gives actual

---

treats each nature as a set of properties, but not discrete particulars. This results in the challenging task of explaining how apparently contradictory properties may exist in the Person of the Son as part of the same particular, not conjoined discrete particulars as the concrete view holds. It is not clear that the communication of idioms from two discrete and concrete natures to the same hypostasis in which they subsist can provide any assistance here. No less formidable philosophers than Alvin Plantinga and Michael Rea have developed philosophical explanations of an abstract view of two natures that do not draw on communication of idioms *in concreto*, but develop strategies that in Plantinga's case especially may serve as a form of communication in the abstract. But as Oliver Crisp demonstrates, both of these solutions entail monothelitism, which I have argued must be rejected on theological grounds. Therefore, I will limit myself to affirming only communication of idioms in the concrete for present purposes to avoid thorny historical and contemporary philosophical problems. Turretin, *Institutes*, XIII.8; Crisp, *Divinity and Humanity*, 50–61.

63. Chemnitz, *The Two Natures in Christ*, 174.

64. Ibid., 190. Similar verses are also cited in the Reformed tradition in a similar manner. For example, Calvin, *Institutes*, II.14.6.

existence and specificity to the nature. In other words, a human nature capable of writing a novel subsists in both Jane Austin and Michael Jordan, but the actual act of novel writing has been made concrete in Jane Austin on numerous occasions, but not in Michael Jordan, who has only written biographical content as far as I can tell. So we can speak of a particularly Austin-esque novel while still affirming that the act of writing emerges from Austin's human nature. This claim will be important when we turn to the question of eternal functional subordination below.

Thus far the doctrine of the communication of idioms provides rules for speaking of the single person of the Son who subsists in two natures, divine and human. One additional claim must be added to avoid implying that at one moment the Son acts as a human, and the next as divine. It is also necessary to show that the hypostatic unity of the natures is more than just a linguistic matter, but is rooted in ontology. Remember that Chemnitz saw a similar union between the two natures in Christ that we see between the Spirit and Christians in sanctification, a divine-human *koinonia*. The doctrine of the communication of idioms shows that, unlike the believer and the Spirit during sanctification, in the hypostatic union the actions of each nature are made concrete in the same subject—the Son. When a Christian is lead by the Spirit, the particular leading work of the Spirit is made concrete in the person of the Spirit, while any fruit of this leading is made concrete in the Christian. Despite this difference, there is a harmony between the divine and human natures in Christ that is similar to the harmony between the Spirit and the Christian. The harmony of the two natures in Christ is of a much greater magnitude than any current harmony between a Christian and the Spirit. Chemnitz summarized:

> For all of these works and blessing pertain to the person of Christ not according to either the divine or the human nature alone but according to both. And the person in carrying out these works possesses activities or operations in both natures and not only in one. These are not things which pertain to the duties and benefits accomplished in only one nature but in, with, and through both.[65]

The harmony of Christ's natures is therefore foundational for the unity of Christ's person, a claim that Chemnitz illustrated through the Son's mediatorial work. The author of Hebrews is clear that "Since therefore the children share in flesh and blood, he himself likewise partook of the same things, that through death he might destroy the one who has the power of death, that is, the devil" (Heb 2:14). Chemnitz understood this to illustrate

65. Ibid., 217.

that the Son assumed a human nature to be able to complete the human act of dying, which is only proper to flesh and blood. On the other hand, Chemnitz knew that the Bible suggests that to defeat death Jesus had to be divine. Here Chemnitz cited 2 Timothy 1:10, which indicates that death was abolished at the "appearing" of the Savior, a purpose established in grace "before the ages began" (1:9), a clear reference to the eternal divine nature. Chemnitz summarized as follows: "The human will in Christ desired, sought, willed, and approved that which Christ did by His divine power in His work, and thus His soul cooperated with conscious mind and conforming will."[66] Chemnitz claimed that the suffering and obedience unto death of redemption is a work of human nature (standing in contrast with those who speak of eternal submission), but this same act is also a defeat of sin's power and Satan, for example, and the defeat is a work of the divine nature. This is of course a very brief treatment of soteriology, which will be explored much more thoroughly next chapter.

What Chemnitz treated in terms of redemption is actually clear across the New Testament. For example, at various points in the Gospels Jesus heals—a divine act—in a manner that involves his human nature. So Jesus spits in the eyes of the blind man at Bethesda to heal him (Mark 8:23), touches the eyes of blind men outside of Jericho to heal them (Matt 20:34), and heals by touching the person injured or dead (Luke 7:14; 8:54). Chemnitz rightly saw such physical involvement—and even the act of speaking—as acts of the human nature cooperating with miraculous work of healing proper to the divine nature. "By deliberate council, he willed to show also his flesh as an organ of deity."[67] More examples could be provided, but the principle is now clear. Any act of the Son is an act accomplished "in, with, and through" each nature, in such a manner that the unity of the person of the Son is insured, while the diversity of the natures is kept intact. Each nature contributes what is proper to it, and when the divine or human natures complete an action proper to that nature, the other nature is not "idle," but wills and acts unitedly with the other nature. Thus, the doctrine of the communication of idioms reveals that we can speak in line with Scripture of the Son sleeping (Mark 4:38 and pars.), crying (John 11:35), being hungry (Mark 11:12), and learning (Luke 2:52) according to his human nature. Even so, we must recognize that the divine nature strengthened Christ in his human acts, such as in times of hunger and temptation during the forty days of fasting in the desert (Luke 4:1–13). The divine nature also ensured that Christ's human learning proceeded at an astonishing rate such that even as a

---

66. Ibid., 220–321.
67. Ibid., 219.

boy Christ amazed his listeners (Luke 2:47). It is worth noting that claiming in the context of dogmatic analysis (standards for popular piety were more lenient) that the Son submits to the Father in his person was historically treated as another example of insufficiently distinguishing the two natures, a violation of the communication of idioms.[68]

Dyothelite Christology and the Eternal Submission of the Son

Most theologians who accept the eternal submission of the Son appear to also affirm dyothelite Christology, but the compatibility of these views is unclear. For example, Wayne Grudem is quite explicit on the matter: "It seems necessary to say that Jesus had two distinct wills . . . and that the wills belong to the two distinct natures of Christ."[69] Yet, though Grudem treats will as a property of nature in his Christology, when he speaks of the Trinity he treats will as a personal property, for example claiming, "The Son is the one who carries out the will of the Father."[70] Bruce Ware insists that Jesus possesses "a full human nature,"[71] and he recognizes that this tradition originates with the Third Council of Constantinople.[72] Ware also follows the precedent of Maximus the Confessor to argue that Christ overcome temptation by virtue of a "perfect obedience"[73] accomplished through "all the resources given to him in his humanity."[74] However, though dyothelite Christology treats will as a property of nature, Ware is prone to cite P. T. Forsyth's claim that the Son has a "yielding will" and the Father an "exigent will,"[75] implying that will is a personal property and not a natural one. As we have seen, Ware explicitly treats will and/or submission as something pertaining to persons, not natures, when responding to the charge of Arianism.

Other theologians who affirm EFS also affirm dyothelite Christology, teaching that Christ possesses a human and divine will. Some recognize the historical claim that will is a property of nature. So Norman Geisler,[76]

---

68. See Agatho of Rome, "The Letter of Pope Agatho," 333; Chemnitz, "The Two Natures of Christ," 236; "The Symbol of Chalcedon," 62–63.
69. Grudem, *Systematic Theology*, 560.
70. Grudem, "Doctrinal Deviations," 41.
71. Ware, *The Man Christ Jesus*, 20.
72. Ibid., 75–76.
73. Ibid., 88.
74. Ibid., 84.
75. Ware, *Father, Son, and Spirit*, 81; cf. Ware, "Equal in Essence," 36.
76. Geisler, *Systematic Theology*, 290–91; Geisler and MacKenzie, *Roman Catholics*

Robert Letham,[77] and J. Scott Horrell[78] present contradictory christological and trinitarian theologies or ambiguous understandings of the divine will. Kyle Claunch is aware of the problem reconciling EFS with dyothelitism[79] to the extent that he will only minimally affirm that "the submission of Christ to the Father, per his human will, is the analogical expression of the immanent trinitarian *taxis* of the one eternal divine will."[80] He rejects language of eternal submission and authority as "too strong."[81] Instead, Claunch argues that "gender complementarity" is grounded in the immanent Trinity only "indirectly."[82]

Widespread affirmation of dyothelite Christology is a good thing, a trend to be expected from evangelical theologians trained in the tradition. However, it should be clear this affirmation does not fit easily with the common affirmation of EFS. As I have just demonstrated, many who speak of the Son's eternal submission use language that implies that the Father and Son have distinct wills, suggesting that will is a personal property, not a natural property. Since there is only a divine person who is the Son, this would mean there is no human will, and Christ would not be fully human. Second, the doctrine of the communication of idioms and the confession of the Third Council of Constantinople treat the natures as sources of actions that subsist in a person. However, the claim that the Son submits to the Father is expressed in a manner that often implies that the persons are

---

and Evangelicals, 73, 76.

77. Letham, "Reply," 343–44. Letham attemps to use Constantinople III in an argument against Giles, and he at times treats the property of will as a property of natures. Nevertheless, Letham defines submission as a "free action chosen willingly by the one who submits," though it is a choice still made in "the unity of his indivisible will." It is never explained how a will shared by all three persons is only used by the Son to willingly submit to the Father.

78. "We may say that there are both one mind and three minds, one will and three wills, as each [person] indwells the other." Horrell here succumbs to the very sort of metaphysical confusion that Maximus castigated. Horell, "Complementarian Trinitarianism," 355.

79. "In order for the Son to submit *willingly* to the *will* of the Father, the two must possess distinct wills. This way of understanding the immanent Trinity does run counter to the pro-Nicene tradition, as well as the medieval, Reformation, and post-Reformation Reformed traditions that grow from it. According to traditional trinitarian theology, the will is predicated of the one undivided divine essence so that there is only one divine will in the immanent Trinity." Claunch then notes that this is connected to dyothelite Christology, and for this reason he will not fully affirm eternal submission. Claunch, "God is the Head of Christ," 88–89.

80. Ibid., 93.

81. Ibid., 91.

82. Ibid., 93.

the source of the action, rather than that all operations or actions are in, with, and through each nature. This incompatibility between dyothelitism and EFS risks the full humanity of Jesus, the possibility of our sanctification in Christ, and the coherence of the christological doctrine developed at Chalcedon. In the face of these problems, few have explained how EFS is compatible with dyothelitism, and existing efforts do not clearly succeed.

Mike Ovey is the theologian who has most extensively addressed the compatibility of dyothelite Christology and the eternal submission of the Son. He summarizes his argument as follows:

> The objection to the Son's eternal subordination might be made that subordination is simply a category error because the Father, Son and Spirit share the same divine natural will, that is will at the level of their common nature (using "nature" in its technical trinitarian sense). In fact, this objection does not refute the point that at the level of personal relationship rather than nature, the Son is subordinate to the Father. This is attested in the prayer in Gethsemane, and is entailed by the Son's unity at the level of person, whereby, although he has two natural wills, they are not opposed to each other. Alternative arguments to the effect that the Son does not obey, or only obeys in the Incarnation both fail to deal with the Gethsemane prayer at the exegetical level and risk dividing the personal unity of the Son.[83]

Because Ovey's argument is the most extensive treatment of dyothelitism by an advocate of EFS, we must treat it in detail. Ovey begins by asserting that Maximus the Confessor argued that the natural will (a technical term for Maximus) was proper to Christ's human and divine natures, but that Maximus ensured the unity of these wills through the unity of the person of the Son. Ovey claims that Maximus distinguishes between natural will as the faculty allowing one to act, and the personal actualization of that will. Given this distinction, Ovey claims that EFS is compatible with Maximus's theology, for EFS does not posit a distinction of natural wills, but a distinction in the way that these wills are actualized.[84]

After distinguishing between a natural will and the personal actualization of a will, Ovey argues that he finds biblical support for his position in Matthew 26:36–46. When Jesus prays for the cup to pass from him, Ovey argues that three elements are present: a "reference to the Father wants/desires/plans/is able to do; a petition on that basis that the Cup pass by; a concluding, over-riding petition that the Father's will be done in preference

83. Ovey, *Your Will Be Done*, 101.
84. Ibid., 104–5.

to Jesus.'"⁸⁵ Ovey considers three possible interpretations of this prayer. First, when Jesus refers to his own will he might be referring only to his natural human will. Ovey rightly notes that this claim would need to be supplemented by a second or third interpretation to make sense of the Father's will, so he sidesteps significant analysis of this option. Second, when Maximus refers to the Father's will Jesus may refer to the shared divine natural will. Ovey objects to this on the grounds that the Gospel authors likely did not have something so precise in mind. Moreover, Matthew 26:39 (NRSV) depicts Jesus praying "not what I want but what you (singular) want." Ovey finds it difficult to reconcile the singular "you" with a reference to the natural will shared by three persons, claiming that this may reveal that the Gospel authors had something else in mind. Even more problematic, in Ovey's mind, is the idea of Christ's human nature submitting to his divine nature: "Submission and obedience seems necessarily to involve the will or desire of another which one prefers to one's own" [emphasis original].⁸⁶ Such otherness is only available at the level of persons, not natures, so Matthew must be referring to something relating to the person of the Father and the person of the Son. Ovey grants that it may be possible for "Jesus the Son to obey in his human nature" according to the natural will, but he dismisses this as "well on the way to Nestorianism." He asks, "In what sense, if Jesus the Son wills one thing in his natural human will and another in his divine natural will, is there a genuine, unified, integrated person?"⁸⁷ In fact, if the human nature was obeying the divine nature all within the single person of Christ, Ovey claims that this would be a conflict of wills undermining personal unity.

After rejecting an interpretation of Jesus's prayer for the cup to pass in the context of a human natural will submitting to a shared divine natural will, Ovey settles on a third option for interpreting the passage: Jesus's references may "be taken as a reference not to natural wills but to actualizations of will at the level of person."⁸⁸ To put it simply, "The reference to what each Person wills is to be taken within the context of personal relation rather than of the common nature/substance."⁸⁹ He insists that his "construal leaves intact the dyothelite theology advocated by Maximus and adopted at Constantinople III (680)."⁹⁰ Here, Ovey's defense is in line with the argu-

85. Ibid., 107.
86. Ibid., 110.
87. Ibid., 111.
88. Ibid., 108.
89. Ibid., 112.
90. Ibid.

ments of Bruce Ware and others considered in chapter 1: the submission of the Son to the Father is at the level of personhood, relation, and hypostasis, not at the level of nature, being, or essence. If Ovey's argument holds, then dyothelitism is quite compatible with EFS.

On closer examination, Ovey's argument is in fact riddled with problems, beginning with his claim that what he has presented is compatible with the dyothelitism of both Maximus and the Third Council of Constantinople. Recall how Maximus in fact disagrees with the Third Council of Constantinople in terms of how he treats the unity of the natural wills, as discussed above. The council teaches that unity is found as "each nature wills and works what is proper to it, in communion with the other."[91] This tradition was in continuity with the *Tome* of Leo canonized at the Council of Chalcedon, and it led to the development of the doctrine of communication of idioms which is explored above with reference to Martin Chemnitz. Ovey is not in fact reconciling EFS to the Third Council of Constantinople, but is at most siding with Maximus the Confessor against the Third Council of Constantinople. Of course, it may be the case that an ecumenical council is wrong, but it is important to be clear that EFS is not siding with the ecumenical councils here against a modern corruption of orthodoxy. The dyothelitism of Maximus is not quite the same as the dyothelitism of the council.

As it turns out, it is not even clear that Ovey is correctly using Maximus here. Rather strangely, Ovey does not cite a single primary source written by Maximus in his analysis of the Confessor, instead relying on a secondary treatment by Demetrios Bathrellos, who, as we noted above, admits a large debate surrounding how, precisely, Maximus treats the unity of the two divine wills.[92] Ovey fails to mention this debate, and instead treats Bathrellos' treatment of Maximus as definitive. What is even more puzzling, though, is that Ovey's summary of Maximus relies almost entirely on pages 74–75 of Bathrellos' *Byzantine Christ*, which is actually a discussion of Sergius' of Constantinople's thought (under the heading "Sergius of Constantinople") with occasional reference to Maximus.[93] So Ovey's demonstration of dyothelitism's compatibility with EFS neglects an important distinction and disagreement between Maximus and Constantinople III, disregards scholarly debate concerning how to interpret the unity of Christ in Maximus's thought, ignores all primary sources, and merely relies on parts of

---

91. "The Statement of Faith of the Third Council of Constantinople," 384.
92. Bathrellos, *Byzantine Christ*, 164.
93. Ibid., 74–75; cf. Ovey, *Your Will be Done*, 103–4.

secondary literature that do not even focus on Maximus. This is hardly a clear proof of Ovey's point.

The problems grow even larger, however, for when Maximus actually addressed the prayer at Gethsemane in *Opusculum 6*, for example, where Maximus first treated the Gethsemane passage, he did not agree with Ovey's interpretation of the passage.[94] In *Opusculum 6*, Maximus treated Christ's prayer at Gethsemane at great length, claiming that the prayer illustrates the "perfect harmony" (*sumphuia*) and "concurrence" (*sunneusis*) of the divine and human wills of Christ.[95] When Jesus prays, "Let not what I will, but what you will prevail" (Matt 26:39), Maximus took this to be "the ultimate concurrence of his human will with his divine will," arising from the wills and operations proper to each nature.[96] Maximus was clear that the "not what I will" portion of verse 39 cannot refer to the divinity, for the shared divine nature "excludes his willing something for himself separately from the Father." Maximus went on, "Since the Father and the Son always share a common will," the negation "not what I will" cannot refer to the divine natural will, for that would ascribe "that declining to [the Father and Son's] common and eternal divinity."[97] Instead, Maximus took the phrase "not what I will" to reveal "harmony between the human will of the Savior and the divine will shared by him and his Father." Simply put, Jesus "was calling on his God and Father in a human manner (*anthrōpoprepōs*)."[98] Though Maximus did not explain the personal unity of the Son here, and one wonders how he might combine his interpretation with his theory of the unity of the divine person, Maximus did offer an interpretation that is precisely what Ovey has rejected. Ovey finds no ally in Maximus the Confessor, especially given that, over time, Maximus' interpretations even more clearly highlighted that the Gethsemane prayer was an issue of *the human natural will submitting to the divine*.[99]

Very well, then. Neither Maximus nor the Third Council of Constantinople appears to agree with Ovey. This does not, of course, mean that Ovey is wrong with his interpretation of Matthew 26, so we must attend to his exegesis. Though Ovey makes much of the singular use of "you" in Matthew 26:39, he also admits that it would be an "anachronistic construction" to

---

94. Wilken, *Early Christian Thought*, 126–31.
95. Maximus the Confessor, *Opusculum 6*, 173.
96. Ibid., 174.
97. Ibid., 175.
98. Ibid., 176.
99. See the discussion in Blowers, *Maximus the Confessor*, 162–64.

interpret Matthew to refer to the "faculty of will arising in the nature."[100] This is certainly the case. As I have argued since the introduction, the doctrines we are considering are not immediately expressed in Scripture, but arise from an effort to synthesize the broad scriptural narrative using a second-order of language that seeks terminological clarity by which the various teachings of Scripture can be upheld. For centuries, Christian theologians have claimed that dyothelite Christology provides exactly this sort of second-order language when it interprets Matthew 26 to refer to Christ's human nature submitting to the divine will shared by the Father and the Son, even granting that the apostle Matthew himself likely did not have this in mind. This same tradition would agree with Ovey that submission requires an "other," though drawing on the doctrine of the communication of idioms, we would say that the Son submits to the Father *according to his human nature*. The person of the Son is the one in whom the operation is concrete, but lest we imply a division of wills in the Godhead, which Maximus treated as tantamount to Arianism (somewhat inaccurately using that title), we add the qualifying "according to his human nature." This theological rule was likely not envisioned by the apostle Matthew, but it allows us to uphold what Matthew says while also making sense of the broad pattern of Scripture that depicts a fully human and fully divine Messiah.

Michael Ovey's proposal that "Not what I will but what you will" refers to the personal actualization of the divine natural will in distinctive ways according to the personal relations is also an anachronistic construction that surely goes well beyond what the apostle Matthew would have understood. However, in this case the proposed interpretation does not result in a second-order of language that provides terminological clarity by which the various teachings of Scripture can be upheld. His proposal lacks terminological clarity because it is unclear how nature and person are distinguished if the classical connection between natures and operations is muddled by also attributing these operations to the persons.[101] This muddled nature is revealed when Ovey affirms dyothelitism and the single natural will of God, and yet claims that "in some sense there is a plurality of wills" in the

---

100. Ovey, *Your Will be Done*, 109.

101. It should be noted that Maximus allowed for a distinction of this sort for human beings, contrasting a natural will proper to each nature with a gnomic or deliberative will proper to the hypostasis or person. However, Maximus denied that the divine persons possess a gnomic will, for there is no need for God to deliberate on how to best use his faculties. Maximus thought that this follows from God's omniscience and omnibenevolence. At any rate, even if we disagree with Maximus here, Ovey does not provide a terminological distinction to help makes his case. Instead, his interpretation adds confusion. Hovorun, *Will, Action, and Freedom*, 134.

Godhead,[102] and insists that submission requires conforming "one's will to the will of another."[103] This is exactly the sort of terminological confusion that Maximus charged the monothelites of fostering when he accused them of crafting a quaternity, of reducing the Trinity to a monad, or of splitting the Trinity into three natures.[104] For Ovey, will (and if we follow this principle to its logical conclusion, all operations) appears to be a property both of nature and person, but this simply blurs the person/nature distinction and risks sacrificing trinitarian metaphysics.

Ovey's solution also does not allow us to affirm the broad patterns of Scripture. His claim that the Son submits to the Father in Gethsemane by "actualizing the same thing as a Person using two different faculties in two different natures." Ovey claims that such unity in actualizing natural wills is "so important if dyothelitism is not to degenerate into Nestorianism."[105] Similar claims are made by others who support EFS, who claim that if the two wills do not coincide or act identically the result is Nestorianism.[106] Consider his proposal in the context of another divine/human act: temptation. Applying Ovey's claims concerning Matthew 26 to Luke 4:1–13 (and pars.), where the Synoptic Gospels teach that Jesus was tempted in the desert, if we want to avoid Nestorianism, we cannot say that the human nature was tempted but the divine nature was not tempted. Rather, the person of the Son must actualize both the divine and human faculties in his single person. But this is impossible, for we know concerning the divine nature that God cannot be tempted (Jas 1:13). Ovey's explanation is not able to uphold both Luke 4 and James 1. Conversely, dyothelite theology—and here I refer to what I summarized in this chapter above, not to Ovey's inaccurate representation—is able to explain both Matthew 26 and the Luke 4/James

---

102. Ibid., 107.

103. Ibid., 110.

104. Maximus the Confessor, "Dispute at Bizya," §4; Maximus the Confessor, *Opuscule 3*, 195–96; Maximus, *Disputation*, §15.

105. Ovey, *Your Will be Done*, 112. Ovey is clear in his treatment that if one nature obeys, the other cannot not obey.

106. So Robert Letham writes that there must be something about the Son making it appropriate that he submit in human form, lest we fall into Nestorianism. The point is granted. Letham then makes the unwarranted jump to the conclusion that Constantinople entails that "the two wills, divine and human, nonetheless coincide. There is no discrepancy, as if one will worked against the other, or as if the human will obeyed and the divine will did not. Jesus would then be some kind of schizoid." Letham, *The Holy Trinity*, 394–96. Letham assumes the hypostatic union requires identical actions by both wills instead of merely cooperative actions that nevertheless remain distinct according to the appropriate differences in natures; cf. Fesko, *Trinity and the Covenant*, 179.

1 combination when coupled with the doctrine of the communication of idioms. Similar problems occur when we think of scriptural accounts of Jesus eating or drinking, for example. Did the divine nature digest the meals that Jesus ate? Of course not, but this need not entail Nestorianism.

As shown above, to avoid Nestorianism the two natures in Christ do not have to will and do the exact same thing; they merely need work in harmony, so that each act of the person of the Son is by, in, and through both the divine and human nature, with each nature working what is proper to it. When Jesus prays for the cup to pass from him, he submits in his human nature, but not in his divine nature—the single divine will prevents this. However, the divine nature contributes the strength proper to it so that the human nature is able to embody so perfect a submission. Similarly, when Jesus is tempted in the desert, it is only the human nature that is tempted, not the divine, for God cannot be tempted. Yet, the act of the Son is in, with, and through both natures, so the divine nature contributes again a grace that empowers the human nature to overcome such temptation. The Gospel authors allude to this in a less philosophically developed form when they note that Jesus was full of the Holy Spirit and was led into the desert by the Holy Spirit (Luke 4:1). Here we have the unity of persons preserved against Nestorianism, but we also avoid a confusion of natures found in miaphysitism, which Ovey's Christology tends toward.

To my knowledge, Michael Ovey's work represents the most extensive treatment of dyothelite Christology and the eternal submission of the Son published as of the time of my writing. However, Ovey's work actually does nothing to show that dyothelitism is in fact compatible with EFS. He argues against the Third Council of Constantinople and inadequately engages Maximus the Confessor such that it is not clear that he fully understands dyothelite Christology or the doctrine of the communication of idioms. Making submission a personal property referring to the personal actualization of a natural will, something akin to the mode of willing discussed in the previous chapter in reference to J. Scott Horrell, results in muddled metaphysics that appear to have problematic consequences for Christology. Claiming that the Father and Son have distinct wills, as other EFS advocates do, and as Ovey himself (mis?)states on occasion, implies that wills are a personal property, which undermines not only trinitarian metaphysics, but also the full humanity of Christ, and therefore the potential for the full sanctification of Christians. As it stands, it simply is not clear that EFS is compatible with dyothelitism, despite the continued affirmation of both dyothelite Christology and eternal submission by many evangelical theologians. There is a great rift between evangelical Christology and much evangelical trinitarian theology. A purportedly eternally submissive Son does not easily fit with "the one man's obedience" (Rom 5:19).

3

Obedient to the Point of Death
Christ's Obedience and the Doctrine of Salvation

"And being found in human form, he humbled himself by becoming obedient to the point of death, even death on a cross." (Phil 2:8)

"If it came not of him freely, it had not been satisfactory; for *satisfaction est redditio voluntaria*, it must be a voluntary payment; and as our disobedience was free, so must his satisfaction be."[1]

—Thomas Goodwin

THE DOCTRINE OF SALVATION is closely related to the question of the Son's obedience to the Father. As explored in the previous chapter, Paul teaches that "by the one man's obedience the many will be made righteous" (Rom 5:19). As systematic theology developed over the centuries, a consensus emerged that the obedience Jesus offered was a *human* obedience requiring a *human will*, which compels us to adopt a dyothelite Christology affirming two wills in Christ, each proper to a distinct nature. The claim that Jesus has a human will and a divine will proper to the human and divine nature creates a problem for those who teach the eternal submission of the Son. However, the problem only begins here, for the question of Christ's person and nature is intricately tied to the theology of Christ's saving work. After all, Paul speaks not only of one *man's* obedience, but of this obedience being the basis by which many will be made righteous.

---

1. Goodwin, *Christ the Mediator*, I.8.

The scriptural connection between Christ's obedience and our salvation is clear in several places across the New Testament.[2] In Philippians chapter 2, Paul teaches that "being found in human form" Christ Jesus "humbled himself by becoming obedient to the point of death, even death on a cross" (2:8). The connection between the Son's obedience and his sacrificial death is also made clear in Hebrews 10, where the author cites Psalm 40:7–8 to put the Psalmist's words in Jesus's mouth:

> "Sacrifices and offerings you have not desired, but a body you have prepared for me; in burnt offerings and in sin offerings you have taken no pleasure. Then I said, 'Behold, I have come to do your will, O God, as it is written of me in the scroll of the book.'" When he said above, 'You have neither desired nor taken pleasure in sacrifices and offerings and burnt offerings and sin offerings: (these are offered according to the law), then he added, "Behold, I have come to do your will." He does away with the first in order to establish the second. And by that will we have been sanctified through the offering of the body of Jesus Christ once for all. (Heb 10:5–10).

Notice that Christ's obedience to God's will is the basis of our salvation, the reason why we are no longer justified by the law but instead sanctified through the offering of Jesus Christ's body. In fact, Christ himself summarizes the reason he has come by pointing to his obedience when he taught that he has come to fulfill the requirements of the law and the prophets (Matt 5:17). This is so important to Christ, that when Peter tries to stop his willful death, Jesus proclaims in Mark 8:33, "Get behind me, Satan!"

The connection between the Son's obedience and salvation is clear in the New Testament, but it is not immediately obvious how this connection works. No single passage of Scripture answers all the theological questions that arise from this connection. Therefore, an important project of systematic theology has been the development of different theological theories that draw on the broad testimony of Scripture to help illuminate the several passages where the connection between obedience and salvation is made clear, though not exhaustively explained.

Given that obedience is central to soteriology and that obedience is the subject of heated debate centering on the question of the eternal submission of the Son, it is only reasonable to enquire as to how claims about God's will in the immanent Trinity relate to soteriology. If Christ's obedience is the

---

2. Actually, if one decides that the Greek phrase *pistis christou* means "the faithfulness of Christ" and not "faith in Christ," then there is a much more prevalent connection. I will leave aside more contentious exegetical debates for present purposes.

basis of our salvation, the current debate about the eternal submission of the Son compels us to explore whether this obedience is eternal or only a result of the incarnation. According to those who affirm EFS, the Son has submitted to the Father from eternity, and the submission of Jesus Christ following the incarnation is only a continuation of what has eternally been true.[3] The same Son who eternally submits to the Father carries this submission into the human life of Jesus of Nazareth and brings about salvation. However, this chapter will argue that the most important models of the atonement present in the history of Christianity in the West disagree with those who uphold EFS. Instead, the theologians who developed these models clearly taught that the obedience required for salvation was a human obedience proper to Christ's human nature. This obedience was voluntarily assumed in time by the Son, who was under no prior obligation to obey the Father in this manner, but who designed this plan for salvation in unity with the Father and the Holy Spirit by virtue of the one, shared will all three possess in the unity of the Godhead. As we will see, to abandon this position creates enormous problems for the doctrine of salvation as well as unintended ethical challenges for the common teaching of evangelicals on salvation.

Varieties of Atonement Theories

Throughout the church's history Christian theologians have attempted to explain the logic behind the atonement, alternately drawing on Scripture, reason, tradition, and experience to explain how Christ's death on the cross resulted in the salvation of those who repent and believe. It is a striking feature of Christian history that no ecumenical councils authoritatively declared one explanation orthodox, to the end that a wide range of theories have circulated throughout the centuries, each finding purchase in different contexts among Christians with different concerns and theological sensibilities. Before we consider the kind of obedience offered by the Son to the Father in the atonement, we must first sort through the various atonement theories on offer.

Broadly speaking, atonement theories fit into three categories: cosmic, revelatory, and transactional. Cosmic theories of the atonement emphasize Scripture passages[4] highlighting the fact that Jesus's death somehow transformed the cosmic order, redeeming the entirety of creation by overcoming the evil powers plaguing the created order. Perhaps the most well-known cosmic atonement theory is Gustaf Aulén's Christus Victor model, which

---

3. Ware, *Father, Son, and Holy Spirit*, 84.
4. For example Colossians 2:15 or 1 Corinthians 15:24–26.

centers the Son's victory over powers of evil such as sin, death, and the devil, with the end result that the created order is restored to communion with God.[5] Revelatory theories emphasize biblical accounts[6] of the Son coming to reveal something about God or humanity to the faithful. For example, Peter Abelard's moral exemplar theory emphasizes how Christ's death reveals the divine love that is the basis of our justification, and Hugo Grotius's governmental theory argues that the cross displays the justice of God that condemns sin.[7] While each of these perspectives rightly (and sometimes incompletely) points to aspects of the work Christ accomplished on the cross and resulting benefits to the faithful, the majority of Protestant theologians throughout history, and likely an even larger majority of evangelicals today, privilege a third variety: transactional theories.[8] Transactional theories emphasize the fact that Christ's death was part of some exchange or transaction between the Father and the Son. Because these models are so important to evangelical theology, and because they tend to focus on biblical themes of obedience more than other models, we must spend time to explain the two most prominent transactional models in greater detail.

Anselm of Canterbury and the Satisfaction Model of the Atonement

Anselm of Canterbury (1033–1109 AD) was the first theologian to use reason to consider the patterns of scriptural teaching on salvation in order to develop an extended treatment of soteriology through a transactional model of the atonement. His explanation of Christ's death has become known as satisfaction theory, which can be summarized (in Anselm's own words) in the following manner:

> No member of the human race except Christ ever gave to God, by dying, anything which that person was not at some time going to lose as a matter of necessity. Nor did anyone ever pay a debt to God which he did not owe. But Christ of his own accord gave to his Father what he was never going to lose as a matter of necessity, and he paid, on behalf of sinners, a debt which he did not owe.... He gave his life, so precious; no, his very self; he

---

5. Aulén, *Christus Victor*.
6. For example John 18:37 or 1 Peter 2:21.
7. Abailard, "Epistle to the Romans," 276–87; Grotius, *The Satisfaction of Christ*.
8. I am inclined to agree with Thomas Schreiner when he writes that, "penal substitution [one particularly influential transactional atonement model] is the heart and soul of God's work in Christ." Schreiner, "Penal Substitution View," 72.

gave his person—think of it—in all its greatness, in an act of his own, supremely great, volition.[9]

Because Christ paid this human debt that was not required, he repaid what was owed by humanity to God as a result of the fall and restored God's honor, satisfying the obligation of humanity before God. Now debt-free, humanity could have a restored relationship with God.

It is important to note that, just like Gregory of Nyssa who wrestled with the doctrine of the Trinity, or Maximus the Confessor who wrestled with the doctrine of Christ, Anselm was attempting to use reason to make sense of the broad scriptural testimony concerning the work of Christ on the cross. In one particularly exegetical passage early in his treatise, Anselm wrestled with various scriptural accounts of the Son's obedience to the Father. He explored Philippians 2:8–9's claim that the Son was obedient to the point of death, Christ's affirmation in John 6:38 that he did not come to do his own will, and Jesus's prayer in Matthew 26:42 that the cup may pass from him, but only according to the Father's will.[10] Anselm's theological explanation of these passages, and the satisfaction model of the atonement that emerges, is in many respects a brilliant product of Anselm's effort to understand how Scripture's testimony to the Son's obedience can result in both a gift to the Father by which we are saved and a corresponding theology of the divine will. As Katherine Sonderegger explains, "Obedience is a matter of the will; and when we have raised the topic of the will, human and divine, we have touched on the nerve center of [Anselm's] whole treatise."[11]

How, then, did Anselm explain the connection between the Son's obedience and our salvation? We can best understand Anselm's theology if we situate the discussion in the context of one of Christ's sayings in the Gospel of John:

> For this reason the Father loves me, because I lay down my life in order to take it up again. No one takes it from me, but I lay it down of my own accord. I have power to lay it down, and I have power to take it up again. I have received this command from my Father. (John 10:17–18 NRSV)

To affirm the logic of this passage, a transactional account of the atonement must make sense of three things. First, a transactional atonement model must explain why the "reason" for the Father's love is the Son laying down

---

9. Anselm of Canterbury, *Why God Became a Man*, II.18.

10. Ibid., I.8–9. Before considering these verses, Anselm's focus had been on dismantling the ransom theory of the atonement.

11. Sonderegger, "Anselm, *Defensor fidei*," 354.

his own life, and what precisely this idea means in relation to broad scriptural themes. Second, the atonement model must explain how the Son lays down his life of his own accord. Third, the atonement model must somehow balance the claim that the Son does this "of my own accord" with the claim that this is the "command" of the Father.[12]

I will consider Anselm's treatment of these three issues working backwards from the third. Anselm balanced the claim that the Son's death is of his own accord with the claim that it is according to the command of the Father by appealing to dyothelite Christology. In his other writings, Anselm followed the precedent established in early trinitarian theology and claims will is an attribute of nature. "In no way does any willing or power belong to the Father and the Son by reason of their proper characteristics themselves, that is fatherhood and sonship," wrote Anselm, "but by reason of the substance of the divine nature, which is common to them."[13] This belief, no doubt combined with his adherence to the Third Council of Constantinople,[14] led Anselm to conclude that with a divine will belonging to the divine nature, the Son eternally wills with the Father and the Holy Spirit that the Son die on the cross. With a human will belonging to his human nature the Son is obedient to the divine command. He interpreted the obedience expressed in passages like John 10:17–18, Philippians 2:8–9, and Matthew 26:42 in the following manner: "That particular *man*, Christ, owed this obedience to God his Father, *and his humanity owed it to his divinity* [emphasis added]."[15] When Christ speaks of obeying his Father's command, he speaks *according to his human will*. Dyothelite Christology serves as the first major presupposition of the satisfaction model of the atonement, balancing the Son's voluntary death with his obedience to the command of the Father.

Claiming that Christ's death was voluntary or of his own accord with respect to the divine nature and will is still too ambiguous. After all,

---

12. This is in fact a pressing task for the interpretation of the Gospel of John as a whole, as similar tension between Christ's obedience and his voluntary or self-initiated act is found in John 14:28, John 1:1–18, 5:1–47, and John 17. C. K. Barrett offers a helpful summary of possible solutions to this tension, though in the end he wrongly rejects the patristic position that is in line with Anselm's theology and the dyothelite Christology discussed in chapter 2. Barrett mistakenly associates his experience of personhood too closely with the personhood of Christ, forgetting that there can be a great disjuncture between mere humanity as possessed by created human persons and perfect humanity united with perfect divinity that is possessed by Christ. Barret, "Subordinationist Christology," 19–36.

13. Anselm, *On the Incarnation*, §2.

14. Given that this council is an ecumenical council, it is inconceivable that Anselm would reject its teachings given his historical milieu.

15. Anselm, *Why God Became a Man*, I.9.

theologians and philosophers throughout history have debated what it means to undertake a voluntary act. A voluntary act may be one that fits the desires of the one acting, or it may refer to something an agent does that could have been otherwise. In what sense, then, did Anselm address the voluntary nature of Christ's death according to his divinity? Anselm explained the voluntary nature of the Son's death by appealing to the idea of consequent necessity.[16] Anselm was clear that "you ought not to say that . . . [the Son] wished to die obligatorily."[17] As God, the Son was under no obligation to die, Anselm argued, for all necessity and obligation are subject to God's will. Thus, Anselm understood "voluntary" to mean not according to any obligation, or in his own words, not due to any "coercive or prohibitive necessity."[18] The Son did not will to die because he was under a necessity or obligation that logically or temporally preceded his will to die, thereby obligating him to will a certain thing. Rather, the Son willed to die, and consequently it was necessary that he die. This is consequent necessity: "It was for no reason that [Christ's atoning death and resurrection] were, other than that he willed it: if he had not so willed, they would not have been." Here Anselm cited John 10:18.[19]

We have now explored how Anselm provided two of three needed answers to the three issues central to a transactional theory of atonement. He balanced the Son's obedience and voluntary death by appealing to dyothelite Christology: as man, Jesus obeys, but as God he voluntarily dies. He explained the nature of Christ's voluntary death through the idea of consequent necessity: the Son's death is voluntary insofar as he is under no obligation to die, and the necessity of his death follows as a consequence of his willing it. How, then, does the non-obligatory death of the God-man result in our salvation? Or, to use John 10's language, how does this death result in the Father's love (10:17)? How is the Son laying down his life for the sheep (10:15)?

Anselm explained the connection between salvation and the Son's death through an idea typically called supererogatory gift—a gift above what is required. Anselm understood justice or righteousness to be a result of being right in heart and will, which he saw evident in Psalm 32:11—"Be glad in the Lord, and rejoice, O righteous, and shout for joy, all you upright in heart."[20] He drew on dyothelite Christology to show that Christ can live a

---

16. See Sonderegger, "Anselm, *Defensor fidei*," 354.
17. Anselm, *Why God Became a Man*, II.16.
18. Ibid., II.17.
19. Ibid.
20. Anselm here understood the parallelism between "O righteous" and "you

life of human righteousness on behalf of humanity, for human righteousness requires being right in human will.[21] However, the human that was obedient to the point of death (think Philippians 2!) is also divine, the eternal Son of God, second person of the Trinity. Because his life is divine life, voluntarily given not under obligation but according to consequent necessity, Anselm concluded, "this life is more loveable than sins are hateful."[22] Only such a supererogatory gift can result in the salvation of humanity, for every other human being already owes God everything, and is therefore incapable of offering to God anything beyond what every human being is already under obligation to give. Jesus Christ, as demonstrated in the notion of consequent necessity, was under no obligation to offer the divine life to God as a sacrifice. Therefore, his willing death brings such great honor to God that humanity is restored to right relationship with the Father, because through dyothelite Christology, this sacrifice also counts as a human offering, as human rectitude of the will.[23]

We can therefore see how Anselm's entire satisfaction theory of the atonement was centered around questions of the single divine will of God. Anselm developed scriptural patterns concerning the repayment of debts, the obedience of the Son, the voluntary death of the Son, and the love of the Father into a theological system that uses the philosophical concepts of dyothelite Christology, consequent necessity, and supererogatory gift to explain the connection between Christ's obedience and our salvation.

Reformed Theologians and the Penal Substitutionary Theory of the Atonement

By the time of the Reformation, Anselm's ideas were well known and had been modified in small ways in dozens of different formulations of the satisfaction theory of the atonement. With the rise of Reformed theology, beginning in particular with the work of John Calvin, a new transactional theory of the atonement developed now known as penal substitution theory. This model offered a corrective to Anselm by highlighting the fact that God's justice cannot allow sin to go unpunished, so a supererogatory gift alone is insufficient to accomplish the atonement. Therefore, Calvin also claimed

---

upright in heart" to provide a definition for righteousness. Anselm of Canterbury, *On Truth*, §12. See the helpful discussion in McGrath, "Rectitude," 205–7.

21. Anselm, *Why God Became a Man*, II.7.

22. Ibid., II.14.

23. Here Anselm's argument relied heavily on the unity of Christ's person. See Anselm, *Why God Became a Man*, II.19.

that, "Christ interposed, took the punishment upon himself, and bore what by the just judgment of God was impending over sinners."[24] Here Calvin stood on solid scriptural ground (i.e., 2 Cor 5:21; Gal 3:13; Isa 53:4–5, etc.). This corrective was usually not a replacement for Anselm's ideas concerning satisfaction, but rather a supplement to it.[25] In fact, Reformed theologians in the Reformation and Post-Reformation Scholastic eras retained Anselm's ideas concerning dyothelite Christology, consequent necessity, and the supererogatory gift while providing more solid scriptural foundations for each idea. They simply added a punitive element to what had previously only been a pecuniary atonement theory.

Reformed theologians consistently claimed that Christ's obedience was the basis for the justification of the Christian. So Zacharius Ursinus, an important early Reformed theologian and commentator on the *Heidelberg Catechism*, taught that Christ's obedience is the formal cause of our justification.[26] Several generations later, John Owen could write, "The righteousness of Christ (in his obedience and suffering for us) imputed unto believers, as they are united unto him by his Spirit, is that righteousness whereon they are justified before God."[27] The consistent connection between Christ's obedience and the justification of the sinner must be interpreted through the lens of dyothelite Christology, for it was Christ's human obedience under the law that counted as obedience for humanity. When John Calvin treated justification, he proceeded in the fashion of most Reformed theologians by saying, "If it is asked, in what way are we justified? Paul answers, by the obedience of Christ." However, immediately before this claim, Calvin argued that it is "certain that he performed all these things in his human nature." He explained that the Son's obedience was a human obedience rendered in "the form of a servant" (here Calvin alludes to Philippians 2:7).[28] Elsewhere, Calvin cited Galatians as proving the same point, for God sent the Son to be

---

24. Calvin, *Institutes*, II.16.2.

25. Robert Letham notes how Luther, Calvin, and key Reformed statements of faith all continue to utilize versions of Anselm's satisfaction theory. Letham, *The Work of Christ*, 165–66. There is, however, a noted exception to this pattern. Charles Hodge distinguished between vindicatory justice and commutative justice. For Hodge, it was not due to the commutative justice ("as paying a sum of money would be") but due to vindicatory justice "which renders necessary the punishment of sin" that brought about satisfaction. This is a deviation from the norm in Reformed theology, and a reduction of the fullness of the gospel to only a single aspect of divine justice. Charles Hodge, *Systematic Theology*, Vol. II., 495. This partly explains why defenders of EFS can find a champion in Hodge. For example see Grudem, *Systematic Theology*, 251.

26. Ursinus, *Commentary on the Heidelberg Catechism*, 330–31.

27. Owen, *Justification*, 208.

28. Calvin, *Institutes*, III.11.9.

"born of woman, born under the law, to redeem those who were under the law" (Gal 4:4–5). Calvin claimed that Christ "removed enmity between God and us ... by the whole course of his obedience," and interpreted Galatians 4 to indicate that the obedience toward deliverance began "from the moment when he assumed the form of a servant."[29] Why is this the case? Because only human beings are subject to the law, so only humans can obey the law and thereby fulfill the covenantal obligations of humanity, providing obedience that is the basis for our justification.[30] The Son was born of Mary so that he can obey the law as a human. As Christ himself taught, he came to fulfill the law (Matt 5:17). Here, Calvin was making dyothelite Christology central to his atonement model, using it to balance the obedience of Christ and the voluntary death of Christ in the exact same manner as Anselm.[31]

Reformed theologians were also widely in agreement that Christ's death must be "voluntary,"[32] a sentiment expressed in some Reformed confessions and catechisms as well.[33] Of course, words like "voluntary," "freely," and "willingly" could have a number of meanings, as I noted above. These words could indicate that Christ could have chosen to do otherwise. Perhaps they were meant to indicate that Christ's atoning death was one he desired to undertake. However, given the context, it is clear that words like "voluntary" were intended to indicate that Christ's obedience was neither obligatory nor antecedently necessary, but was instead self-assumed.[34] This

---

29. Ibid., II.16.5.

30. This was a widespread argument among Reformed theologians. Jonathan Edwards is a prime example. Edwards wrote, "For Christ merely as God was not capable either of that obedience or suffering that was needful. The divine nature is not capable of suffering, for it is impassable and infinitely above all suffering; neither is it capable of obedience to that law that was given to man." Edwards, *A History of the Work of Redemption*, 295; cf. Wollebius, *Compendium*, 107; Archibald Alexander Hodge, *The Atonement*, 199; Owen, *Justification*, 256.

31. Robert Peterson aptly summarizes Calvin's appeal to dyothelite Christology here: "If Christ's deity serves to emphasize the voluntary nature of His obedience, His humanity underlines the reality of that submission to the Father's will." Peterson, *Calvin's Doctrine of the Atonement*, 44.

32. Similar words such as "spontaneously," "freely," or "willingly" are often used. Calvin, *Institutes*, II.16.5; Heppe, *Reformed Dogmatics*, xviii.16; Archibald Alexander Hodge, *The Atonement*, 199; Wollebius, *Compendium*, 103; Turretin, *Institutes*, Vol. 2, XIV.13.16.

33. The Heidelberg Catechism teaches that Christ was "freely given unto us for complete redemption." The Westminster Confession of Faith claims, "This [mediatorial] office the Lord Jesus did most willingly undertake." Schaff, *The Heidelberg Catechism*, Q 18; Schaff, *The Westminster Confession*, VIII.3.

34. Besides examples discussed below, see Calvin, *Institutes*, II.12.1. Calvin rejected claims that the Son was mediator by absolute necessity, implying consequent necessity.

is clear from the fact that, though many Reformed theologians left terms like "voluntary" unexplained, those who did explain the use of this word and parallels deployed the same concepts as Anselm to explain satisfaction: consequent necessity and supererogatory gift.

Though many Reformed theologians only employed the notion of consequent necessity implicitly, some explicitly used language parallel to Anselm's own. Francis Turretin is one example of a theologian who understood Christ's voluntary death as a non-obligatory death rooted in the consequent necessity of the mutual decision by Father, Son, and Spirit that Christ atone for sins. He argued that Christ's obedience was a result of that "voluntary dispensation from the office of the Mediator and in virtue of an agreement entered into with the Father himself."[35] In other words, Christ was not subject to this obedience under an obligation, but was willingly obedient through the voluntary assumption of humanity according to the eternal agreement of the *pactum salutis,* the covenant of redemption. Like Anselm, Turretin believed the eternal agreement between the persons of the Trinity in the *pactum salutis* resulted in the consequent necessity of the incarnation of the Son ("the decree of God concerning the redemption of men being supposed").[36] In fact, Turretin was clear that the only thing God willed under antecedent necessity was his own existence. God could not but will his existence. God's other acts are free in the sense that they are willed spontaneously, meaning "without coaction," and with "the liberty of indifference" so that he could will otherwise. Therefore, the only way that God's voluntary acts are necessary is through "hypothetical necessity"—Turretin's equivalent for Anselm's term "consequent necessity"—where something follows necessarily on the supposition of God willing it.[37] Turretin was equally clear that the decrees arise from God's will, and that "the will of God . . . is nothing else than the essence itself willing."[38] (Here Turretin's theology followed the classical understanding of God's one will as a property of the divine essence, as discussed in chapter 1.) In other words, Turretin explained that the satisfaction provided by the Son was a result of a commitment that is only obligatory insofar as it is accepted by the Son through hypothetical necessity. Satisfaction was not a result of the Father imposing such a

---

35. Turretin, *Institutes*, XIV.13.15–16.

36. Ibid., XIII.3.14. In other words, the necessity is dependent upon a prior contingent condition.

37. Turretin, *Institutes*, Vol. 1, III.14.2–6.

38. Ibid., IV.1.7.

commitment on the Son, but rather because of the willing of the divine essence that simply is Father, Son, and Spirit.[39]

Other Reformed theologians offered a similar theology, incorporating some equivalent to consequent necessity to safeguard satisfaction. Zacharias Ursinus claimed that satisfaction depended on "a conditional necessity."[40] John Owen viewed the fundamental obligation to human obedience that Christ fulfills as being "necessary in this relative state" arising from "free acts of the will of God."[41] Drawing on Matthew 11:26, Psalm 115:3 and 135:6, William Ames interpreted the "good pleasure of God" as not only referring to God decreeing "saving good," but also to all of God's works.[42] God's single will shared by Father, Son, and Spirit[43] is "truly free" and "most free," meaning that "it wills not by necessity of nature, but by counsel,"[44] where such counsel involves purpose, plan, and agreement of the will.[45] When Ames taught that the Son's death was "voluntary and not compelled," citing John 10:17–18, he likely had in mind both the willing human obedience of the Son to the Father through the human nature, and the counsel of the Father, Son, and Spirit through the divine nature deriving from the agreement of divine will.[46] Though he does not explicitly use the technical terminology of consequent necessity, Herman Witsius explained at great length that the entire Trinity voluntarily adopted the covenant of grace in eternity and that the Son was under no "necessity" except for that of his own free will. However, once the covenant was made, God's trustworthiness ensured it must be fulfilled.[47]

There is equally strong evidence that Reformed theologians understood the obedience of the Son to result in salvation through a supererogatory gift. This is evident in Johannes Wollebius, who noted that Christ was obedient

39. Ibid., XVII.i.3.

40. Ursinus, *Commentary on the Heidelberg Catechism*, 81.

41. Owen, *Justification*, 240. Note that Owen repeatedly insisted that Jesus's obedience is only a human obedience. So where he did not explicitly connect the idea of relative necessity, his equivalent of consequent necessity, with satisfaction proper, he does treat the entire need for satisfaction as resulting from relative or consequent necessity.

42. Ames, *The Marrow of Theology*, VII.33, 37.

43. Ames affirmed both a single will in God, and that all operations *ad extra* proceed from the Father through the Son in the Spirit. Ibid., IV.58, IV.28.

44. Ibid., VII.34–35.

45. Ibid., VII.11.

46. Ibid., XXII.2. Ames affirmed the doctrine of communication of idioms explained in chapter 2. Ames saw a "communion or concurrence in the same operations, so that things are performed together by each nature but according to the distinct properties of each." Ibid., XVIII.21.

47. Witsius, II.3.21–25.

either for himself or in our place, before arguing that Christ certainly had no need to be obedient for himself. Therefore, his obedience counted in our stead. The logic here mirrors Anselm's: Christ rendered an obedience he need not give, a supererogatory obedience, that as our representative this obedience may be credited to us as righteousness. Citing Leviticus 18:5 and Luke 10:28, Wollebius claimed that life arises through Christ's obedience to the law because the reward for such obedience is life.[48] B. B. Warfield even more clearly relied on Anselm's notion of supererogatory gift. He argued that "the biblical doctrine of the sacrifice of Christ" is properly summarized "in no other construction" than one recognizing Christ's death "of intrinsic value ample for the expiation of our guilt." He explained that this doctrine "was first given scientific statement by Anselm."[49] Examples could be multiplied.

We have seen that Reformed treatments of penal substitution generally maintained the basic three aspects of Anselm's theology of the single divine will in atonement. Dyothelite Christology allows Reformed theologians to balance the fact that Christ was obedient with the fact that the Son voluntarily lays down his life. The voluntary nature of Christ's death is preserved through an appeal to consequent necessity (under various names, or even explained yet unnamed). Because Christ's obedience was a human obedience due to dyothelite Christology, it can count on our behalf. Because this was the obedience of the God-man, who as the second person of the Trinity was under no obligation to obey to the point of death, Christ's death counts a supererogatory gift to God, and his merit can count as our merit, the basis of Christian justification. These three ideas are the fundamental contours of the most important transactional atonement models in systematic theology.

Eternal Functional Subordination and the Problem of Satisfaction

I turn now to consider the theological consequences of claiming that the Son eternally submits to the Father on the models of the atonement considered above. To put the matter bluntly, EFS threatens to unravel the entirety of the theological system we have addressed in Anselm and Reformed theologians, putting dyothelite Christology at risk, eliminating the notion of consequent necessity for an antecedent necessity rooted in the Father's command, and thereby eliminating the possibility of a supererogatory gift being the foundation of the justification of Christians.

48. Wollebius, *Compendium*, 107.
49. Warfield, "Atonement," 278–79.

It is important to connect the christological concerns raised in chapter 2 with their significance for transactional atonement theories. Bruce Ware argues, "the Son's property of eternally submitting to the Father is a relational property that pertains to his distinctive personhood and *not to his essence* [emphasis added],"[50] and that this property is "strictly and *only* a personal property [emphasis added]."[51] We have seen that this claim works against traditional notions of both will and energies/activities as proper to natures, but now the full consequences of this shift from classical metaphysics becomes clear. If obedience and submission are only personal properties, and if the incarnate Son had a human nature but not a human person, then it is not possible for the incarnate Son to render a human obedience to God. This should be troubling to Ware, given that he writes elsewhere that Christ overcame temptation by virtue of a "perfect obedience"[52] accomplished through "all the resources given to him in his humanity."[53] Ware's Christology aligns well with the claim that Jesus's obedience and defeat of sin must have been human obedience and human sinlessness, but Ware's EFS doctrine of the Trinity does not.

Without human obedience, the entire notion of satisfaction found in both Anselm's model and the Reformed model of the atonement falls apart entirely. As Paul Dafydd Jones remarks,

> On one level, Anselm's dyothelitism is a necessary corollary of his belief that humanity ought to render obedience to God. Were God to impose obedience upon Christ—say, by coercively superintending the humanity that the Son assumes—the soteriological fabric of *Cur Deus Homo* would unravel. Only because Christ lives and dies humanly, offering a human "compensation" to God, are God and humanity set in right relationship.[54]

Dyothelite Christology is so important to Reformed notions of satisfaction that we actually see occasional arguments against EFS, even though the teaching that the Son eternally submits to the Father was not a prominent feature of theology during this period. "By undertaking to perform this obedience, in the human nature, in its proper time," Herman Witsius wrote, "the Son, as God, did no more subject himself to the Father, than the Father with respect to the Son, to the owing that reward of debt, which he promised

---

50. Ware, "A Denial of *Homoousios*?" 243.
51. Ibid., 244.
52. Ware, *The Man Jesus Christ*, 88.
53. Ibid., 84.
54. Jones, "Barth and Anselm," 267.

him a right to claim."[55] Witsius even more clearly stated that "the divine nature, as subsisting in the Son, could not truly and really be subject."[56] This follows logically from the long-held claim that God has a single will that is proper to the shared divine nature, the very thing that Ware rejects. It also safeguards the possibility that Christ die "for us" (Rom 5:8; 1 Cor 15:1–3; 1 John 3:16; 1 Pet 2:21, etc), something not easily explained if Jesus lacked human obedience.

Here two responses from those who affirm the eternal submission of the Son must be addressed. First, Michael Ovey offers an argument that is the exact opposite of the one developed above. He claims that in a situation where theologians claim the Son was only obedient in his humanity "questions arise as to how Jesus can be the righteous man through whom many are justified (Rom 5:19)." Questions certainly do arise, and I have spent considerable effort explaining how Anselm and Reformed theologians answered these questions by appealing to dyothelite Christology, consequent necessity, and supererogatory gift. Surprisingly, Ovey neglects these answers and instead argues that claiming Jesus was obedient in his humanity means "Jesus would not save by his obedience." He defends this claim by arguing that Jesus is not submitting to another if we have the shared natural will of Father and Son in mind. He adds the argument that if we posit two natural wills in God "actualizing incompatible things for himself in those two different natural faculties of will," then we lack a "genuine, unified, integrated person."[57]

Ovey's objections are serious ones, and this is why they are treated within the same traditions explored above. When Anselm addressed the incarnate Son's actions, he does so in line with the theology introduced in chapter 2—"this was the action of the man of whom we have spoken" but "*it may be said* that God did it, in view of the unity of his person [emphasis added]."[58] We also see this same pattern in the Reformed tradition. John Owen wrote that the "principle of operation"[59] in obedience is the human nature, but the "perfecting efficacy of them"[60] was in his person, who was the subject of the action.[61] The underlying principle here is that of the communication of idioms. (Note how Anselm provided a rule for speaking of God's actions, and recall that the traditional rule developed was the

---

55. Witsius, *Economy*, II.3.7.
56. Ibid., II.3.17.
57. Ovey, *Your Will Be Done*, 111.
58. Anselm, *Why God Became a Man*, II.19.
59. Owen also used the more technical term *energēmata*.
60. Owen also used the technical term *apotelesmata*.
61. Owen, *Justification*, 255.

communication of attributes). Nestorianism posited a human nature doing human acts apart from Christ's divinity. This is what Ovey fears in his objection. Monothelite Christology, on the other hand, posited that Jesus's actions arose indiscriminately from his divinity and humanity, with the great problems outlined in chapter 2. The theological tradition deemed orthodox chose a middle path: the divine and human natures remain distinct in their operations, against the monothelites. However the attributes and actions of a nature are communicated or attributed to a person in the concrete, against the Nestorians.[62] So when Christ in his humanity submits to the Father, this action that is proper to the human nature simply is the action of the Son by virtue of the communication of idioms. The action is possible because of the human nature, but the Son does the action. This action is offered to the Father, who does not have a human nature and who receives this obedience as given by another person (the Son) with a distinct will (Christ's human will).[63] As we have seen, in his confused treatment of dyothelite Christology, Ovey instead argues that Jesus "actualizes the same thing as a Person using two different faculties in two different natures," so that the Son obeys both as a human and as God.[64] This retains the monothelite intermingling of operations, wills, and natures that Maximus and others sought to overcome. Therefore, despite his protests, it is not clear how his theology resolves either the soteriological or christological questions surrounding the divine will.

A second objection that I have briefly addressed in chapters 1 and 2 could be raised here, namely, that "submission" or "functional subordination" could refer to a mode of willing while retaining wills as properties of natures. As previously indicated, chapter 4 will treat this question at great length in the context of the doctrine of God. However, one soteriological problem with this possibility should be mentioned here. In traditional versions of transactional atonement theories, human obedience is required for satisfaction. Supposing that obedience is a mode of willing proper to the persons, this still causes a theological challenge insofar as in Christ there is only a divine person, so it is not immediately clear how there could be human obedience. To my knowledge, no theologian supporting EFS has adequately treated that subject, though it is so central to the doctrine of salvation. I am willing to grant that there may be a solution to this problem, but its absence reflects the poor fit between current formulations of EFS and classical soteriology. Without this clarifying work, any appeal to "modes of

---

62. See the helpful summary in Chemnitz, *The Two Natures in Christ*, 173–75.

63. Dyothelite Christology clearly played a role here. If Christ did not obey in his humanity and human will, Ovey's objection might carry more weight.

64. Ovey, *Your Will be Done*, 112.

willing" faces the same problems as Bruce Ware's theology of submission as only a personal property.

Even if theologians affirming the eternal submission of the Son are able to integrate the idea of "submission" as a "mode of willing" into dyothelite Chrsitology, eternal submission creates far more significant problems in the areas of consequent necessity and supererogatory gift. Throughout *Why God became a Man*, Anselm took great pains to insist that "the Father did not force the Son to die against His will; nor did He permit Him to be put to death against His will. Instead, that man willingly underwent death in order to save men."[65] Indeed, "the requirement of obedience did not constrain Him, but His mighty wisdom disposed Him."[66] The reason Anselm insisted that Christ's obedience is not obligatory or due to eternal obedience is in order to preserve the notion of supererogatory gift. If the Father eternally commanded the Son to die, then the Son was eternally obligated to die. If this is the case, then Christ's death did not offer anything supererogatory to God, nor anything above what was required. Instead, when Christ died he gave to God precisely what was due: obedience. He did nothing to earn merit on our behalf for he obeyed for his own sake. This is why even a more contemporary Reformed theologian like Louis Berkhof can write that vicarious atonement is only possible under the condition "that the person enduring the penalty is not himself already indebted to justice, and does not owe all his services to the [divine] government."[67]

Theologians within the tradition are well aware of this problem. John Owen, for example, responded to an objection of the Socinians, who argued that, "What was necessary unto [Christ] himself, and done for himself, cannot be said to be done for us, so as to be imputed for us."[68] Owen granted that this is the case, claiming that if Christ obeyed "on the necessity of his condition," then there is "no foundation left to assert his merit upon."[69] Owen then proceeded to show that Christ was not obedient for himself for six reasons, three of which are particularly pertinent here. First, as the eternal Son of God, Christ was never "made under the law in his whole person, for the divine nature cannot be subjected to an outward work of its own," which is the law.[70] Second, though Christ is subject to the law in his humanity, he is only subject to this law voluntarily. Owen explicitly rejected the idea that obedi-

---

65. Anselm, *Why God Became a Man*, I.8.
66. Anselm of Canterbury, *A Meditation on Human Redemption*, 3:140.
67. Berkhof, *Systematic Theology*, 376.
68. Owen, *Justification*, 252.
69. Ibid., 253.
70. Ibid., 256.

ence "belongs to the necessary constitution of his person, with respect to his mediatory work."[71] And note here, is this not precisely what advocates of EFS commonly argue? When the so-called "role" of eternal submission is treated as the ontological basis for the constitution of the Son, then the obedience of the Son is indeed necessary and obligatory, and hence no longer an obedience for us as the basis of our salvation. Owen's third argument reiterates the basic point by arguing that the human nature of the Son does not need to be obedient to be glorified and brought into right relationship with God, for this glory is granted through the human nature's union with the person of the Son, whose glory does not depend upon any obedience. Indeed, Owen dismissed as "a Socinian fiction" the idea that "the first foundation of the glory of Christ was laid in his obedience."[72] Here again, in the context of soteriology, we see a clear Reformed objection to EFS.

In his discussion of the atonement in his widely read *Systematic Theology*, Wayne Grudem, a leading advocate of EFS, appears to be aware of the need for Christ's death to be voluntary and not obligatory. He writes:

> It might be argued that Christ had to live a life of perfect righteousness for his own sake, not for ours, before he could be a sinless sacrifice for us. But Jesus had no need to live a life of perfect obedience for his own sake—he had shared love and fellowship with the Father for all eternity and was in his own character eternally worthy of the Father's good pleasure and delight. He rather had to "fulfill all righteousness" for our sake; that is, for the sake of the people whom he was representing as their head. Unless he had done this for us, we would have no record of obedience by which we would merit God's favor and merit eternal life with him.[73]

When he speaks of atonement Grudem is quite clear: "Jesus had no need to live a life of perfect obedience for his own sake." How different this statement is from Grudem's own trinitarian claim, that "if we do not have economic subordination . . . we do not have the three distinct persons existing as Father, Son, and Holy Spirit for all eternity."[74] In other words, in Grudem's trinitarian

---

71. Ibid., 258.

72. Ibid., 259.

73. Grudem, *Systematic Theology*, 571. Other EFS defenders recognize the same truth. So Mike Ovey and his co-authors can write, "The principle of inseparable operation underlines that the Father and Son share a unity of will and purpose. Penal substitution does not imply that the Father is unwillingly coerced into an attitude of forgiveness, or that the Son is unwillingly coerced into offering himself." Jeffery, Ovey, and Sach, *Pierced for Our Transgressions*, 131–32.

74. Ibid., 251. I should note here that at the 2016 Annual Meeting of the Evangelical

theology the Son *did* have a need to live an eternal and perfect life of obedience for his own sake, for the sake of his own hypostatic existence. Notice as well that Grudem rightly recognizes here that Christ had to be obedient for our sake as the ground of our justification. Grudem rightly states the connection between Christ's obedience and our justification, but he fails to articulate the logic behind this connection with the rigor offered by Anselm and the Reformed theologians. There is no account of consequent necessity, and so Grudem apparently fails to recognize the inconsistency between soteriology and the Trinity present at the heart of his theology.

Consequent necessity is of central importance to transactional models of atonement insofar as it preserves the non-obligatory and voluntary death of Christ by claiming that the necessity of Christ's death is a consequence of and thus consequent to the shared eternal decision of Father, Son, and Spirit to send the Son to die for the salvation of the faithful.[75] As long as Christ's death is not fulfilling an obligation to the Father, it can count as a supererogatory gift, earning the merit which serves as the basis of our justification. However, when we posit (as advocates of EFS do) that in all divine acts the Son submits to the Father,[76] then the Son is obligated to obey according to an antecedent necessity—the command of the Father that obligates the Son to obey for his own sake.

The eternal submission of the Son simply does not fit with an atonement theory rooting our justification in the supererogatory obedience of Christ. EFS undermines the metaphysics of transactional atonement theories by putting Christ's human obedience in question through a rejection or distortion of dyothelite Christology. In so doing, it resists the best theological attempts to explain the biblical testimony that Christ's human obedience is the foundation of our salvation (i.e., Rom 5:19; Heb 10:5–10). Where EFS insists that the Son always acts in obedience to the Father, it undermines the logic of consequent necessity that safeguards the voluntary nature of the Son's death. EFS theologians tend to neglect John 10:17–18 altogether in their works, but when they do engage it they often read the passage in an

---

Theological Society, Grudem pledged to change this portion of his *Systematic Theology*, admitting for the first time that there is validity to the idea of eternal generation. However, given the vast quantity of books sold with Grudem's previous position, it is still important to respond to his arguments as written.

75. This is why Johannes Wollebius, for example, asserted that the efficient cause of the Son's mediatorial work was not the Father alone, but the entire Trinity. Wollebius, *Compendium*, 96.

76. For example, see Grudem, *Systematic Theology*, 250–51. Grudem treats the functional subordination of the Son as the basis for personal distinction, and based on the unchangeableness of God argues that these relationships do not change (i.e., in all things the Son submits).

imbalanced way, emphasizing the command of the Father without offering an adequate explanation for the fact that the Son lays down his life of his own accord.[77] Rejecting consequent necessity also undermines the traditional understanding of how the Son died *for us*, as widely attested to in the Scriptures (Rom 5:8; 1 Cor 15:1–3; 1 John 3:16; 1 Pet 2:21, etc.). Finally, if the Son was obligated to die, he did not offer a supererogatory gift to God. This eliminates the dominant explanation for satisfaction in transactional atonement theories, and with it the majority interpretation of scriptural passages claiming that Christ's death purchased our salvation (Mark 10:44; 1 Cor 7:23; 1 Pet 1:18–19, etc.). I cannot think of many theological claims that could disrupt the metaphysics of transactional atonement theories more than the claim that the Son eternally submits to the Father.

The Ethics of Atonement and EFS

Modern theologians frequently question the penal substitutionary model of the atonement for its ethical implications, something that bears on our current discussion of the eternal submission of the Son. Hans Boersma summarizes his own concerns in a manner that represents widely held views. "In Reformed scholasticism," the perspective on penal substitution discussed above, "the violence of the economy of exchange came to dominate the understanding of the cross."[78] As violence became so centralized, a number of problems purportedly emerged. Elizabeth Johnson calls for theologians to repudiate:

> ... an interpretation of the death of Jesus as required by God in repayment for sin. Today, such a view is virtually inseparable

---

77. For example, John Starke reads this passage and Augustine's interpretation of it as evidence that the Son is omnipotent, yet still eternally submissive. Starke, "Augustine," 165–66. While I do not believe that John intends this passage to explain the eternal relationship between the Father and Son, in terms of either obedience or a single shared operation, at least one feature of the text does push back against an EFS reading of this passage. As addressed extensively in chapter 1, John tends to speak of the Son doing nothing apart from the Father. Frequently this is expressed by an open denial that the Son does anything of his own accord (*ap' emautou*), as in John 5:30; 7:28; 8:28, 42; and 14:10. However, uniquely here in 10:18, Jesus claims that he lays down his life of his own accord (*ap' emautou*). This unique emphasis on the Son acting on his own fits well with Anselm's claim that the Son acts under no necessity but his own free choice. This language fits well with a non-obligatory atonement. On the uniqueness of John's wording here, see Westcott, *John*, 156.

78. Boersma, *Violence, Hospitality, and the Cross*, 170. Boersma is particularly concerned about the individualizing, de-historicizing, and juridicizing aspects of Reformed scholasticism.

from an underlying image of God as an angry, bloodthirsty, sadistic father, reflecting the very worst kind of male behavior.[79]

Johnson wholeheartedly rejects "Jesus' necessary passive victimization."[80] Summarizing Mary Daly, Darby Kathleen Ray voices a similar objection. "The qualities extolled in Jesus by traditional theology—such as obedience, selflessness, and sacrificial love—are those of a victim," Ray writes. She is adamant that we should not glorify these qualities in the context of a culture where women are so frequently victimized.[81] Gregory Boyd sees an "insurmountable difficulty" in any claim that God necessarily punishes, for "how are we to reconcile the idea that the Father needs to exact payment from or on behalf of his enemies with Jesus's teaching (and example) that we are to love unconditionally and forgive without demanding payment?"[82] Rosemary Radford Reuther argues that emphasizing submission, obedience, and unjust suffering encourages the suffering faced by abused women, "since by sweetly accepting unjust suffering they become Christlike," to quote Rosemary Radford Reuther. Here penal substitution is treated as a "tool for justifying domestic violence."[83]

I have claimed above that there is scriptural warrant for a penal dimension to the atonement. This alone is enough to require an evangelical defense of penal substitution. The question simply becomes what sort of defense should be made. Presumably, any defense would rely upon scriptural support for the doctrine, but theologians can supplement this support in one of two different ways, depending on whether they accept the eternal submission of the Son. For ease of understanding, I will call the first supplementary defense the "difference in roles" defense. This is the sort of defense that is found at the center of Bruce Ware's *Father, Son, and Holy Spirit*. Ware crafts his entire discussion of the Son's submission in eternity past as a response to those who "find the very notion of authority and submission objectionable."[84] Ware claims that submission and authority are central to the Godhead, arguing that a difference in role does not entail inferiority in nature of the one who submits, and that we must embrace submission joyfully.[85] This "difference in roles" defense could be used to suggest that submission to authority, as displayed by Christ on the cross, need not entail

79. Johnson, "Redeeming the Name of Christ," 124.
80. Ibid.
81. Ray, *Deceiving the Devil*, 58.
82. Boyd, "Christus Victor Response," 104.
83. Reuther, *Introducing Redemption*, 99.
84. Ware, *Father, Son, and Holy Spirit*, 77.
85. Ibid., 138.

inferiority, and so women and children who submit should be treated with dignity. Indeed, Ware is careful to state that those in authority should not be "heavy-handed, mean-spirited, harsh, and demanding in unloving and selfish ways."[86] From this standpoint, Christians can affirm the (eternal) submission of the Son to the point of death while simultaneously rejecting dehumanizing of women and children as well as any universal rejection of submission as leading to violence.

Before I comment on the success of such a strategy, let me outline a second possible defense. Those who reject EFS cannot use the "difference in roles" defense to argue that authority is not intrinsically bad, for they reject an eternal difference of roles in the Trinity.[87] Those who reject EFS instead can appeal to what I will call the "single will" defense, a strategy unavailable to advocates of eternal submission who must posit either three wills in the Trinity, or three modes of willing. This defense argues that a division in the divine will lies at the heart of claims that the penal substitution model leads to abuse.[88] Stephen Holmes deploys this defense in the following manner:

> The criticisms [against penal substitution as abuse] assume an improper separation between Father and Son (and no account of the Spirit, usually.) If we do not realize that God is on the cross, that God is taking the suffering on himself, then we have not begun to understand what is going on. . . . The story is not of a vengeful Father punishing an innocent Son, but of a loving and holy God, Father, Son and Spirit, bearing himself the pain of our failures.[89]

Elizabeth Johnson objects to "Jesus' necessary passive victimization" because it causes violence against women and children, but the theology of satisfaction I have outlined above does not easily fit her description. If Jesus shares the divine will with the Father, by which he voluntarily decided with a consequent necessity to die for humankind, he is not passive in his death but rather the active, voluntary agent of his death.[90] Nor is he victimized by someone in authority who commands his death, for he dies not due to

---

86. Ibid., 142.

87. As I will argue in chapter 4, this does not logically entail any stance about authority in the created order. Analyzing such authority would proceed from a doctrinal locus different from the Trinity.

88. Johnson, "Penal Substitution," 53.

89. Holmes, *The Wondrous Cross*, 109.

90. I should note here that Johnson may be using "passive" in an older sense referring to the sufferings of Christ. Though it is not perfectly clear in context, it seems more likely Johnson refers to "passive" in the sense of inactive.

obligation from an external command, but as a supererogatory gift to the Father of his own accord. Many theologians' critiques of penal substitution assume that the Father has a distinct will and operation with which he orders the Son to die, and the Son then chooses to accept this pain that is imposed upon him. This is a caricature of the transactional atonement theories outlined above, and the "single will" defense can easily point this out, simultaneously rejecting various forms of real victimization that are categorically different from the atonement.[91]

When evaluating these two defenses, it is important to recognize that the best forms of the modern objection to certain transactional theories of the atonement do not argue for a necessary and direct causal link between a penal substitutionary view of the atonement and violence against women and children. Leanne Van Dyk notes that the motivations of abusers are complicated and not easily explained in terms of their religious dimensions, but the testimonies of abused women do often suggest a religious component that may be linked to certain theological views.[92] While affirming penal substitution may not require men to deduce by logic that they should act violently toward their wives, for example, the thought world within which penal substitution is interpreted will have some impact on how images of the atonement effect assumptions about gender roles, ethics, and social norms. Therefore, the images behind each defense will be the primary focus of my analysis.

The "single will" defense can argue that penal substitution is not an image of child abuse or a violent and abusive power dynamic, but an image of self-sacrifice by an authority. In this case the Son voluntarily (according to consequent necessity) takes upon himself suffering and sacrifice, not because he is under obligation to any authority, but because he is offering a voluntary gift beyond what is expected or required. In light of this example of self-sacrifice, a pastor could speak against abusive dynamics by proclaiming that even in Christ's example suffering is not something we are obligated to do, and that in a marital relationship the individual in authority should be the one making sacrifices, not a person in a role of submission. This is only a provisional first step of a theological response to abuse, but such an image of self-sacrifice does not obviously support abusive power dynamics in relationships. Indeed, some theologians who voice concerns

---

91. So, for example, Shirley Guthrie uses this argument to reject any view of Jesus the loving God saving us from the angry Father God. "The doctrine of the Trinity means that the will and action of God the Son in our behalf are not opposed to the will and action of God the Father; they *are* the Father's will and action." Guthrie, *Christian Doctrine*, 84.

92. Van Dyk, "How Does Jesus Make a Difference?" 211 n. 17.

about violence in penal substitutionary models are even open to this image as potentially acceptable. For example, Sally Alsford notes that there can be a distinction between "self-sacrifice" of the weak as enabled by an overemphasis on penal substitution, and "self-giving." The latter "is genuinely a choice, and it presupposes prior possession of that which is given. Self-giving can then be an act of self-assertion." While "hesitant" to embrace this way of thinking, Alsford cautiously endorses it.[93] Similarly, though J. Denny Weaver considers penal substitution unsalvageable because of its emphasis on violence, he is willing to grant that appeals to the Trinity "may serve to mitigate" the problem.[94] The "single will" defense thus offers a potential defense against one modern objection[95] to penal substitution and creates fundamental images of the atonement that need not reinforce abuse when properly explained.

In the case of the "difference in roles" defense, the underlying images of the atonement may in fact reinforce abusive patterns. Let me illustrate by again addressing Ware's treatment. Once he explains the difference of roles, he further comments on the relationship between husbands and wives by appealing to Ephesians 5. Ware offers the normal complementarian interpretation of the passage,[96] interpreting it to support a wife's "glad-hearted and consistent submission" to her husband, as unto the Lord.[97] Husbands, Ephesians 5 teaches, are to love their wives "as Christ loved the church and gave himself up for her" (5:25), something Ware highlights for the reader. Notice the pattern here: in appealing to Ephesians 5 in this manner, Ware depicts the husband as an authority over his wife in a manner reflecting Christ's authority over the church. Christ sacrificed for the church and suffered for the church. Here (as in the case of the "single will" defense), the one in authority is the same one who sacrifices and suffers for the one in submission. Unfortunately, an appeal to eternal submission between Father and Son results in a very different image than does a complementarian appeal to Ephesians 5. When appealing to the Trinity as understood in EFS, the husband is compared to the Father and the Son to the wife. In this case the Father is in authority, but the submissive Son is the one who suffers

---

93. Alsford, "Sin and Atonement," 162–64.

94. Weaver, *Nonviolent Atonement*, 321.

95. Other objections, such as concerns about glorifying death in an inappropriate way, still require a different response.

96. Many egalitarians would interpret the passage to affirm mutual submission between husbands and wives, emphasizing verse 21. For present purposes, it is not necessary to decide whether the complementarian or egalitarian reading of Ephesians 5 is correct.

97. Ware, *Father, Son, and Holy Spirit*, 145.

and sacrifices. Applying this parallel to marital relationships conveys a very different meaning than a complementarian read of Ephesians 5 or the "single will" defense. Whereas in Ephesians 5 the one in authority is the one who sacrifices and suffers, in an appeal to eternal submission the one who submits is the one who sacrifices and suffers at the command of another.[98]

This shift in images is troubling for two reasons. First, this image seems to be the opposite of the normal scriptural depiction of Christian ethics. Jesus teaches an apocalyptic ethic where "the first will be last and the last first" (Mark 10:31 and pars.). He not only teaches this ethic, but he embodies it by voluntarily taking on death in the form of a servant—at least in traditional versions of transactional atonement theories as explained above. For EFS, the eternally submissive Son is never first, and so never forsakes his authority to become last. This can play out in gender ethics. Whereas egalitarianism and what may be called Ephesians 5 complementarianism can call on spouses who are in authority (whether male headship or shared authority is in mind) to sacrifice for the one they love, "differences in role" complementarianism and EFS both treat the one who is first commanding the subordinate to sacrifice as the norm of gender ethics. Where Philippians 2 teaches us to follow the example of Christ who forsook power to humble himself for the salvation of the powerless, EFS implicitly teaches the powerless to submit themselves to the powerful even to the point of death. In an ethical vision derived from the theology of EFS, the least of these are no longer served for Jesus's sake (Matt 25:34–40) but sacrificed in his imitation, and the power of God is no longer made evident in the weakness of self-humbling (2 Cor 12:9) but in the authority of one who can subdue the weak. We are left with a pastoral theology centering the authority of the Father over the Son, whose obedience does not clearly establish redemption under traditional transactional models. For EFS, the eternally submissive Son's death in weakness at the command of the authority of the Father alone erases the moral horizon within which penal substitution fits the biblical picture of the divine goodness. In short, the image implied in the way theologians appeal to the eternal submission of the Son often rejects the biblical picture of ethics.

The second problem that arises concerns ethical outcomes. While the "difference-in-roles" defense argues that the submission of the wife to the husband need not entail inferiority in nature, it is certainly easy to imagine

---

98. Ware seems unaware of the opposite nature of these defenses, and in his defense of the submission of wives he concludes his discussion of Ephesians 5 and the role of a husband by saying, "Just as there is rightful authority and submission in the Trinity, husbands must accept and embrace this God-given mandate to undertake leadership." Ibid., 141.

how a controlling metaphor of the husband/wife relationship that depicts the submissive party suffering and sacrificing could be a harmful metaphor in situations of spousal abuse. Moreover, in this case it is more difficult to respond to theologians who see penal substitution as an abusive relationship between a Father in authority and a Son in obedience. Such an offense would either have to grant that, yes, this is abusive, but at least the Father and Son remain equal in nature, or else it would have to argue that, no, a person in authority compelling a (functional) subordinate to suffer is not abusive. Neither response bodes well for the physical and emotional security of Christian women and children in a context where the "difference in roles" defense is deployed.

The argument I am making here is not that there are negative ethical consequences to EFS, and so it is wrong. For present purposes, I am setting aside any treatment of whether doctrines can be evaluated for their truth content based on their ethical outcomes. Instead, I argued earlier in the chapter that EFS is wrong on dogmatic grounds, and, even worse, I now suggest in this section that this false doctrine may have significant harmful consequences for Christian women. I hope that recognizing this will drive us to even greater urgency in rejecting any notion of the eternal submission of the Son.

Obedience unto Death, But Not Eternal Obedience

In this chapter, I have explored the connection between eternal functional subordination and soteriology. I have paid particular attention to transactional atonement theories. Anselm and the Reformed tradition developed specific answers to how it is that the Son's obedience resulted in salvation for the faithful. Dyothelite Christology ensures that the Son can offer human obedience for human obligations, and consequent necessity ensures that the Son's death is still voluntary. As a result, the Son's voluntary death on behalf of humanity serves as a supererogatory gift to the Father, one that merits Christian salvation. Anselm and Reformed theologians were not the first to highlight these theological themes,[99] but they do provide a more sophisti-

---

99. For example, Cyril of Alexandria, whose theology served as a precursor to dyothelite Christology, could write: "If he conquered as God, to us it is nothing; but if he conquered as man we conquered in Him. For he is to us the second Adam according to the Scriptures" (*Commentary on John*, 13.36). Anselm gave systematic voice to this impulse by showing how Christ could offer voluntary human obedience as a supererogatory gift. Wilken, *Early Christian Thought*, 121. To cite another example, Ephrem the Syrian offered a precursor to consequent necessity when he writes, "'Blessed is He Whom freedom crucified, when He permitted it." Ephrem the Syrian, *Ephrem the Syrian: Hymns*, 84. Examples could be multiplied.

cated systematic explanation of the many scriptural passages that connect the Son's obedience with salvation, or his death with a payment of human debt. I have shown that claiming the Son eternally submits to the Father threatens to undermine all of the elements that Anselm and his successors offered to explain the atonement. If one claims, as Bruce Ware does, that obedience is only a personal property, then it is not clear how Christ can offer human obedience, unless we reject the christological synthesis offered at Chalcedon and Constantinople III. Claiming that the Son always and eternally acts in obedience to the Father undermines consequent necessity and the voluntary nature of the Son's death. This in turn destroys the notion that Christ's death is a supererogatory gift to the Father. In short, EFS destroys the possibility of transactional atonement.[100] Here again, we see dramatic consequences for theology as a result of moving away from the claim that God has a single operation and will.

---

100. Of course, other varieties of atonement theory do not fare much better. It is not easy to see how the Son can serve as a human moral example without a human will or human obedience in revelatory models, for example. Many cosmic atonement models depend upon the Son assuming full humanity to redeem the entirety of human nature, which is again threatened when dyothelite Christology is undermined. Nevertheless, my focus remains on transactional atonement modes since these are so central to biblical pictures of salvation.

4

God's Good, Pleasing, and Perfect Will

The Doctrine of God and the Divine Will

"Do not be conformed to this age, but be transformed by the renewing of your mind, so that you may discern what is the good, pleasing, and perfect will of God." (Rom 12:2 CSB)

"We think of man's generation in one way; we surmise of the divine generation in another.... When it comes to the divine generation the mind rejects ... everything else which our argument contemplated as taking place in human generation; and he who enters on divine topics with no carnal conceptions will not fall down again to the level of any of those debasing thoughts, but seeks for one in keeping with the majesty of the thing to be expressed."[1]

—Gregory of Nyssa

WHEN THE BIBLE SPEAKS of the will of God, particular divine acts of willing, or any other divine operation, it does so in the context of a larger biblical account of God's nature. God reveals who God is through the historical acts God has taken on behalf of his people. God is known through his covenant with the family of Abraham, so he is "the God of Abraham, the God of Isaac, and the God of Jacob" (Exod 3:6). He is "the Lord your God, who brought you out of the land of Egypt" (Exod 20:2). God is "he who raised the Lord Jesus" (2 Cor 4:14). We also know who God is through the divine attri-

---

1. Gregory of Nyssa, *Against Eunomius*, I.39.

butes. God is immutable or unchanging (Mal 3:6, Jas 1:17). He is eternal (Ps 90:2), omnipresent (Jer 23:23-4, 1 Kgs 8:27), omnipotent and omniscient (Ps 147:5). Whenever theologians try to explain how the Father, Son, and Holy Spirit are one God, yet also eternally distinct from one another, they must explain these distinctions in a manner consistent with God's nature as revealed through redemptive history and in the divine attributes. In the context of the present debate, when we speak about the will of God and whether the Son eternally submits to the Father's will, we must always have in mind the fact that the Son is God. Therefore, any talk of the Son submitting or yielding in his will must fit with what we know about God elsewhere in the Bible. In other words, the question of whether the Son may submit cannot be answered in isolation from the Bible's teaching about who God is. God is good and perfect, and so we ought not be surprised to find language of God's "good, pleasing, and perfect will" (Rom 12:2).

Theologians who affirm EFS attempt to explain eternal submission in the context of who God has revealed himself to be in redemption history. Here many EFS advocates appeal to what is known as Rahner's rule, or the *grundaxiom*.[2] To simplify matters, this rule states that God eternally is what God has revealed himself to be in history.[3] Most EFS advocates who appeal to this concept seek to make a more nuanced connection than Rahner is sometimes interpreted to be making. Thus, Kyle Claunch denies that there is a "strict identification" between who God eternally is and how God is revealed in history. Rather, "the relationship between God's being and God's revelation is analogical."[4] Similarly, J. Scott Horrell writes, "Scripture's record of God's revelation in human history . . . should inform and control how we think about the eternal relations of the Godhead."[5] However, Horrell rejects "too narrow a correspondence."[6] On this softer account, the Son's submission in history reveals something about the eternal relationship between the Father and the Son, even if the historical manifestation of submission remains distinct from the eternal relationship.[7]

I grant that Rahner's rule applies such that the incarnate Son reveals to us certain truths about the immanent Trinity, yet I deny that Rahner's rule applies exhaustively such that all aspects of the life of Jesus Christ point to

2. See Rahner, *The Trinity*, 21–24.

3. LaCugna, *God for Us*, 212–21. LaCugna offers a brief survey of major figures in Catholic debates surrounding Rahner's rule. An exhaustive treatment of debates around Rahner's rule would be far more extensive.

4. Claunch, "God is the Head of Christ," 85–86.

5. Horrell, "The Eternal Son," 47.

6. Ibid., 73.

7. Ibid., 91.

eternal truths about the Trinity. For example, the incarnate Son's human acts of eating or sleeping teach us nothing about the trinitarian divine life. I have argued in previous chapters that it is better to interpret Christ's submission as a human submission performed in his human nature to offer a human obedience toward the satisfaction of human debt and obligations to God. As a human act, the incarnate Son's submission need not reveal any more about the eternal Father/Son relationship than does a human act like eating. My argument challenges the claim that these historical acts reveal anything about the eternal Father/Son relationship or the nature of God. This chapter, however, will pursue a different line of argumentation. I will grant for the sake of argument that the Son's submission on earth might reveal an eternal submission, and will turn to ask an important question: What would it even mean to say that the Son eternally submits to the Father? Few EFS theologians have done the careful work required to explain how the Son's earthly submission is different from the action these theologians speak of under the name of "eternal submission." Any explanation of the correlation between earthly and eternal submission would be quite challenging given classical explanations of the divine attributes.

When we consider the claim that the Son eternally submits in light of what we know about the divine attributes, it becomes clear that EFS conflicts with the doctrine of God. It is not at all clear how the Son can eternally submit given the fact that God is simple, eternal, omnipotent, omniscient, and immutable. In the context of such divine attributes, the word "submission" loses nearly all of its meaning. It is far more helpful, and more scripturally warranted, to use language of eternal generation and eternal procession to explain the eternal relationships between Father, Son, and Holy Spirit. Historically significant theologians have done a far better job at explaining what words such as generation mean and how they are compatible with the divine attributes than advocates of EFS have done to explain how the Son might eternally submit. Such clarity is particularly evident in the medieval scholastic and reformed orthodox scholastic eras. This chapter will demonstrate the incompatibility of EFS and the divine attributes by contrasting accounts of eternal generation offered in Thomas Aquinas and Francis Turretin with evangelical accounts of eternal submission, paying particular attention to how Aquinas, Turretin, and other scholastic theologians explain the divine attributes.

The Doctrine of Analogy: A Theological Foundation for the Doctrine of God

Before turning to the question of the divine processions and their relationship with the divine attributes, we must pause to consider what theologians are doing when they speak about God. There are three basic theories concerning how human language relates to the divine nature: univocity, equivocity, and analogy.[8] Aquinas and Turretin affirm the theory of analogy. The theory of univocity assumes that when theologians use words to describe God, they are able to use those words as if they bear the same meaning when said of God that they do when said of created reality. Of course, there will be a difference in magnitude so that God's strength, for example, is far greater than human strength, but a theologian who affirms univocity understands the word "strength" to retain the same fundamental meaning when said of God or of a human being. Aquinas quite clearly rejects the idea that it is possible to speak of God univocally.[9] Creatures cannot properly know what God's essence or being is, but only what it is not. This limit to human knowledge is rooted in the fact that God is infinite while we are finite, and that God's being is of a different sort than human being because it is not time-bound, material, or characterized by composition that would need to be explained by appeal to a higher Creator.[10] Because God is fundamentally different from creation, words have different meanings when used of God and of creation, for these words are not predicated of "the same mode of being."[11]

Where univocity assumes a fundamental similarity between God and the world, the theory of equivocity denies any similarity between God and the world. God is radically different from the world and stands in opposition to all of created reality as its Creator, so there is no common ground that would allow using the same words of both God and creation. Aquinas notes that in the theory of equivocity, identical words signify two things for which "There is no order or reference to one another."[12] The word "boxing," which can refer to placing something in a cardboard cube used to package things or to a combative athletic event, illustrates an equivocal use of words. The athletic event and act of packaging are named with the same word, but (to my knowledge) there is no underlying relationship or connection between them. Aquinas rejects the theory of equivocity because words used

---

8. Each of these possibilities may be further subdivided into additional theories.
9. Aquinas, *Summa Theologica*, PP Q13 A5.
10. Gilson, *Philosophy of St. Thomas*, 108.
11. Aquinas, *Summa Contra Gentiles*, I.32.3.
12. Ibid., I.33.2.

in common between God and creatures are not said based on an order or relationship, which equivocity denies. Rather, we speak on the basis of a correlation between a cause and an effect.[13] Furthermore, a pure theory of equivocation would prevent any creaturely knowledge of God, but Aquinas cites Romans 1:20 to argue that some knowledge is possible, so there must be some correlation between creation and Creator.[14]

Aquinas affirms a theory of analogy based on the causal relationship between God and creation. He writes, "Whatever is said of God and creatures, is said according to the relation of a creature to God as its principle and cause, wherein all perfections of things pre-exist excellently." Aquinas admits that this analogy is imperfect,[15] and he insists that all names of God are predicated first and most truly of God, and only secondarily in terms of created realities. In other words, God is more truly Father than are human fathers.[16] There is much dispute over how precisely the analogy between God and creation works, but at a minimum it seems we must affirm that this doctrine relates both to the logic necessary for accurate theological speaking and to the underlying relationship between created beings and the Being of God.[17] The Thomist view of analogy thus requires two things. First, when speaking of God we must recognize that our words bear a different yet related meaning when used of God as they do when used of created realities. Second, we ought to recognize an underlying connection between created beings and God, such that all properties that beings have are theirs only insofar as they participate analogically in what is more properly God's. Thomas's views have had a lasting impact on the Roman Catholic Church. The Fourth Lateran Council in 1215 affirmed the doctrine of analogy, and Pope Leo XIII's papal encyclical *Aeterni Patris* endorsed Aquinas (and hence analogy) as exemplary of Christian theology.[18]

Francis Turretin affirms a version of the doctrine of analogy, though it plays a lesser role in his theology. An exemplar of the Reformed Scholastic

13. See the concise summary in Wippel, "Metaphysics," 116–17.

14. Aquinas, *Summa Theologica*, PP Q13 A5; cf. Aquinas, *Summa Contra Gentiles*, I.33.5.

15. Aquinas, *Suma Theologica*, PP Q13 A5.

16. Ibid., PP Q13 A6.

17. Hütter, *Dust Bound for Heaven*, 354. Hütter helpfully distinguished between predicamental analogy, which governs theological language and is rooted in Aristotle, from transcendental analogy, which concerns the participation of created beings in God as the basis for their existence and properties, an idea more Platonic in nature.

18. Denzinger, *The Sources of Catholic Dogma*, 171. Admittedly, aspects of the participatory aspect of analogy met some resistance shortly after Thomas's life in the form of the condemnations of 1277. The ultimate victory went to Aquinas. See Pabst, *Metaphysics*, 273–77.

tradition,[19] Turretin's reticence may predict the wider skepticism among later and particularly modern Reformed theologians toward the idea of an analogy between God and creatures rooted in the relationship between cause and effect.[20] Often Reformed theologians, and especially those of a Neo-Orthodox orientation, object to establishing any necessary condition for God-talk (including analogy) apart from consideration of the content of revelation. Therefore, when affirming any analogical limits to theological language, they speak of an analogy of faith. This approach is ultimately compatible with the Thomist alternative in its broad strokes, and the details need not detain us here.[21] Turretin himself does not address these eventual concerns, rather affirming a doctrine of analogy derived from "way of eminence or causality."[22] The way of eminence claims that any good attribute in creation can be predicated of God once sufficiently purified and amplified. The way of causality, previously deployed by Aquinas, seeks to understand God's attributes on the basis of creation because effects resemble their causes. Turretin affirms analogy "of similitude," meaning that there is some likeness between God and creation. It is also "of attribution," meaning that words can be said of both God and creation, but they are primarily and preeminently said of God and only secondarily of creatures.[23] Citing 2 Peter 1:4, Turretin also affirms that creatures participate analogically in the being of God, not by sharing in the essence of God, but rather according to God's will and through his work by producing creaturely effects and works similar in form to those of God.[24]

The doctrine of analogy is a seemingly abstract and obscure doctrine that has a significant practical implication for the debate surrounding the eternal submission of the Son. If words are used in an analogical sense when speaking of the Godhead, then theologians can clarify any statement by paying attention to the analogy. Any word predicated of God possesses a meaning both similar and dissimilar from the meaning normally associated with that word when used of created reality. To illustrate with a simple example, when calling God powerful theologians intend to describe the fact that God has more expansive capabilities than he would were he

---

19. It is important to recognize diversity in trinitarian thought among Reformed Scholastics, just as among Roman Catholic theologians. Despite this, there is a more fundamental unity.

20. This reticence is most clearly expressed in Karl Barth, who rejected the *analogia entis* as a creation of the anti-Christ. Barth, *Church Dogmatics* I/1, 10.

21. See Alan J. Torrance, *Persons in Communion*, 149–50, 162–67.

22. Turretin, *Principles of Elenctic Theology*, Vol. 1, VI.7.2.

23. Ibid., VI.7.4.

24. Ibid., VI.7.1, 5.

not powerful. The word powerful conveys a similar meaning when used of created reality. A powerful truck, for example, can pull more than a truck with less power. However, there are also a number of differences between a powerful truck and our powerful God. One difference is that the power of a truck depends upon certain material configurations—a strong engine and chassis, for example. God's power has no material basis. The concept of power could be further clarified, but the practical implication of analogy should now be clear. Any claim that the Son eternally submits to the Father is subject to the same analogical task, such that theologians ought to be able to explain how this submission is different from any created submission. Without a sufficiently clear explanation, using the language of "submission" to speak of God remains questionable at best.

Many EFS advocates openly accept a version of the doctrine of analogy, but they fail to explain adequately how the word "submission" functions when used of God. Wayne Grudem is quite clear on the matter: "The names 'Father' and 'Son' are not 'univocal.' . . . Yet the names 'father' and 'son' [sic] must mean *something* when applied to God. In other words, the names 'Father' and 'Son' must be *analogous* to *some* human experiences of being a father and being a son."[25] J. Scott Horrell, Kyle Claunch, Norman Geisler, Tom Smail, and John Frame all openly accept the doctrine of analogy.[26] Others implicitly accept the doctrine of analogy by rightly explaining it without critique when discussing historical theology, yet without a clear endorsement.[27] I know of no EFS supporter who explicitly rejects analogy. Such widespread support should be no surprise given the fact that an analogical view (in various forms) has been prevalent among theologians since the patristic era.[28] What is surprising, however, is how little time theologians who accept EFS spend explaining what exactly it would mean for the Son to submit eternally and how this submission differs from the submission

---

25. Grudem, "Biblical Evidence," 227.

26. Horrell, "Complementarian Trinitarianism," 342; Claunch, "God is the Head of Christ," 85–86; Geisler, *Systematic Theology,* 22. Smail does not directly use the terminology of analogy, but affirms that humans bearing the image of God means that "the massive difference between Creator and creature remains, but within that difference there is a similarity which the one bestows on the other in the act of creation." In its essence, this is the doctrine of analogy. Smail, *Like Father, Like Son,* 47. John Frame provides the briefest possible treatment in his massive *Systematic Theology,* merely noting that words like love are only analogous in meaning when used of God and humans. Frame, *Systematic Theology,* 232.

27. Letham, *The Holy Trinity,* 136–37.

28. For example Athanasius adopted a theology of the symbols applied to Christ such as wisdom that required acknowledging both similarity and dissimilarity between how these words are used of created reality and of God. Anatolios, *Retrieving Nicaea,* 113

found among created human beings. This stands in stark contrast with the precision found in earlier forms of speaking about the divine persons using the language of generation and procession.

Eternal Procession in Thomas Aquinas and Francis Turretin

Aquinas and Turretin put forward different explanations of the divine processions that are the basis for the eternal distinction between the Father and the Son, but both shared a similar methodological commitment. Each sought to explain eternal generation in contrast with mere human generation of a child. Each also sought to clarify the analogical relationship between human and eternal generation by referring to the divine attributes. The relationship between the divine attributes and eternal generation is clear in Thomas Aquinas's *Summa Theologica*, a text whose theology of God and the divine attributes is later used, in the words of D. Stephen Long, to "norm trinitarian language to avoid speaking poorly of God."[29] Among Reformed Scholastics, including Turretin, the connection between the divine attributes and eternal generation was the basis for the typical Reformed application of the way of negation to the divine processions. Reformed theologians negated all ideas of change, time, division, materiality, and imperfection when speaking of eternal generation to relate this divine generation to human generation analogically.[30] Such negation was grounded in a particular understanding of the divine attributes. The particular account of eternal generation offered by Aquinas and Turretin will establish a model for how any account of eternal submission would need to unfold.

Aquinas treated the eternal action of the divine processions as the basis for differentiating the persons of the Father, Son, and Spirit, so he had to offer an account of eternal generation and eternal spiration that clearly allowed for a distinction between Son and Holy Spirit.[31] To establish such a distinction, Aquinas drew on a psychological analogy in the tradition of Augustine of Hippo. Matthew Levering summarizes Aquinas well: "The Son's proper mode of procession is as 'Word' and thus as 'Image' (by way of likeness), whereas the Spirit's proper mode of procession is as 'Love' and

---

29. Long, *Triune God*, 48.
30. Muller, *Reformed Dogmatics*, Vol. 4, 287.
31. Emery, *Trinitarian Theology of St. Thomas Aquinas*, 55. Though Aquinas pursues different arguments and deploys different sources and formats in the *Summa Theologica* and the *Summa Contra Gentiles*, the basic steps of his argument are the same. Both texts begin with the divine processions.

thus as 'Gift' (by way of imprint)."[32] This explanation provided a way of distinguishing the persons, but it is important to recognize that it does not indicate any form of subordination or submission.[33]

When Aquinas affirmed that processions do exist in God, he recognized that such a claim seemed to be contrary to what he had established concerning God's divine attributes in the preceding treatise *de Deo Uno*, but he explained how divine processions are dissimilar from created processions to justify the ancient teaching concerning the Trinity. It would seem that procession could not occur in God because it suggests diversity where God is simple. Such procession also appears to challenge the infinite nature of God because it seems to entail movement outside of God, but what can move beyond the limits of an infinite being? Aquinas explained that procession is not an outward procession but an inward one, analogous to "a conception issuing from our intellectual power."[34] Just as a thought proceeds from the mind while remaining internal to the mind, so too, in an analogous way the Son proceeds from the Father without being external to God.[35] Divine procession is therefore akin to "an intelligible emanation," an inward procession that does not require diversity and so is compatible with divine simplicity and the infinite essence of God.[36] Aquinas noted that it may seem that procession in God would also jeopardize divine monarchy, the notion that God is the source and explanation of all things. If God proceeds from something, it would seem that there must be some explanation for God that is not God. However, an inward procession does not jeopardize divine monarchy because an inward procession does not require a source beyond that thing itself. In this case, God the Father is the principle of the Son and Holy Spirit, so there is no principle outside of God and divine monarchy is preserved.

Turning to the specific procession of the Son, Aquinas explained that eternal generation relates to created generation analogically. This fact allowed Aquinas to explain the generation of the Son in a manner that is compatible with the divine attributes. Generation among created things entails a shift from non-existence to existence in a manner that the proceeding thing has the likeness of the one from which it proceeds. When a human child

32. Levering, *Doctrine of the Holy Spirit*, 107.

33. Ibid.

34. Aquinas, *Summa Theologica*, PP Q27 A1.

35. Emery, *Trinitarian Theology of St. Thomas Aquinas*, 55. Here Aquinas draws on an Aristotelian distinction between a transitive action whose term is outside a subject, and an immanent action whose term is within the subject. Divine procession is an immanent action.

36. Aquinas, *Summa Theologica*, PP Q27 A1.

is generated, for example, it comes from non-existence into existence and bears the likeness of its parents. Aquinas explained that eternal generation includes the notion of similitude, but not of a move into existence from non-existence. In this way, eternal generation is compatible with the eternal and self-subsistent nature of God.[37]

Aquinas next explained how eternal generation differs from the procession of the Holy Spirit. Following precedent set by Augustine of Hippo, Aquinas again appealed to the analogy of a human mind. Where the Son proceeds by way of likeness as a procession of the intellect as Word, the Holy Spirit proceeds by way of imprint as a procession of the divine will as Love.[38] This distinction is shaped by scriptural terminology. It is fitting to argue that the Son who is eternal Word of God (John 1:1–18) proceeds as a procession of the intellect, while the Spirit who is the love of God proceeds from the will. In the *Summa Contra Gentiles*, Aquinas drew on a number of scriptural passages to justify connecting the Spirit with the love of God (for example Rom 8:14; 2 Cor 5:14; Rom 5:5, and 1 John 4:10).[39] Though he interpreted these passages in a different manner from many modern exegetes, he was in line with earlier interpretations, notably Augustine's.[40]

While critics may believe that this account relies only on Aristotelian psychology, Aquinas actually based this analogy in broad scriptural patterns.[41] Jesus himself claims that he proceeded from the Father in the incarnation (John 8:42), and several texts read as prophetically applying to the Son also speak of eternal begetting or generation (Ps 2:7; Prov. 8:24).[42] Here Rahner's rule would seem to apply: the fact that the Son proceeds from the Father in the incarnation reveals an eternal procession. If Aquinas only

---

37. Aquinas, *Summa Theologica*, PP Q27 A2.

38. Ibid., PP Q27 A4.

39. Aquinas, *Summa Contra Gentiles*, IV.19.11, IV.21.1–3.

40. Levering, *Doctrine of the Holy Spirit*, 55–67. Augustine interprets 1 John 4:8's claim that "God is love" in light of 1 John 4:7–8 teaching that love is also from God. Something that is God of God is either the Holy Spirit or the Son. Augustine favors the interpretation that the Spirit is the love which is God of God in light of 1 John 4:10–13's teaching that if we love, God abides in us, and that if we love God has given us his Spirit.

41. Davies, *Thought of Thomas Aquinas*, 196–97. John 1 appears to influence Aquinas more than Aristotelian psychology. In his commentary on Boethius's *De Trinitate* I.4, Aquinas notes that in a simple God such psychology would not require intellect and the object of the intellect to be a real distinction, but in the psychological analogy Aquinas pushes against this psychology and affirms a real distinction between the Father as intellect and Son as object of the intellect on the basis of scriptural accounts to a real distinction.

42. Aquinas, *Summa Theologica*, PP Q27 A2. For a recent analysis of the use of Proverbs 8:24 in trinitarian theology see Emerson, "Role of Proverbs 8."

briefly treated Scripture in his account of the processions in the *Summa Theologica*, this was more a result of genre than any neglect of Scripture.[43] In fact, Aquinas's commentary on John offers a similar account of the Trinity with an exhaustive exegetical foundation.[44] Similarly, the *Summa Contra Gentiles* begins with a survey of biblical texts implying that there is eternal generation in God. Aquinas also believed that such generation follows from the names "Father" and "Son."[45] Even in the *Summa Theologica*, Thomas still treated the Bible as the most important source for the development of his trinitarian theology above any other author from the tradition.[46] It is clear that the Thomistic account of eternal generation is a second-order reflection on the broad pattern of Scripture, an attempt to clarify using reason patterns present in the biblical text.[47] In this case, the clarification carefully explains generation as analogous to human generation because it establishes difference and likeness between the Father and Son. Eternal generation is different from human generation in order to be compatible with divine monarchy, simplicity, infinity, and eternality as well as the self-subsistence of God.

Francis Turretin's account of the divine processions differs from that of Aquinas in many details, but it is similar in its broad contours. Whereas Aquinas saw the distinction between the persons and essence as a notional distinction, Turretin proposed that the distinction is a modal distinction (*distinctione modali*), though he admitted disagreement among theologians. The persons are not different things from that thing which is the divine essence, but they differ from the essence as a mode from the thing.[48] Each mode is also distinct from the other modes as a result of personal properties: the Father is unbegotten, the Son begotten, and the Holy Spirit

---

43. As Stephen Holmes remarks, "The [*Summa Theologica*] presentation is no doubt an attempt to aid conceptual clarity, but it is in danger of obscuring the exegetical basis of Thomas's doctrine if it is read in abstraction from the other treatments." Holmes, *Quest for the Trinity*, 156–57.

44. Emery, *Trinitarian Theology of St. Thomas Aquinas*, 18–22.

45. Aquinas, *Summa Contra Gentiles*, IV.2.

46. Long, *Triune God*, 67–69. Aquinas cites the Old Testament 148 times and the New Testament 191 times in this portion of the *Summa Theologica*. His argument always unfolds from the *sed contra* of each article, where he cites the Bible 112 of 233 times.

47. Matthew Levering explains that Aquinas's account "is not a rationalistic claim ... [but] manifests the intelligibility of the data of revelation, which attest to two processions, and it deploys the appropriateness of John's use of the name 'Word.'" Levering, *Doctrine of the Holy Spirit*, 98.

48. Turretin, *Institutes*, I.iii.27.2–3.

proceeding.[49] Turretin differed from Aquinas in that he did not want to explain how the processions occur—he deployed no account of procession by way of likeness and by way of imprint, and hence no psychological analogy.[50] Despite this methodological difference, Aquinas and Turretin shared much common ground. Like Aquinas, Turretin sought to explain eternal generation analogically, carefully exploring the similarities and differences between human and divine generation. Also like Aquinas, Turretin used the divine attributes as a means of clarifying this analogical explanation of eternal generation. Despite their differences, both theologians presented a relatively similar account of the divine processions.

Turretin's *Institutes* were written with various theological opponents in mind, a fact that shaped Turretin's argument. His treatment of the Trinity focused on antitrinitarian Socinians, who often rejected the doctrine of the Trinity as a non-scriptural by-product of mistakes in patristic theology. Most reformed scholastics, Turretin included, responded to the rise of antitrinitarianism by affirming *sola scriptura* in a stance against Roman Catholic theological method, while accepting patristic insights into the Trinity as a helpful *testes veritatis*—a test of the truth of a given interpretation of Scripture. Interpretations that go against the fathers are likely to be mistaken, because early pro-Nicene theologians and their medieval descendants develop terminology and concepts that are non-biblical, and yet which helpfully summarize the content of Scripture.[51] Translating this claim into language I have used elsewhere in this book, Turretin argued that early pro-Nicene concepts are valid second-order reflections that provide conceptual clarity concerning biblical patterns.

Turretin presented the idea of eternal generation as a valid inference from the Scriptures, particularly Psalm 2:7—"I will tell of the decree: The Lord said to me, 'You are my Son; today I have begotten you.'" Turretin explained that the New Testament clearly applies this text to Jesus Christ (Acts 4:25; 13:33; Heb 1:5).[52] Psalm 2 concerns the provision of an eternal kingdom to a son of God, and Turretin saw the eternal generation of the Son as "the foundation upon which the universal kingdom (granted to him) is built." Had Christ not been eternal Son, he could not have been appointed mediator and received the eternal kingdom.[53] Turretin also cited a favorite text of pro-Nicene theologians: Proverbs 8:22-30, which speaks of the

49. Ibid., I.iii.27.10-17.
50. Ibid., I.iii.27.16-20.
51. Meijering, "The Fathers and Calvinist Orthodoxy," 869-71.
52. Turretin, *Institutes*, I.iii.29.8.
53. Ibid., I.iii.29.9.

wisdom possessed by the Father at the beginning of the world, a wisdom brought forth before the earth began. Turretin argued that this passage must refer to Christ, who is called the Wisdom of God (Luke 7:35; 1 Cor 1:24), and who as Word of God was with God in the beginning (John 1:1). It was also clear to Turretin that the acts attributed to Wisdom in Proverbs 8 can only be performed by the Son.[54] Therefore, we must speak of the Father bringing forth a Son before the creation of the world, which theologians explore under the name eternal generation.

When explaining eternal generation in an effort to clarify these passages of Scripture, Turretin carefully ensured the doctrine's compatibility with the divine attributes. Reformed scholastic theologians commonly treated eternal generation as "hyperphysical," such that, using the way of negation, all change, time, division, and imperfection are excluded from this procession.[55] Turretin was no exception.[56] God is eternal, so divine generation possesses no "priority or posteriority of duration," but is unceasing.[57] God is infinite and uncircumscribed (without spatial limits), so divine generation is not to a place outside of God; generation is without place (*achōristos*). God is immutable and impassible, so generation is "without any passion or change, either in the Father or in the Son, since that he begat denotes no imperfection."[58] God is perfect, so any perfections of material generation must be attributed to eternal generation, while any imperfections must be ignored.[59] God is simple, so eternal generation does not result in division or composition in God.[60] The divine attributes greatly restrict the meaning of eternal generation.

With wrong interpretations of eternal generation negated as is necessary based on the divine attributes, Turretin provided a precise, analogical definition of eternal generation. Like human generation, divine generation is "a communication of essence from the Father." In human generation, only part of the essence is communicated, but in divine generation the entire essence is communicated indivisibly.[61] With New Testament language of the Son as the image of the Father in mind (Col 1:15; Heb 1:3), Turretin concluded that there is a "true generation" by which the one begotten is "the im-

---

54. Ibid., I.iii.29.10–12.
55. Muller, *Reformed Dogmatics*, Vol. 4, 287.
56. Turretin, *Institutes*, I.iii.29.5.
57. Ibid., I.iii.27.5, I.iii.27.7.
58. Ibid., I.iii.27.5.
59. Ibid., I.iii.29.29.
60. Ibid., I.iii.27.4, I.iii.29.4.
61. Ibid., I.iii.29.4.

age of the begetter."[62] Unlike human, physical generation, eternal generation is perfect and internal, implying no change, time, location, division, composition, place, or imperfection. Eternal generation simply denotes likeness, shared essence, and differentiation. Turretin was quite similar to Aquinas in his definition of generation. Both Aquinas and Turretin provide a clear example of how to speak carefully of the eternal relationships between Father, Son, and Spirit.

EFS advocates who speak of the Son eternally submitting to the Father do not spend time carefully explaining how the word "submit" applies in an analogical sense to the Godhead. In this respect, they differ significantly from their theological predecessors like Aquinas and Turretin who clarified the doctrine of eternal generation using the principle of analogical language about God to explain how such generation was compatible with the divine attributes. When Turretin and Aquinas speak of eternal generation, it is quite clear what they mean by the terminology, and there is no obvious contradiction between eternal generation and the divine attributes as classically construed. When EFS advocates speak of eternal submission, the only clarification comes from the adjective "eternal" adjoined to the idea of submission. Otherwise, it remains unclear how submission is compatible with any of the divine attributes. Of course, this is partly because some theologians who are most vocal in defending EFS tend to have dedicated far less time writing on the doctrine of God's attributes. Michael Ovey and Robert Letham come to mind here. Other theologians have dedicated significant time to the divine attributes but spend far less time exploring eternal submission. Norman Geisler and John Frame fit this category. Only Bruce Ware and Wayne Grudem have dedicated extensive time to exploring both the doctrine of God and of eternal submission. They have simply neglected to connect their teaching on the two subjects. Therefore, as I explore whether it is appropriate to speak of eternal submission in an analogical sense in light of the divine attributes, I will pay particular attention to Ware's and Grudem's writings. I will supplement this with reference to the doctrine of God presented by theologians like Frame and Geisler, and will assume that the common cause of EFS theologians implies at least a degree of overlap in their theology of God and understanding of submission so that this limited survey is applicable to a larger group of theologians. This survey will show that the language of "submission" is entirely inappropriate, for the language of submission is incompatible with the divine attributes, and any attempt to make the concept of submission compatible would render that word nearly meaningless.

62. Turretin, *Institutes*, I.iii.29.17.

Eternal Submission and the Divine Attributes

The word submission must possess a different meaning when applied to God than when applied to human beings, a difference that the divine attributes help to illuminate. However, when the divine attributes of simplicity, omnipotence, omniscience, immutability, eternity, and omnibenevolence are applied to the concept of submission, a major problem results. The word "submit," if used of God, would possess a meaning so different from its normal meaning that it would no longer share any helpful semantic overlap. In other words, using the word "submit" of God would simply be imprecise theological language. I will illustrate this claim by demonstrating the widespread agreement found among medieval and Reformed scholastics concerning the divine attributes as they pertain to submission. Such classical definitions prohibit any notion of submission. Of course, the theological arguments presented in previous chapters also prohibit using the word "submit" of God with the same meaning that word bears in created relationships, but I will delay addressing those insights until the end of the chapter.

Divine Simplicity

Divine simplicity was one of the most central beliefs in the medieval and Reformed scholastic approaches to the doctrine of God, but it is also one of the more contested doctrines in modern theology.[63] If the classical view is maintained, it causes serious problems for EFS. Even certain revised modern accounts may cause trouble. In its most basic form, the doctrine of simplicity argues that God is not composed of parts. The doctrine of simplicity is a second-order reflection on scriptural patterns, a concept derived from the use of reason and tradition in light of biblical teaching. For example, the Reformed theologian Amandus Polanus offered seven different arguments for divine simplicity, four of which I will highlight here. First, Polanus noted that any composition must be explained—parts do not come together without cause. If God were composed of parts, we would need an explanation outside of God for how God's parts came together. God is the ultimate explanation and cause of all things (John 1:3; Col 1:16), so no such explanation possibly exists. Therefore, God must be simple. Second, God is spirit (John 4:24), but only matter can be divided into parts. Therefore, God is simple. Third, God is immutable and unchanging (Mal 3:6; Jas 1:17), but

---

63. For a good survey of the debate defending simplicity, see Long, *The Perfectly Simple Triune God*. Among scholars who contest divine simplicity, see for example: Hinlicky, *Divine Complexity*.

anything with parts is capable of change. Therefore, God must be simple. Fourth, God is both logically and temporally first (Rev 22:13), the ultimate foundation of all knowledge and being. However, if God had parts, those parts would be both logically and temporally before him. Therefore, God must be simple.[64] Taken together, such arguments offer a compelling case for the idea that God is not composed of parts in the form of a second-order reflection on broad patterns of Scripture. The Bible itself does not affirm simplicity, but simplicity is a reasonable inference from the Bible. It is not surprising that the doctrine of simplicity was central to both Turretin's and Aquinas' theological systems, and we have seen that both theologians explain the divine processions in a manner that preserves simplicity.[65]

Explaining what it means to say that God is not composed of parts is far more challenging than merely arguing that God does not have parts. What constitutes a part? Few theologians would claim that God is characterized by material composition, but beyond this consensus things are a bit more contested. Aquinas denied a real distinction between God's essence and God's existence in his explanation of divine simplicity. God's essence—those attributes that inhere in God in all possible circumstances—simply *is* God's existence. God necessarily exists. Turretin agreed.[66] Aquinas believed this follows logically from God's role as the cause of all things. He argued, "if the existence of a thing differs from its essence, this existence must be caused either by some exterior agent or by its essential principles." No exterior agent could have caused God, for God is the first cause of all things. God's essence could not have caused God's existence, for "nothing can be the sufficient cause of its own existence."[67] Therefore, Aquinas concluded that God's essence must not differ from his existence. God is the pure act of existence. This means that God is existence itself. As Brian Davies summarizes,

> God is not a creature. Creatures, Aquinas thinks, "have" existence, for their natures (*what* they are) do not suffice to guarantee their existence (*that* they are). But with God this is not so. He does not "have" existence; his existence is not received or derived from another. He is his own existence and the reason why others have it.[68]

64. Dolf te Velde and Roelf te Velde, *Doctrine of God*, 141–42.
65. Muller, *Reformed Dogmatics*, Vol. 3, 275; Long, *Triune God*, 23. For Turretin, the centrality of divine simplicity was partly a polemical move against the Socinians. Aquinas appealed to the doctrine as the basis for how God can be one while still possessing real relations between Father, Son, and Holy Spirit.
66. Turretin, *Institutes*, I.iii.7.5.
67. Aquinas, *Summa Theologica*, PP Q3 A4.
68. Davies, *Thought of Thomas Aquinas*, 55.

This conclusion returns us to the doctrine of analogy: All contingent beings analogically participate in the existence and being of God. God, on the other hand, necessarily exists, for his essence and existence are simple and indivisible.

Many theologians who affirm EFS accept a version of divine simplicity. Wayne Grudem affirms the traditional doctrine of simplicity, though he prefers to use the term "unity." Grudem argues that each attribute of God is characteristic of all of God, and no attribute is "something external from God's real being or real self."[69] Presumably, existence and the other operations would fall within this argument. Norman Geisler offers extensive exegetical and historical arguments for divine simplicity and for what he calls "God's pure actuality," the idea that God is "existence, pure and simple."[70] John Frame agrees with Aquinas that God's nature is not characterized by physical composition and that each attribute refers to the entirety of God, yet differs in one important area. Aquinas claimed that the divine attributes are only notionally distinct, for simplicity denies real distinctions between God's attributes. In other words, attributes like "omnipotence" and "goodness" are distinct in the human mind, but not truly distinct things in God's nature. Not fully understanding Aquinas, Frame rejects this as neo-Platonic and contrary to the Trinity.[71] I have been unable to find anything in Bruce Ware's writings on the doctrine of simplicity, but given that he modifies the classical doctrine divine immutability, as we shall see, his theology is likely more compatible with some kind of (non-material) composition in God.[72]

The doctrine of divine simplicity poses serious questions for some theologians who accept EFS. Those who distinguish between function and being to suggest that the Son is functionally subordinate but not subordinate in being are particularly puzzling. Such a distinction appears to be a rejection of divine simplicity because being and function have a real distinction, requiring composition in God. Those theologians who deny simplicity,

---

69. Grudem, *Systematic Theology*, 178–79.

70. Geisler, *Systematic Theology*, 11, 39–50. Geisler's terminology appears to be informed by Aristotle or his Christian theological heirs.

71. Frame, *Systematic Theology*, 429–31. Frame fails to situate Aquinas' claim that there is no real distinction between the divine attributes within Aquinas' larger analogical conception of God. Moreover, Frame, like many evangelicals we have seen in chapter 1, conflates God's essence/substance with the essential/accidental distinction where anything necessary to God is essential. However, Aquinas does not use Aristotle's distinction in this manner, so would not treat the persons as essential in the same way that Frame does. The persons are the essence, but more properly they are subsistences of the essence relationally distinguished by opposition. Aquinas, *Suma Theologica*, PP Q39 A1.

72. Ware, "A Modified Calvinist Doctrine of God," 90–92.

either partially or completely, would not view this consequence of eternal submission as a problem. Such EFS advocates would then need to provide answers for the sorts of arguments found in Aquinas, Polanus, and others. If God's functions are distinct from the divine being, what explanation exists for why God has these functions? If the divine functions are different from the divine being, can God change these functions without changing the divine being and attributes? If God is composed of distinct functions and being, are not the categories of function and being logically prior to God? Are they not the ultimate basis of all knowledge, rather than God himself being the foundation? I have not seen EFS advocates who distinguish between function and being provide satisfactory answers to these questions.

Though some EFS theologians may simply weaken divine simplicity, others may prefer to associate a distinction in function to the divine persons. EFS advocates have very clearly argued that submission pertains only to the divine persons. Presumably, functions must also refer to the persons. Horrell explains that functions are "an operation in a characteristically proper or particular way.... The function of each member of the Godhead is the active expression of each persons [sic] of the Trinity's distinguishing personal characteristics."[73] Since the time of Anselm of Canterbury, Western theologians traditionally do allow for personal distinctions despite divine simplicity where there are relations of opposition, namely relational properties that require a correlate that is logically incompatible with the relational property.[74] Consider the Father/Son relationship: the Father begets and the Son is begotten. The Son's property of being begotten has an opposite correlate in the Father, who is unbegotten. Eternal generation is relationship between the Father and Son that requires a relational distinction between the two, a distinction granted despite simplicity.

It is not clear that relational opposition would work in the case of EFS. Submission is an act of the will, but the faculty of will is not relational and does not require opposition with an opposite correlate. Therefore, theologians traditionally have attributed a single will to the simple essence of God, as we have seen throughout this book.[75] Theologians who speak of multiple wills in God run into problems in Christology and soteriology, as we have seen. Perhaps reference to submission as a "mode of willing" could be compatible with the notion of relational opposition, but no theologian to my knowledge has yet defended EFS with any reference to how this might work. At the very least, the doctrine of divine simplicity shows how EFS is under-

---

73. Horrell, "Complementarian Trinitarianism," 352.
74. Anselm of Canterbury, *On the Procession of the Holy Spirit*, 392–93.
75. Jowers, "A Simple God," 384.

developed for those theologians who affirm a version of divine simplicity. At worst, EFS may be incompatible with simplicity.

Divine Omnipotence

Where simplicity is a contested doctrine among evangelicals, the doctrine of divine omnipotence is widely accepted. I am unaware of pre-modern theologians who reject the idea that God is omnipotent, nor of any EFS advocates who would deny this claim. Grudem defines God's omnipotence as the fact that "God is able to do all his holy will."[76] Frame defines omnipotence as the claim that "God can do what he can do."[77] Geisler writes that "God can do whatever is possible to do."[78] While earlier theologians often spoke like Geisler of God's ability to do anything logically possible, even evangelical definitions found in Grudem and Frame are a robust affirmation in line with scholastic theology.

Medieval and Reformed Scholastic accounts of omnipotence denied the possibility of there being more than one omnipotent being. Often this argument derives from the idea that more than one omnipotent being prevents unity in governing creation. (Such unity is often called divine monarchy.) Francis Turretin argued that if there was more than one omnipotent being, either these multiple beings would be equal, which would mean that "neither would be first and most perfect," or else they would not be equal, in which case one would be inferior and not omnipotent. If both are equal and neither is first, there may not be unity in governance of the world.[79] Aquinas raised a similar concern. "He to whom rulership belongs should have unity. Hence, we must admit that God, Who is the cause of all things, is absolutely one."[80] The problem these theologians are addressing is more clearly articulated in the writings of Zacharius Ursinus. When Ursinus addressed unity, he began by citing the Scriptures (Deut 6:4; 32:39; Isa 44:6; 1 Cor 8:4; 1 Tim 2:5). God "alone reigns over all," but there can be only one who reigns over all, and this one is God. Moreover, "There cannot be more than one being that is omnipotent, for if there were many, they would mutually hinder and oppose each other, and so would not be omnipotent. It is by this argument that the monarchy of the world is ascribed to one God in the prophecy of Daniel, where it is said, 'No one can stay his hand, or resist

---

76. Grudem, *Systematic Theology*, 216.
77. Frame, *Systematic Theology*, 343.
78. Geisler, *Systematic Theology*, 159.
79. Turretin, *Institutes*, I.iii.3.6.
80. Aquinas, *Summa Contra Gentiles*, I.42.20.

his will' (Dan 4:35)."[81] There can only be one power and one will behind the divine monarchy.

Bonaventure offered a different argument for why there can only be one omnipotent being. He treated omnipotence as "the ability to do all things and to be the cause all power." In other words, God's omnipotence is the exemplary cause for all created power and operations, which have power only insofar as they correspond to an exemplar.[82] Bonaventure notes that there can only be one cause of all power, one exemplar, so there can only be one omnipotent God.[83] If there were two causes, than none would be the exemplary cause of all powers. Protestants speak of something similar to what Bonaventure meant by omnipotence under the heading of meticulous providence. There are certain differences, but both ideas affirm that omnipotence implies both God's ability and the fact that all other powers depend upon him.[84]

Bonaventure considered an objection that directly pertains to the issue of EFS and that challenges EFS at its root. Some might argue that claiming there can only be one who is omnipotent undermines the doctrine of the Trinity, for there are three persons in the Trinity. Bonaventure replied, "there is one nature and power and wisdom and goodness and influence and causality" shared by the three persons.[85] By appealing to inseparable operations and by treating will and power as properties of the single divine nature, Bonaventure preserved a single omnipotent essence that is Father, Son, and Spirit. Using the pro-Nicene formula we can say that any divine act proceeds from the Father, through the Son, to the Spirit as the act of

---

81. Ursinus, *Commentary on the Heidelberg Catechism*, 128.

82. Bonaventure's argument is rooted in a form of exemplarism, where God is the exemplary cause of all things who reflect their exemplar in lesser degree. Bonaventure believes that the pursuit of the one exemplar is at the heart of metaphysics, so it is not surprising to see this theme appear in his analysis of divine omnipotence. Gilson, *The Philosophy of St. Bonaventure*, 127–28.

83. Bonaventure, *Disputed Questions on the Trinity*, Q. 2, A. 1, arg. 3.

84. Bruce Ware's definition of providence is comparable to Bonaventure's definition of omnipotence. "God continually oversees and directs all things pertaining to the created order in such a way that 1) he preserves in existence and provides for the creation that he has brought into being, and 2) he governs and reigns supremely over the entirety of the whole of creation in order to fulfill all of his intended purposes in it and through it." Ware, *God's Greater Glory*, 17. A key distinction here is that language of meticulous providence tends toward nominalism instead of realism. All things have power because God's power wills and causes their own, not because God serves as an exemplary cause. Structurally, though, the common ground of treating omnipotence not just as unrestricted ability but also as a direct connection with creation whose power depends upon God remains.

85. Ibid., Q. 2, A. 1, resp. 2.

a single omnipotent God. Theologians who speak of eternal submission reject inseparable operations by speaking of distinct acts of willing and of the Father commanding and the Son submitting and obeying. Whereas Bonaventure claimed that there is only one omnipotent God because of united action, EFS would demand that there are three omnipotents, which is logically contradictory given classical notions of omnipotence.

The easiest way that evangelicals could defend the idea of eternal submission is by positing that it is logically impossible for the Son to disagree with the Father. Assuming such an account of logical impossibility was satisfactorily developed, the problem would be resolved. Both Son and Father would be omnipotent, in the sense of being able to do everything that they willed and everything that is logically possible. The divine attribute of omnipotence would thus require that submission when spoken of humans requires the possibility of dissent, but when spoken of God does not. On the other hand, even this solution does not fix the problem of omnipotence as the basis for all powers, and the question of whether it is the Father or Son who causes all things (by decree or in an exemplary manner) remains unanswered.

Immutability

Most theologians who affirm EFS affirm God's immutability. Ware distinguishes between "ontological immutability," "ethical immutability" and "relational mutability," affirming the prior two kinds of immutability, but denying relational immutability. What this means is that God cannot change his character or nature, but can change in relations to creatures. Here Ware provides the example of relenting and not destroying Ninevah (Jonah 3:10).[86] Grudem affirms God's "unchangeableness." He writes, "God is unchanging in his being, perfections, purposes, and promises, yet God does act and feel emotions, and he acts and feels differently in response to different situations."[87] Ware and Grudem appear to present their definitions as if they differ from the tradition, but classical depictions do not deny that God acts or has emotions as suggested, although such ideas are certainly clarified through analogical predication.[88] Instead, the doctrine implies that God acts and feels as God wills, but is not compelled to any action or feeling apart from that will.[89] As classically expressed, the divine immutability

---

86. Ware, "A Modified Calvinist Doctrine of God," 90–92.
87. Grudem, *Systematic Theology*, 163.
88. Muller, *Reformed Dogmatics*, Vol. 3, 308–9.
89. See Lister, *God Is Impassible and Impassioned*.

drew on biblical patterns speaking of God's unchanging will (Jas 1:17; Ps 102:29; Isa 46:10; Heb 6:17, etc.), to deny any change in God's nature, will, or knowledge.[90] Reformed and medieval scholastic theologians nearly unanimously rejected the possibility of God changing his will.[91] When Grudem points to God's unchanging purposes and promises, something similar is implied, though some ambiguity remains. Ware's affirmation of ethical immutability at least suggests that God does not change his will when acting in any situation with ethical significance. Given most definitions of simplicity, ontological immutability would also deny any other change in God's will, because God's will simply is the divine essence.[92] This is true even if we posit will as a personal property, for the persons simply are the essence as well.

The attribute of omnipotence precludes the possibility that eternal submission could involve the Son disagreeing with the Father, but divine immutability precludes "submission" signifying any other sort of change in the Son's will. This means that submission could not even be a change from the Son being indifferent toward an action and then willingly accepting it, submitting to the Father's command. Even if we soften immutability to allow for "relational mutability" and reject divine simplicity such that the Son's will is distinct from the divine essence, the Son could only move from a position of indifference to the Father to a position of submission for decisions that are morally neutral. Change concerning any morally significant decision would imply a move toward or away from the highest moral character, which even Ware denies under the title of "ethical immutability."

Eternality

Most classical theologians believed that God was eternal. Turretin, for example, wrote against the Socinians to argue that God is eternal both in the sense of having no beginning or end and in the sense of having no succession. He noted that the hills (Deut 33:15) and the covenants (Gen 17:7) are called eternal in the Bible, but in these cases, the idea of eternity points to a duration without end. Both hills and covenants experience the succession of passing time. When the Bible speaks of the eternal nature of God, it insists that he is always the same (Ps 102:27), but "he is not always the same from whom almost every moment something anteriorly is removed and by whom

---

90. Muller, *Reformed Dogmatics*, Vol. 3, 309, 314.

91. For example: Turretin, *Institutes*, I.iii.11; Ursinus, *Commentary on the Heidelberg Catechism*, 126; Ames, *Marrow of Theology*, VII.4; Wollebius, *Compendium*, 39, 47; Aquinas, *Summa Theologica*, PP Q19 A7; Anselm, *Why God Became a Man*, 327–28.

92. Aquinas, *Summa Contra Gentiles*, I.73.

posteriorly something is added," as would be the case were God subject to succession. Similarly, James 1:17 teaches that God "does not change like shifting shadows." Turretin read this as biblical grounds for rejecting succession in God.[93]

While Turretin's argument was rooted in patterns of Scripture, the language of the eternity or timelessness of God as a denial of succession moves beyond scriptural categories. Once again we see a theologian offering a second-order reflection on biblical patterns attempting to provide conceptual clarity unavailable through pure exegesis. In this case, the second-order language also connects with other divine attributes, namely divine simplicity and immutability. A simple and immutable God cannot change, so God's eternality must entail a rejection of any sort of succession, which would itself be change.[94] Some later theologians softened this claim. Charles Hodge, for example, followed an ancient precedent set by Boethius when he denied that there is any succession in God in terms of external events, for God sees all times simultaneously. However, unlike some of his predecessors Hodge argued that internal to God there appear to be "successive exercises of the divine efficiency." Most notable here is the notion that God answers prayer. Hodge was cautious here, and he admitted that we may not be able to understand God's consciousness and how he might experience internal succession, but whatever we conclude, "we are not to deny that God is an intelligent being, that he actually thinks and feels, to get over the difficulty."[95]

Following the trajectory set by Hodge, some contemporary evangelicals prefer to speak of God being everlasting but not eternal, thereby allowing for succession in God. Others suggest that there is an eternal aspect of God and a temporal aspect of God. Bruce Ware, for example, suggests that "God existed in himself, apart from any spatiotemporal reality, in the fullness of his infinite and glorious existence . . . being essentially (i.e., in his essence or nature) nonspatial and nontempral."[96] In the eternal inward life of the Trinity, God is timeless. However, Ware suggests that when God created a universe characterized by space and time, God chose to "'fill' all of the space and time he created," becoming "omnitemporal" or everlasting.[97] On Ware's account, then, submission could only imply succession in terms of God's presence in creation, not in terms of the timeless life within the Trinity. At most there could be a succession in the pre-incarnate but

---

93. Turretin, *Institutes*, I.iii.10.1–3.
94. Ibid., I.iii.10.5.
95. Charles Hodge, *Systematic Theology*, Vol. I, 387–89.
96. Ware, "A Modified Calvinist Doctrine of God," 89.
97. Ibid., 89.

post-creation economic work of the Son. In God's inward life as Father, Son, and Holy Spirit, there would be no succession, so "eternal submission" as a characteristic role that distinguishes the persons of the Trinity could not imply that the Father first wills and then the Son obeys, as Ware often suggests. For example, in *Father, Son, & Holy Spirit*, he characterizes submission as "before the creation of the world,"[98] yet still speaks of distinct divine acts of command and obedience or submission, a succession. Others who affirm eternal submission, like Norman Geisler, insist that eternity means timelessness or lack of succession, without making any distinction of the sort found in Hodge or Ware.[99] This version of divine eternality would rule out any succession when using the word "submission" of the Son.

Omniscience

Omniscience is another uncontested divine attribute among evangelicals who affirm EFS. In fact, Bruce Ware has dedicated a significant portion of his career to combatting open theism, a perspective claiming that divine omniscience is limited by God's choice to create a world with libertarian freedom, such that God cannot know the future except through his predictive power.[100] Ware has compellingly shown on scriptural grounds that this account is mistaken. In contrast to open theism, classical views of divine omniscience since the patristic era (Boethius was particularly influential) have suggested that God knows all thing simultaneously. Aquinas wrote, "God sees all things together, and not successively."[101] Wayne Grudem affirms the same principle when we writes that God "does not experience a succession of moments."[102] Other EFS advocates agree with this definition of omniscience.[103]

---

98. Ware, *Father, Son and Holy Spirit*, 79.

99. Geisler, *Systematic Theology*, 94; Grudem, *Systematic Theology*, 168–69. Grudem denies any "succession of moments" in God's being, and insists that time "has no effect on God's . . . purposes or promises," his shorthand for the divine actions. It is difficult to see how Grudem could affirm succession in the divine will even within the economy of redemption.

100. Sanders calls this version of omniscience "dynamic omniscience," through which "God knows all that can be known given the sort of world he chose to create," namely, the past and present. Sanders, *The God Who Risks*, 15. Ware rejects any such limit to divine knowledge. Ware, *God's Greater Glory*, 218–38.

101. Aquinas, *Summa Theologica*, PP Q14 A7.

102. Grudem, *Systematic Theology*, 170.

103. Geisler, *Systematic Theology*, 182.

Divine omniscience as classically defined would severely restrict the possible meaning of "submission" when predicated of the Son. Because God knows all times simultaneously without succession, the Son's submission could not entail any sort of process whereby he became aware of the Father's will. There would also never be a time when the Son would not know that he would "submit" to God. Aquinas took things a step further, denying any sort of discursive reasoning or deliberation in God's will. After all, deliberation requires succession, which God's timelessness and omniscience has precluded.[104] Earlier theologians had already reached similar conclusions. For example, though Maximus the Confessor affirmed that Jesus had a human and a divine will, he denied that this will was *gnomic,* or a deliberative will, because such a will would make the Son like us, deliberating over the decision due to a lack of knowledge.[105] The fullness of God's knowledge prohibits any such deliberation. Human submission generally includes such deliberation, as the one submitting must seek to understand a command, judge its moral character (no one is obligated to follow a command contrary to Scripture), and, frequently, evaluate whether one will decide to willingly submit. This would be another significant difference between divine and human submission.

Clarification Arising from Other Doctrines

The divine attributes of simplicity, immutability, omnipotence, omniscience, and eternality have each revealed clear points where using the word "submit" eternally of the Son must differ analogically in meaning from when that word is used of human submission. The doctrinal problems addressed previously in this work add further restrictions. If an EFS advocate seeks to preserve pro-Nicene trinitarianism and dyothelitism, the Son could not submit to the Father using a distinct will from the Father's own will. If an EFS advocate wanted to preserve classical versions of satisfaction and penal substitutionary atonement theories, then God's command to the Son would imply no obligation, and the Son would submit in a non-obligatory manner. No doubt other doctrines not explored in this work would offer additional points of clarification.

---

104. Aquinas, *Summa Theologica,* PP Q14 A7.
105. Bathrellos, *Byzantine Christ,* 157.

"Eternal Submission" as Imprecise Theological Language

Using the method of analogy informed by the divine attributes, it is clear that if the word "submission" if used of the Son eternally it must bear a very different meaning than when used of creatures. Accepting the classical definitions of the divine attributes, claiming that the Son eternally submits cannot include any idea of possible disagreement, for this would contradict divine omnipotence. The Son's submission could include no succession or change, which would contradict divine immutability and simplicity. Nor could the Son's submission include any process or deliberation, which would run contrary to divine omniscience. Even under modified accounts of the divine attributes, speaking of "eternal submission" cannot indicate any disagreement, succession *in se* (in the life of the Trinity apart from creation), change in any morally significant manner, or deliberation. In light of other doctrines we have considered, it is clear that the language of "eternal submission" should not include the idea of different wills or different actions, for this would jeopardize dyothelite Christology and undermine the pro-Nicene doctrine of inseparable operations. "Eternal submission" also could not suggest any obligation for the Son to obey, lest the idea of satisfaction be undermined. For those EFS advocates who affirm the most robust versions of divine simplicity coupled with relational opposition, it is not even clear how one would be able to speak of any distinction between persons when using the word "submission" at all.

A careful analogical analysis of the word "submission" indicates that the word fails to provide any helpful insight into the eternal relations that cannot be better expressed using different terminology. Human submission involves one person changing their numerically distinct will across a succession of time often after a process of deliberation and sometimes in light of an obligation. None of this meaning can remain if theologians try to use the word "submission" of the Son. All that remains, as far as I can tell, is an affirmation of ordering and difference, and this is not the meaning of "submission" at all. When speaking of submission, EFS advocates emphasize that there is a divine order to God, a *taxis*, and the divine attributes do not preclude such a possibility as far as I can tell.[106] Furthermore, EFS advocates insist that "eternal submission" is related to the personal distinctions of the persons.[107] The divine attributes cannot be explained in a manner that undermines such distinctions, which are fundamental to the biblical narrative. However, the idea of order and difference is already included in the

---

106. Ware, *Father, Son and Holy Spirit*, 72–73; Claunch, "God is the Head of Christ," 90–93; Letham, *The Holy Trinity*, 482–83.

107. See my discussion in chapter 1.

traditional language of eternal generation and spiration/procession. When explained by Turretin and Aquinas, these doctrines do not undermine divine simplicity, they do not challenge inseparable operations or jeopardize dyothelite Christology and satisfaction theory. Furthermore, they provide additional dimensions of meaning, denoting likeness and consubstantiality. The eternal processions allow theologians to distinguish how the Father is source of the Son and Spirit from how he is source of creation—acts of generation and procession are different than acts of creation. The language of eternal generation and procession also suggests intimacy. Therefore, I am convinced that the language of "eternal submission" is an inferior alternative to language of eternal generation and procession. Saying, "the Son submits" and "a human submits" would be far too dissimilar in meaning when used of God and humanity to be of any assistance. When this word is used by EFS advocates, especially without the careful analysis I have tried to offer in this chapter, language of submission is prone to confuse and distort theology. It is simply imprecise and inferior theological language.

Some theologians who defend EFS (and some who oppose it) have rejected the idea of eternal generation and procession in their publications.[108] In his bestselling *Systematic Theology*, Grudem fails to engage authors like Aquinas and Turretin to explore eternal generation, feebly claiming, "'begetting' has never been defined very clearly."[109] He prefers to avoid this language and speak of difference in role,[110] and notes that "it would seem more helpful if the language of 'eternal begetting of the Son' (also called 'eternal generation of the Son') were not retained in any modern theological formulations."[111] In his *Father, Son, & Holy Spirit*, a foundational text for EFS, Bruce Ware writes, "The conceptions of both the 'eternal begetting of the Son' and 'eternal procession of the Spirit' seem to me highly speculative and not grounded in biblical teaching."[112] This chapter has demonstrated that language of eternal generation and procession is scripturally grounded, far more precise, and considerably more compatible with traditional notions of the doctrine of God than the language of eternal submission. Ware and Grudem have recently verbally recanted their hesitance to use the traditional terminology, though their widely disseminated publications that deny eternal generation remain influential. I suspect that their initial rejection of this doctrine partly explains their acceptance of EFS as an alternative

---

108. See the helpful summary in Giles, *The Eternal Generation of the Son*, 29–33.
109. Grudem, *Systematic Theology*, 244.
110. Ibid., 254 n. 38.
111. Ibid., 1234.
112. Ware, *Father, Son, and Holy Spirit*, 162 n. 3.

means of differentiating the divine persons. For this reason, I am especially thankful for theologians like Kevin Giles and Robert Letham on both sides of the debate who have defended eternal generation and procession.[113]

I have argued that claiming the Son eternally submits to the Father is a deviation from pro-Nicene theology. This deviation either requires positing will as proper to the persons, which jeopardizes dyothelite Christology, or it requires talk of distinct modes of willing for each person, which still undermines the non-obligatory satisfaction offered by the Son that is the basis of classical transactional atonement theories. On top of these problems, it is now evident that any talk of eternal submission of the Son is far less precise than talk of eternal generation as a means of distinguishing the persons—indeed predicating "submission" of the Son could bear almost no common meaning to the same word when used of human beings. I expect that some EFS readers have two remaining objections, which I will address in the duration of this work. First, EFS theologians commonly claim that eternal submission is the basis for human gender roles. Is this an additional level of meaning added by the language of "eternal submission"? I challenge this problematic theological move in excursus 2. Following a quick rebuttal of this position, I will engage the more substantive second objection in chapter 5: eternal submission is purportedly biblical. Does this scriptural foundation warrant our use of the word "submission" of the eternal relation of the Son to the Father? As we will see, the scriptural case for EFS is significantly weaker than is often claimed, such that "eternal submission" must be regarded as a second-order theological claim derived from Scripture but not explicitly contained therein. Given that the alternative theological language of eternal generation offers far more precision while creating far fewer theological problems, evangelicals would do well to affirm the classical theology of the divine processions and reject eternal submission as imprecise and problematic theological language.

---

113. Giles, *The Eternal Generation of the Son*; Letham, "Eternal Generation in the Church Fathers."

Excursus

EFS and Theological Anthropology

IT MAY SURPRISE SOME readers to see that I do not dedicate an entire chapter to theological anthropology. After all, there is more agreement among EFS theologians that the Trinity somehow correlates with the submission of wives to their husbands than there is agreement on appropriate terminology for speaking of the Son's eternal submission. I am convinced that there is actually limited direct overlap between theological anthropology and EFS.[1] To make my case I need to pause briefly to address two questions: First, can the Trinity function as an analogy for spousal relationships? Second, is a move away from EFS a result of a distorted theological anthropology, namely "evangelical feminism"?

Against Using the Trinity as a Basis for Ethics

Augustine of Hippo once argued that all things are to be used to orient us to God, except for God, who alone is to be enjoyed, never used for another end.[2] Augustine's argument has been largely ignored in modern theological ethics. One can easily find theologians using the Trinity to justify any number of ethical commitments. To illustrate the problem, consider the discipline of economic theology, where we see numerous arguments that treat the Trinity

---

1. Insofar as he is the perfect human, the christological questions already explored in chapter 2 will have some bearing on theological anthropology. So, too, will questions concerning how we define terms like person and essence. However, these connections are far less central than many in the EFS debate assume.

2. Augustine of Hippo, *On Christian Teaching*, I.2–6.

as an analogy of ideal human relations without any real consensus. Leonardo Boff challenges hierarchical capitalism that excludes the poor because of the eternal relations of Father, Son, and Spirit,[3] while M. Douglas Meeks argues that the Trinity "demythologizes" the God-concepts behind capitalism, an economic system that purportedly favors autonomous rational individuals and exclusive property claims because it has unwittingly incorporated certain flawed assumptions about divinity.[4] On the other hand, Victor Claar argues that the distinctive and yet cooperative missions of the Son and Spirit affirm capitalism's emphasis on freely working together to meet one another's needs through markets.[5] Michael Novak is prone to see the Trinity as exemplary of numerous aspects of capitalism. He claims that distinctive work through specialization and trade mirrors the Trinity as differentiated yet one,[6] and that capitalism is superior to socialism because it is "trinitarian." By this he means that capitalism allows for a distinction between political, economic, and cultural systems that are not allowed in more "monistic" socialism.[7] Turning beyond the field of economic theology, the Trinity is also used to justify certain fundamental principles of political ethics,[8] to advocate queering of gender roles,[9] and, as we have seen, to defend complementarian gender roles. Given the fact that these arguments are mutually exclusive, at least some appeals to the Trinity are not valid. For methodological reasons, I am convinced that no such appeal to the Trinity as an analogy is actually valid.

Two significant problems hinder using the Trinity as a basis for social ethics, whether in economic ethics, political ethics, or family ethics. The first problem facing the use of the Trinity in theological ethics is that language used of God is analogical (as explained at length in chapter 4). This means that any comparison between God and creation may contain some similarities, but

3. Boff, *Trinity and Society*.

4. Meeks develops three types of correlation between God and the economy: (1) disclosive correlation asks how "god concepts" influence the economy, (2) critical correlation asks how the economy has influenced "god concepts," and (3) transformative correlation asks how our God concepts compel us to a change in praxis in the economy. Meeks, *God the Economist*, 41–42.

5. Claar, "Markets and the Economists Who Study Them," 36.

6. Novak, *The Spirit of Democratic Capitalism*, 337–40.

7. Novak, "Seven Theological Facets," 113.

8. Moltmann sees the unity of the Trinity as a social unity derived from the monarchy of the Father, centering through perichoretic unity on the Son, and illuminated through the mutuality of the Spirit. Moltmann claims that this concept of the Trinity overcomes sorts of monotheism that inhibit human freedom, such that politically and individually human freedom must be affirmed as participation in the God who is freedom. Moltmann, *Trinity and the Kingdom*, 177–78, 191–222.

9. Cheng, "Three-Part Sinfonia."

will also contain dissimilarities. Such is the nature of analogy. Appealing to the Trinity as the analogical basis for an ethical claim disregards the dramatic dissimilarities between God and the world. Ethicists would do well to remember the definition of the Fourth Lateran Council (1215): "between the Creator and the creature so great a likeness cannot be noted without the necessity of noting a greater dissimilarity between them."[10] This methodological caution is prudent given widespread scriptural testimony to the sheer difference between God and the world (i.e., Isa 55:8–9; Ps 86:8; Rom 11:13, etc.). Lateran IV cautions us when attempting to use the Trinity in theological ethics—any commonality between economy, family, or state and the Trinity will likely face even larger differences. This should mute our optimism concerning any analogy between the Trinity and created reality.

A second problem facing the use of the Trinity in theological ethics is that of theological innovation. When the Trinity is the foundation for an ethical claim based on an analogy between the Trinity and some ideal, be it economic or marital, the analogy is typically based on a theological innovation. Chapter 1 demonstrated that claims of eternal submission deviate in significant ways from pro-Nicene trinitarianism by utilizing a novel understanding of *ousia* that does not include will/operation, by rejecting inseparable operations, by often challenging eternal generation, and by using novel terminology like "function" and "role." Other efforts to deploy the Trinity as an exemplar for the economy or government also tend to deviate from traditional trinitarian thought. For example, Boff offers the innovative claim that the Father is from the Son and Spirit, as well as the Spirit being from the Father and Son.[11] Moltmann's political use of the Trinity deviates from classical understandings of *perichoresis*, the mutual interpenetration of the divine persons.[12] In light of the fact that appeals to the Trinity to establish an ethical standard for the ideal family, government, or economy rely on such innovation, one wonders if these authors are (perhaps unconsciously) using the doctrine of the Trinity for their own social purposes rather than drawing conclusions from their enjoyment of the Triune God as self-revealed. In other words, in violating Augustine's advice not to use the Trinity, such theologies may succumb to projection more than they reach valid theological conclusions.

10. Denzinger, *The Sources of Catholic Dogma*, 171.

11. "Everything in God is triadic, everything is *Patreque, Filioque* and *Spirituque*." Boff, *Trinity and Society*, 146.

12. Whereas Moltmann uses *perichoresis* throughout his corpus to establish everything from the unity of the Trinity to panentheism, this was not the traditional use for the doctrine. See the discussions in Durand, *La périchorèse*, 26–35; Gifford, *Perichoretic Salvation*, 21.

EXCURSUS: EFS AND THEOLOGICAL ANTHROPOLOGY 153

There is a clear exception to the above problems facing an analogical use of the Trinity in ethics. Where God has explicitly revealed a correlation between the Trinity and created realities Christians can speak of an analogy with confidence. This happens clearly in John 17:22, where Jesus grounds the unity of the church in the unity of the Father and Son. Many EFS advocates believe that the Bible explicitly endorses an analogy between the Trinity and gender roles, which would allow them to speak with similar confidence. These theologians often appeal to 1 Corinthians 11:3 and Genesis 1:26–27. I will treat the former passage in detail in the next chapter. I will argue that there is nothing in 1 Corinthians 11:3 that indicates Paul is speaking of the eternal relation between Father and Son rather than an aspect of the Father/Son relationship assumed in the incarnation. I will now consider Genesis 1:27 at more length.

Many EFS advocates understand the image of God in Genesis 1:27 to be manifest in spousal and/or familial relationships. Genesis 1:27 reads, "God created man in his own image, in the image of God he created them; male and female he created them." Appealing to Genesis 1:27, Owen Strachan and Gavin Peacock argue that God is the perfect community, and that this community is reflected in God creating humanity male and female.[13] Therefore, the submission of wives to husbands reflects the eternal submission of Christ to the Father. Perfect family reflects perfect Trinity, and "there is not Holy Trinity without the order of authority and submission."[14] Tom Smail points to the juxtaposition of the ideas of image and likeness (1:26, 27a) with gender (1:27b) and dominion (1:28) to conclude that likeness and image are expressed in the different ways that each gender fulfills dominion.[15] Smail affirms "functional subordination,"[16] by which he partly means, "As the Son depends on the Father for both his being and his vocation, so the woman depends on the man for her being and vocation."[17] Grudem appeals to the plural "let us make man in our image" (Gen 1:26), which he calls "the first explicit indication of plurality of persons within the Godhead." He claims that the image is therefore a reflection of the Trinity, including submission.[18]

Though I must admit that there is historical precedent for seeing the image as rooted in gender or in the community of human family, significant problems face theologians attempting to root the image in complementarian

---

13. Strachan and Peacock, *Grand Design*, 92.
14. Ibid., 93.
15. Smail, *Like Father, Like Son*, 66.
16. Ibid., 44.
17. Ibid., 249.
18. Grudem, *Systematic Theology*, 455.

gender roles. The juxtaposition of terminology of image and likeness with humans created male and female in poetic parallelism (Gen 1:27) does not necessarily mean that the two ideas are related. Parallelism in Hebrew writing can conjoin completely unrelated concepts.[19] In this instance, it is quite unlikely that the parallelism between image and gender intends to establish similarity, given that Israel is unusual among its ancient Near Eastern peers in rejecting gender and sexual relationships in its view of God.[20] Suppose for the sake of argument that gender does somehow uniquely image God. If this were the case, we could not automatically assume that the submission of women is the particular feature of gender that images God. In fact, if we assume that a trait of human gender images God, Genesis 5:3's emphasis on Adam passing the image and likeness to his son Seth would suggest that the ability to create offspring, not authority relationships, are central to the image.[21] After all, the fruitful multiplication of humankind is a central theme of Genesis, where submission is not. Even if the image of God is rooted in a structural analogy between some human trait embodied in gender roles and God, one might apply this analogy toward egalitarian ends. As I have shown, there is strong theological warrant for the equality and single will of the Father, Son, and Spirit. If gender roles image God, inseparable operations might suggest that human gender roles are equal and united, a theological argument I would consider equally unwarranted.[22] If the image of God is based on a structural analogy between a human trait and God, this still provides little consolation for EFS advocates.

There are ultimately methodological flaws with any attempt to identify a structural analogy between some human trait and God as the basis of the divine image, whether we consider the trait of submission, equality, or reproduction. Any structural analogy assumes that humans share some unique trait with God, and that this trait is the reason why they are made in the image of God. No clear connection between any capacity and the image is ever established in the Bible. In fact, a distinctive human trait that could

19. Petersen, *The Prophetic Literature*, 25–28.

20. Von Rad, *Old Testament Theology, Vol. 1*, 146.

21. Garr, *Image and Likeness*, 131–32, 154. Besides the context of Genesis 5:3, the canonical context of Luke's genealogy that calls Adam son of God (Luke 3:38) is also noteworthy.

22. Even if one adopted a complementarian view of present gender roles, I would think an analogical interpretation of Genesis 1:27 that emphasized the trait of authority would necessitate an egalitarian view of relationships before the fall, such that women's submission is a byproduct of the curse. Complementarianism would thus become a side effect of losing/damaging the image of God. The theological evidence for the equal authority of the Father and Son is too strong and the exegetical evidence in Genesis 1 is too weak to conclude otherwise.

serve as the basis of the image may not exist. Scientists increasingly question whether many traits are in fact unique to human beings. For example, some animal social habits include patterns of behavior similar to submission and authority, suggesting that humanity's unique status as image bearers cannot be a result of submission and authority alone. Moreover, the Bible teaches that the entirety of creation itself somehow images God (see Ps 19:1; Rom 1:19, etc.), even if the precise terminology is not present. This fact implies that the ability to image God is not rooted in any characteristic but is a potential feature of all of creation with its various traits. God may have simply chosen to manifest his image maximally in humans.[23]

Recent biblical scholarship supports an alternative view of the image and likeness of God that rejects any reference to gender roles or submission: these terms more properly depict human ability to manifest the presence of God. Interpreting the image and likeness in Genesis 1:26–27 as an ability to manifest God's presence is strongly warranted given the contexts of ancient Near Eastern religion, other Old Testament writings, and New Testament theology. Randall Garr demonstrates that in various Mesopotamian contexts, "image" refers to persons, idols, or constellations which "communicate divine presence in its real-world setting,"[24] a meaning attested archaeologically "in Sryia-Palestine, during the biblical period, in extrabiblical sources."[25] Garr shows how the term "likeness" is frequently used of God's personal self-disclosure throughout the book of Ezekiel (Ezek 1:28, 8:2, 10:1–10). In Ezekiel the term "implicates God, his divine presence, his royal seat, and his thronebearers."[26] In the New Testament, Christ is the true image of God (Col 1:15), but he is also the one in whom God is fully present (Col 2:9; John 10:38).[27] There is also a clear connection between the image and likeness and the manifestation of divine glory in the New Testament (1 Cor 11:7; 2 Cor 3:18, 4:4–6).[28] Evidence favoring the image as a capacity to manifest God's presence combined with arguments against a structural

---

23. See Cortez, *Theological Anthropology*, 18–21.

24. Garr, *Image and Likeness*, 144. In light of this, Garr claims that the image establishes a "theophany" (132). J. R. Daniel Kirk offers a similar interpretation: "*Salmu* in Assyro-Babylonian antiquity suggests that images in at least some ancient Near Eastern contexts were viewed as constitutive of the reality that they represented, rather than representing a true reality on some other plane." We can therefore claim that humanity was "created to be some sort of theophany." Kirk, *A Man Attested by God*, 51.

25. Garr, *Image and Likeness*, 149.

26. Ibid., 123. cf. Matthews, *Genesis*, 168. Citing Genesis 18:1–2 as an example, Matthews adds, "theophany usually involves a human form."

27. Cortez, *Theological Anthropology*, 32–33.

28. See the discussion in Matthews, *Genesis*, 170–71.

interpretation of the image rooted in a common trait indicate that Genesis 1:26–27 is teaching that God's presence is manifest in human beings,[29] both male and female,[30] not that wifely submission is somehow reflected in the eternal submission of the Son. Therefore, lacking clear scriptural warrant, no analogy between gender roles and the Trinity is appropriate. Any such application risks projection given the great dissimilarity between God and creation and the lack of scriptural guidance. Theological anthropology is not directly related to the Trinity.

"Evangelical Feminism" and the Trinity

I first heard of the doctrine of eternal submission in the Trinity when I attended a series of lectures in a local church with one of my pastors. To thunderous applause, the speaker explained that theologians denied eternal submission because they were corrupted by "feminism." To many in the audience, this theological stain apparently closed the matter for discussion. Labelling opponents of eternal submission as "evangelical feminists" is a widespread tactic used by defenders of EFS. For example, Robert Letham argues that feminism, defined as the rejection of the authority of men over women, "is incompatible with the historical Christian doctrines of God and man."[31] Letham distinguishes between evangelical feminists, who hold to the authority of Scripture, and Christian feminism, which may not.[32] When other advocates of EFS accuse "evangelical feminists" in later contexts they rarely note Letham's assurance that such figures affirm biblical authority.[33] Labelling opponents of EFS as "evangelical feminists" is a rhetorical strategy meant to predispose readers against their perspectives, but it is neither accurate nor just.

Feminist theology is a fluid term signifying contributions from hundreds of different scholars, so establishing a clear definition of the field is so complex that it must remain a task beyond the scope of this work. However, contrary to Letham's usage, many who identify themselves as feminist theologians understand their project to be far more extensive in scope than merely challenging male authority. Consider the work of Elizabeth Johnson, for example. Johnson's *She Who Is* represents the self-conscious efforts of an

---

29. This fits well with New Testament emphasis on the Father, Son, and Spirit each indwelling Christians.

30. Smail has virtually the same insight, without connecting this idea to gender. Smail, *Like Father, Like Son*, 45–46.

31. Letham, "Man-Woman Debate," 66.

32. Ibid.

33. For example, Grudem, "Doctrinal Deviations," 17.

influential theologian to "speak a good word about the mystery of God recognizable within the contours of Christian faith that will serve the emancipatory praxis of women and men."[34] Johnson seeks material from what she labels classical theology that "when read with a feminist hermeneutic . . . could serve a discourse about divine mystery that would further the emancipation of women."[35] This project commits Johnson to appeal to women's experience in an effort to avoid patriarchy and androcentrism so that she can deconstruct existing doctrines that contribute to sexism, identify suppressed theological alternatives, and reconstruct a new theology.[36] The product of her work is an alternative vision of the Trinity, one that incorporates the feminine imagery of wisdom (Greek *sophia*) to speak of Spirit-Sophia, Jesus-Sophia, and Mother-Sophia. Johnson also prioritizes images of communion and perichoresis, affirms the idea of a suffering God, and argues that the Trinity calls for human communities of radical equality.[37]

Johnson's theology does not compare with the trinitarian theology put forward by some egalitarian evangelicals to combat EFS. While there are certainly differences among feminist theologians writing on the Trinity, they generally share with Johnson an emphasis on the lived experience of women as a theological resource, on retrieving certain alternative formations of the doctrine of the Trinity, on fighting sexism, and frequently on using alternative names for God.[38] Appeals to experience run contrary to fundamental evangelical assumptions about the primacy of Scripture in theology—should theological alternatives to received interpretations of classical theology be pursued due to ethical concerns, or only when the retrieval is prompted by a return to Scripture? Labelling opponents of EFS "evangelical feminists" thus associates them with certain moves that run contrary to the heart of evangelical identity and theology. This is despite the fact that the egalitarians (and increasingly also complementarians) who oppose EFS never affirm these troubling moves

34. Johnson, *She Who Is*, 8.
35. Ibid., 9.
36. Ibid., 29–30.
37. Ibid., 124–87, 266–69, 218–19.
38. For example see Coakley, *God, Sexuality, and the Self*. Though Sarah Coakley avoids earlier feminist methods for appropriating human experience, she still sees a "necessary and *intrinsic* entanglement of human sexuality and spirituality" such that "questions of right contemplation of God, right speech about God, and right ordering of desire all hang together" (1–2). This causes her to draw on gender theory, which is itself informed by experience as well as scientific and sociological study. She pursues a "rereading of the formative, patristic sources" (4) to uncover what she eventually describes as "that elusive goal of inner trinitarian *radical* equality" (310). Coakley insists, however, that the feminist must use the term Father for God, "for it lies with her alone to do the kneeling work that ultimately slays patriarchy at its root" (327).

and generally reject the label "evangelical feminist" as an accurate representation of their perspectives.[39] Calling opponents of EFS "evangelical feminists" is an inaccurate title that serves to predispose lay evangelicals to reject any claims made against eternal submission. In this respect the title functions much like Athanasius's term "Arian," which he coined to describe any anti-Nicene theology, a strategy that predisposed orthodox Christians to reject anti-Nicene thought even though, in their specific details, later theologians like Eunomius or Basil of Ancyra had very little in common with Arius.[40] While any grouping of theologians into a category will necessarily overlook certain differences (my use of "EFS advocates" has this shortcoming), intentionally crafting a category that is inaccurately associated with a widely rejected position or person is an unethical and manipulative rhetorical strategy. Opponents of EFS are not evangelical feminists and should not be silenced by labelling them as feminists.

The fact that labels can so often be used in evangelical theology to marginalize entire perspectives also reveals an injustice among evangelicals toward non-evangelical perspectives. I reject many of the methodological assumptions and resulting conclusions found in many feminist theologians. Nevertheless, it is a grave mistake and injustice to disregard automatically the work of a scholar simply because that individual is a feminist theologian. Feminist theologians have had and will continue to have important insights that can offer a needed corrective to evangelical thinking. For example, where Strachan and Peacock argue that God "is exclusively identified in Scripture in masculine terms,"[41] Johnson challenges them to be more scriptural when she points to Old Testament depictions of God in labor or giving birth (Isa 42:14; Deut 32:18), comforting like a mother comforts (Isa 63:13), or playing the role of a midwife (Ps 22:1, 9–10).[42] One need not accept Johnson's proposal and speak of God as "Mother-Sophia" to see that she has demonstrated that Strachan and Peacock are not considering the whole counsel of God. Evangelicals would benefit from considering how to incorporate analysis of devotional and ascetic practices into trinitarian reflection, as Sarah Coakley has done in her feminist trinitarian theology far more successfully than any evangelical theologian I know.[43] Coakley is also one of the first theologians to attempt to engage game theory theologically,

---

39. I would certainly deny this title, and I have confirmed in personal correspondence with Kevin Giles that he rejects it as well. I have never seen any opponent of EFS adopt this terminology.

40. Ayres, *Nicaea and Its Legacy*, 106–7.

41. Strachan and Peacock, *Grand Design*, 23.

42. Johnson, *She Who Is*, 100–103.

43. Coakley, *God, Sexuality, and the Self*.

and she has facilitated and contributed to important research into Gregory of Nyssa's theology.[44] Are we to automatically discount her scholarly contributions because she is not evangelical? Certainly not! When it comes to questions of abuse in the church, many feminists are light years ahead of evangelicals in identifying practices that may harm women. Feminist theology is an important dialogue partner. Few evangelicals will likely ever overcome substantive disagreements with feminist theology, but we have much to learn. In fact, if EFS advocates had listened to Catherine Mowry LaCugna's insistence that discussions of gender roles are more appropriately directed to the social teachings and life of the early church than to the Trinity, this entire book might be unnecessary![45]

In sum, there is no valid connection between theological anthropology and the Trinity. There are strong arguments against using the Trinity as an analogical ideal for human relationships, except where there is clear biblical teaching. Appeals to Genesis 1:26–7 in an effort to ground complementarianism in the Trinity fail to convincingly interpret the text. Nor is a rejection of EFS somehow indicative of feminist inroads into evangelical thinking. The term "evangelical feminist" used by those who uphold EFS tells us far more about evangelical refusal to listen to non-evangelical voices and about evangelical scapegoating than it actually tells us about the views of those who condemn eternal submission.

---

44. Coakley and Nowak, eds., *Evolution, Games, and God*; Coakley, ed., *Rethinking Gregory of Nyssa*.

45. LaCugna notes that *perichoresis* is an appealing model for feminists who might want to establish gender roles, but "the central claim of feminist theology—that a human community structured by relationships of equality and mutuality rather than hierarchy is a true icon of God's relational life—could be more trenchantly and more convincingly made by sidestepping the methodological starting point—and ending point—of Latin theology *in divinis*, and returning to the economy of salvation and the revelation of the concrete forms of human community proclaimed by Jesus as characteristic of the reign of God. Otherwise it seems that feminism, as much as patriarchy, projects its vision of what it wishes would happen in the human sphere, on to God, or onto a transeconomic, transexperiential realm of intradivine relations." LaCugna, *God for Us*, 274. Here Ware and Starke not only fail to listen to LaCugna, but also completely misrepresent her: "Feminist theologians like . . . Catherine LaCugna . . . labored to eliminate anything appearing to give credence to the Son's submitting to the Father from eternity. They thereby gave ontological reinforcement to a completely egalitarian relationship between male and female." Ware and Starke, "Preface," 12.

5

His Counsel Revealed to the Prophets
The Missing Scriptural Case for Eternal Submission

> "Surely the Lord GOD does nothing unless he reveals his counsel to his servants the prophets." (Amos 3:7 NASB)

> "The doctrine of the Trinity . . . [is] not identical with a bit of the text of the Bible witness to revelation. The text of the doctrine of the Trinity is throughout connected with texts in the Bible witness to revelation, it includes also certain concepts taken from that text, but it does so just as an interpretation does, i.e., it translates and expounds that text, and that, e.g., involves its availing itself of other concepts than those contained in the text before it."[1]
>
> —Karl Barth

During the course of this book, I have developed a scriptural case against eternal functional subordination, albeit an indirect one. I have deployed various dogmatic formulas that derive from second-order reflection on the broad scope of the Bible, attempting to synthesize key themes while providing conceptual clarity. Seen in this light, the pro-Nicene account of inseparable operations is also an indirect scriptural case against EFS. The doctrine of inseparable operations attempts to make sense of the scriptural pattern of shared operations between Father, Son, and Holy Spirit, as well as key scriptural texts such as John 5:17–30. To the extent that the doctrine of

---

1. Barth, *Church Dogmatics* I.1, 354.

inseparable operations faithfully represents these patterns in Scripture, there is scriptural warrant for rejecting EFS. Where claims of eternal submission conflicts with dyothelite Christology, satisfaction theory, or classical depictions of the divine attributes, EFS advocates must offer a different account of the scriptural patterns from which these doctrines arrive. When EFS theologians differ from traditional theological interpretations of key texts that led to the development of these doctrines, for example John 10:17–18 and consequent necessity, they must offer a more compelling account of the passage's meaning and theological doctrines that arise indirectly from the passage. If no such accounts are offered, or if offered accounts are not compelling, then there is scriptural warrant for rejecting EFS. This warrant is of an indirect nature—there is no single biblical passage that serves as a basis for rejecting the doctrine of the eternal submission of Christ. Yet it may still be the reasonable doctrinal conclusion to abandon EFS on the basis of reflection on the broad patterns of the biblical testimony in an attempt to provide conceptual clarity. I believe that I have made a strong case for precisely this conclusion.

One possible problem could undermine my entire argument. Where I offer non-scriptural language and concepts, doctrines that derive from Scripture and arguably fit Scripture, but that nevertheless are not explicitly explained in the Bible, I offer an argument that is weaker than an explicit teaching of the Bible. If a doctrine makes sense of scriptural patterns, provides conceptual clarity, and does not contradict the explicit teaching of the Bible, there is strong warrant for accepting it. However, a doctrine may make sense of some patterns in the Bible while contradicting explicit teachings elsewhere, in which case the doctrine is flawed. For example, early Docetists believed that Jesus only appeared to be human but was actually something more of a phantasm. This doctrinal claim does admittedly make sense of some biblical evidence—for example how Jesus violated laws of nature by walking on water (Mark 6:48–9) or how he appeared to the disciples despite the doors being locked (John 20:19). However, Docetism is also an explanation that is contrary to the clear teaching of the Bible that "the Word was made flesh" (John 1:14), that he was "born of a woman" (Gal 4:4), and that he "suffered in the flesh" (1 Pet 4:1). Any conceptual clarity that Docetism provides concerning Jesus walking on water has no validity in the face of verses that explicitly teach that Jesus actually took on flesh. What I have termed second-order systematic theological reflections have less authority than first-order explicit biblical teachings. All participants in the debate affirm that the Bible is the highest authority in theological debate. I certainly accept this principle.

Many who advocate EFS see eternal submission as an explicit first-order teaching of the Bible. Such theologians believe EFS is necessary due to biblical exegesis, or at least due to biblical theology. If this is the case, then this book cannot serve as an argument against eternal submission. Instead, I have merely exposed the incompatibility of much of classical theology with the explicit teaching of the Bible on the question of the number of wills in the Godhead and the eternal submission of the Son. However, most of the texts that EFS advocates put forward are contentious. If there were multiple verses that clearly teach the eternal submission of the Son, then my theological case against EFS fails. If, however, there are multiple verses that may *possibly* teach eternal submission, but that may also be interpreted in a different manner without doing injustice to the author's intentions and words, then the strength of my argument against EFS grows as the weight of the evidence in favor of EFS interpretations of such passages diminishes. My ambitions for this chapter are therefore modest. I do not intent to disprove EFS by appealing to scriptural texts that explicitly reject this doctrine. I do not even intend to prove the less ambitious claim that no text in the Bible could possibly support eternal submission. Rather, I intend to show that some passages of the Bible could be compatible with eternal submission, but that *none of these passages indisputably teach this doctrine*. In fact, as I will show, though some passages may be taken to affirm EFS, the weight of the evidence actually favors the classical interpretation. Lacking explicit endorsement in the Bible, EFS becomes a second-order inference from Scripture, but I have demonstrated in previous chapters that EFS fails to be an adequate second-order account of Scripture, for it neither provides conceptual clarity, fits scriptural patterns well, nor offers precision of theological language. In other words, I hope to show that the weight of the biblical evidence for eternal submission is insufficient to justify overturning centuries of theological tradition.

1 Corinthians 15 and the Case for Eternal Submission

Theologians who accept EFS appeal to a wide range of biblical passages to make their case, but one passage is clearly most important. There is only one passage in the New Testament that uses the Greek word for the verb "to submit" (*hypotassō*) of the Son in a context that is clearly either before the incarnation or after the ascension: 1 Corinthians 15:28. Other uses of this word during the incarnate life of Christ could easily refer to human submission with a human will, so this passage is particularly important. In context, the passage reads,

12 Now if Christ is proclaimed as raised from the dead, how can some of you say that there is no resurrection of the dead? 13 But if there is no resurrection of the dead, then not even Christ has been raised. 14 And if Christ has not been raised, then our preaching is in vain and your faith is in vain. 15 We are even found to be misrepresenting God, because we testified about God that he raised Christ, whom he did not raise if it is true that the dead are not raised. 16 For if the dead are not raised, not even Christ has been raised. 17 And if Christ has not been raised, your faith is futile and you are still in your sins. 18 Then those also who have fallen asleep in Christ have perished. 19 If in Christ we have hope in this life only, we are of all people most to be pitied.

20 But in fact Christ has been raised from the dead, the firstfruits of those who have fallen asleep. 21 For as by a man came death, by a man has come also the resurrection of the dead. 22 For as in Adam all die, so also in Christ shall all be made alive. 23 But each in his own order: Christ the firstfruits, then at his coming those who belong to Christ. 24 Then comes the end, when he delivers the kingdom to God the Father after destroying every rule and every authority and power. 25 For he must reign until he has put all his enemies under his feet. 26 The last enemy to be destroyed is death. 27 For "God has put all things in subjection under his feet." But when it says, "all things are put in subjection," it is plain that he is excepted who put all things in subjection under him. 28 When all things are subjected to him, then the Son himself will also be subjected to him who put all things in subjection under him, that God may be all in all.

Bruce Ware treats 1 Corinthians 15:24–28 as evidence of "the Son's submission to the Father in eternity future."[2] Wayne Grudem goes even farther, arguing that the phrase "he is excepted who put all things in subjection under him" (15:27) reveals that "it was the Father who always had ultimate authority," while Paul's claim that "the Son himself will also be subjected" (15:28) reveals "that the Son will continue to be subject to the authority of the Father forever."[3]

As the only verse explicitly using the word that can be translated "to submit" or "to be put into subjection" (the latter being used by the ESV as quoted above), the weight of the EFS argument must lie particularly heavily on this passage. It serves as a central pillar of the scriptural case for EFS.

2. Ware, *Father, Son, and Spirit*, 83.
3. Grudem, "Biblical Evidence," 252.

Despite this, most theologians debating EFS on both sides have only treated the passage in brief. Grudem, Ware, Millard Erickson, and Kevin Giles[4] only examine 15:24–28, ignoring the wider context of 1 Corinthians 15. Though such cursory treatment is somewhat understandable given the wide scope of the debate, it is still rather surprising that such a central passage is not treated with greater exegetical clarity. Given the brevity of standard treatments, James Hamilton wisely published a chapter defending 1 Corinthians 15:28 as an important piece of the argument for EFS, considered in the context of Paul's argument, and also in canonical context.[5] Because Hamilton has elevated the level of exegetical analysis of this passage, my treatment will largely occur in dialogue with him, only briefly referencing other figures in the EFS debate.

The purpose of 1 Corinthians 15 is to address a controversy surrounding the resurrection. The problem at Corinth may have been a diversity of false beliefs: claims that the general resurrection had already occurred, rejection of bodily resurrection in its entirety, and/or perhaps even denial of afterlife altogether. Paul responds to this problem with what Thiselton characterizes as "clear and careful logical argument, coherence, and constructive use of resources from the best Roman rhetoric of the times."[6] We should expect coherence between what is said in 15:28 and the larger scope of chapter 15. Thus far, Hamilton would agree. He also rightly notes that 1 Corinthians 15:5–11 establishes the centrality of Christ's resurrection to the gospel, and 15:12–19 establishes problems with claiming that there is no resurrection, for this would entail that even Christ is not raised![7] This is significant for Paul, because "if Christ has not been raised, your faith is futile and you are still in your sins" (15:17). The gospel that was passed down from the disciples concerning Christ's resurrection is fundamentally linked to the salvation announced in the gospel.

After setting the scene in 15:1–19, Paul explains in 15:20–28 how it is that Jesus's resurrection is so central to the gospel. First, we must note that Jesus is the firstfruits of the resurrection. Hamilton explains that defending this claim is Paul's purpose in verses 20–28.[8] The term "firstfruits" indicates that the resurrection of Christ is the first installment of a crop, something

---

4. Ware, *Father, Son, and Holy Spirit*, 83–84; Grudem, "Biblical Evidence," 252; Erickson, *Who's Tampering?* 114–15, 164; Giles, *Jesus and the Father*, 112–15.

5. See Hamilton, "All in All," 95–108.

6. Thiselton, *1 Corinthians*, 253–54. See Ibid., 255 for Corinthian views.

7. Hamilton, "All in All," 96–97.

8. Ibid., 97.

serving as proof of the fuller harvest to come.[9] Paul's subsequent treatment of the relationship between Adam and Christ explains why this is the case. Paul writes, "by a man came death, by a man has come also the resurrection of the dead. For as in Adam all die, so also in Christ shall all be made alive" (15:21-2). Here, Paul is making a connection between Adam and Jesus Christ that is central to his Christology. Paul offers another extended treatment of how Christ's obedience undoes Adam's disobedience in Romans 5:12-21. Thomas Schreiner argues that Paul's language calling Christians to put off the old man and put on the new (Eph 2:15; 4:22; Col 3:9-11) also is intended to point to Christ's role as the second or last Adam.[10] This plausible argument would have old man/new man language functioning in a similar fashion to 1 Cor 15:22, "in Adam all die, so also in Christ all shall be made alive."

Hamilton notes the "firstfruits" and new Adam language of 1 Corinthians 15, but does not tarry to consider the significance of this trope in Paul's writing or in the present argument. Instead, Hamilton quickly moves to consider Paul's argument in a wider canonical context, attempting to "synthesize" Paul's claims with the depiction of the end discussed in Revelation 20. The bulk of the remainder of Hamilton's treatment thus becomes an effort to determine precisely the chronology of the events described in Revelation and 1 Corinthians 15. The "first resurrection" of Revelation 20:5-6 parallels the resurrection of believers in 1 Corinthians 15:23, the reign of Christ putting enemies under his feet (1 Cor 15:25) with the millennial reign of Christ (Rev 20:1-6), and the destruction of death (1 Cor 15:26) corresponds with Hades giving up the dead (Rev 20:13-14). As a result, Hamilton concludes that, "Paul does not appear to be discussing the difference between the human Jesus and the divine Jesus. . . . He is discussing the order of the events at the end."[11] Hamilton reduces 1 Cor 15:27-28 to an aside meant to prevent "a possible misunderstanding of the idea that everything will be put in subjection to Christ."[12] The Father is never subject to Christ; he is the one who put all things into subjection under Christ, and the one to whom the Son eternally is subject. Hamilton concludes by endorsing EFS.

---

9. Ibid., 98; cf. Barrett, *First Epistle to the Corinthians*, 350-51.

10. Schreiner, *Paul*, 154-55. Schreiner notes that the same verb calling us to put on the new man (*endysasthai*) is used in Rom 13:14 to urge believers to put on Christ, suggesting that the "new man" is in fact Christ, a title serving as shorthand for "the second Adam." Schreiner also links Rom 13:14 to this similar collection of texts, perhaps less plausibly.

11. Hamilton, "All in All," 98-100.

12. Ibid., 100.

While it is an interesting question how 1 Corinthians 15 lines up with the chronology of Revelation 19–20, and while Hamilton offers a noteworthy opinion on how these passages may relate given certain hermeneutic assumptions,[13] it is not at all clear that Revelation 19–20 provide the hermeneutic lynchpin for determining Paul's meaning in this passage. Hamilton moves from the parallel in chronology between the Corinthian correspondence and Revelation to conclude what Paul is and is not doing in the passage. A far better approach would consider what Paul is doing elsewhere when he treats Christ as second Adam, and then use this insight to help clarify what Paul is doing in 1 Corinthians 15, while retaining an emphasis on the flow of the argument in chapter 15 itself. Hamilton's methodology causes him to miss entirely the heart of the passage.

When Paul appeals to Christ as the "last Adam" (1 Cor 15:45), or treats Adam as a "type" of Christ (Rom 5:14), or contrasts the "old man" and the "new man" (Eph 2:15; 4:22; Col 3:9–11; Rom 13:14), he is establishing something central to the work of Christ. In Romans, perhaps Paul's most systematic work, he explains the human condition in terms of Genesis 1–3. Romans 1:18–32 with its introduction to the sinful state of humanity likely alludes to Adam. As James D. G. Dunn remarks, "The claim to be wise, which in direct contrast plunged into folly, recalls the current understanding of the tree of the knowledge of good and evil."[14] Similarly, Romans 3:23's claim that "all have sinned and fall short of the glory of God" is a concise summary of how Paul's contemporaries would have understood the legacy of Adam.[15] Enter Romans 5:12–21, which even more explicitly explains the human predicament as a consequence of one man's disobedience. Here Paul treats Christ as the new Adam, whose death and resurrection affects his spiritual offspring in a similar manner to how the first Adam's sin negatively affected his offspring. Adam was a type of Christ (Rom 5:14), and Christ is the new Adam who overcomes the legacy of the old Adam. Jesus, like Adam, is representative of humanity, but the consequences of his obedience are the opposite of Adam's disobedience.[16] In Romans 6–8 Paul then explains how the work of Christ results in a shift from the dominion of "the flesh"

---

13. Not least of which concerns how we ought to read the genre of apocalyptic, a heated debate well beyond the scope of this work. For a strong argument against Hamilton, see: Ridderbos, *Paul*, 556–60.

14. Dunn, *Theology of Paul*, 91–92.

15. Ibid., 93.

16. The representative nature of Christ as last Adam is acknowledged by both the New and Lutheran perspectives on Paul. See Dunn, *Theology of Paul*, 200; Moo, *Epistle to the Romans*, 339–49.

polluted by Adam into life "in the Spirit" in the dominion of Christ, the new Adam.[17]

Paul also frequently establishes Christ's identity in Adamic terms. Besides the Adam/Christ typology just discussed, Adamic Christology exists across the Pauline corpus. A parallel between Christ and Adam likely lies behind Paul's treatment of the Son as "the image of the invisible God, the firstborn over all creation" (Col 1:15).[18] In context this passage certainly implies the divinity of Christ, but this divinity is predicated of one who, like Adam, is also said to bear God's image and who will have the prerogatives of the firstborn over creation. Paul apparently partly has in mind the viceregency and dominion granted to the firstborn Adam after his creation (Gen 1:29-30; cf. Rom 8:29).[19] Similarly, Philippians 2 likely plays on a contrast between Adam and Christ, where Adam saw equality with God as something to be seized and thus was punished, while Christ instead humbled himself and was given the title of Lord.[20] If this parallel holds, then the one exalted and "given the name that is above every name" (Phil 2:9) is the second Adam. The one in human form (2:7) is also Lord. Jewish apocalyptic expectations reveal the hope that the faithful would receive the glory and dominion belonging to Adam on the last day.[21]

Given Paul's emphasis on Adamic Christology and his Adam-influenced soteriology, we can expect Paul's appeal to Adam/Christ typology in 1 Corinthians 15 to be an important clue as to his overall meaning. In Romans 5:15-19, the contrast between Adam and Jesus, the new Adam, is a contrast between life and justification through obedience on the one hand, and death and condemnation through disobedience on the other. In 1 Corinthians 15, Paul maintains the parallel life through the last Adam but death through the first Adam: "in Adam all die, so also in Christ shall

---

17. Strom, *Reframing Paul*, 87-95.

18. Schreiner, *Paul*, 155-6.

19. So Peter T O'Brien agrees that Adamic Christology is in view here, but also views wisdom Christology as an important background element. Moo points out that the Wisdom tradition itself draws on Genesis 1's depiction of humanity bearing the image of God. It is noteworthy, Romans 8:29 depicts Christ as firstborn in the sense that he will have many brothers and sisters, serving as the head of a new humanity, as new Adam. That term may more clearly denote an Adamic Christology than the language of "image." O'Brien, *Colossians, Philemon*, 43-44; Moo, *Colossians and Philemon*, 117-18.

20. Brown, *New Testament Christology*, 134-35; Thomas Schreiner, *Paul*, 172.

21. Wright, *The New Testament and the People of God*, 265-66. Wright suggests a similar concept lies behind the apocalyptic vision in Daniel 7. This may be the case, though Adamic connections are explicit and indisputable in the Qumran manuscripts, so it is better to focus the argument there. See also the longer treatment in Kirk, *Man Attested*, 61-70.

all be made alive" (15:21). However, unlike in Romans 5, Paul incorporates another important aspect of Adamic Christology: the eschatological human viceregency fulfilling the dominion of Adam that was destroyed through the sin of the first Adam. As second Adam, Christ "must reign until he has put all his enemies under his feet" (1 Cor 15:25), a direct citation of Psalm 110:1. In 15:27, Paul cites Psalm 8:6, "God has put all things in subjection under his feet." These two scriptural citations provide further insight as to Paul's meaning in 15:28. These two texts together suggest that Paul's purpose here is to connect the significance of Jesus's bodily resurrection to the expected viceregency of the second Adam.

Psalm 110, often seen as an enthronement psalm, was likely written to depict a divine promise to David, or perhaps to a subsequent king of Judah.[22] By the time of the Synoptic Gospels, 110:1 was treated as referring to the Messiah. In a telling series of passages in the Synoptic Gospels, Jesus is challenged by his theological opponents in various attempts to trap him into compromising himself. At the end of this sequence, Jesus presents his own question to his interlocutors:

> How can the scribes say that the Christ is the son of David? David himself, in the Holy Spirit, declared, "The Lord said to my Lord, 'Sit at my right hand, until I put your enemies under your feet.'" David himself calls him Lord. So how is he his son? (Mark 12:35–37; Matt 22:41–46; Luke 20:41–44)

Jesus is challenging his opponents to declare the Messiah to be more than the son of David. He is also David's *lord*.[23] When on trial in front of Pilate, Jesus will also claim that Pilate will see the Son of Man "sitting at the right hand of power," citing Psalm 110:1, "and coming with the clouds of heaven," drawing on imagery from Daniel 7:14–15 (Mark 14:61–2; cf. Matt 26:63–64; Luke 22:67–70). In the Synoptic Gospels, Psalm 110:1 coalesces several key titles: son of David, Messiah, and Son of Man.[24] Each title has a human

---

22. Allen, *Psalms 101–50*, 111–13. Allen helpfully surveys a scholarship on the psalm to reveal a broad consensus on this interpretation.

23. For Matthew and Luke, at least, it is clear that they do not reject the title "son of David" as appropriate for the Messiah, given their efforts to tie Jesus to David in each gospel's respective genealogy (Luke 3:31; Matt 1:6).

24. Bates, *The Birth of the Trinity*, 44–50; Beale and Carson, eds. *New Testament Use of the Old Testament*, 745. There is some debate concerning precisely how the psalm is serving in the synoptics. Matthew Bates believes that Jesus is using prosopological exegesis here, such that the Spirit is seen working through the Psalmist (presumed to be David), so that he can prophetically speak on behalf of the person of God to the person of Christ in a divine theodrama looking beyond the timeframe in which the psalm was written. G. K. Beale and D. A. Carson classify Paul's use of Psalm 110 and 8

referent, though not a *merely* human referent.[25] This canonical context provides exegetical help in determining Paul's meaning in 1 Corinthians 15.

Psalm 8 is treated throughout the New Testament as an important passage for understanding the eschatological role of Christ as second Adam. The Psalm itself reads:

> When I look at your heavens, the work of your fingers,
> > the moon and the stars, which you have set in place,
> > what is man that you are mindful of him,
> > > and the son of man that you care for him?
>
> Yet you have made him a little lower than the heavenly beings
> > and crowned him with glory and honor.
> You have given him dominion over the works of your hands;
> > you have put all things under his feet.

In the first century this passage was read as speaking of humanity in Adamic terms: we have inherited dominion through Adam and Eve (Gen 1:26–27). Though Adamic dominion is still partially exercised by human beings, by the time of the New Testament we see an increasing expectation of a second Adam figure receiving full dominion and being crowned with the glory Adam had before the fall.[26] In Ephesians 1 Paul writes that God raised Christ from the dead and sat him at his right hand (1:20), giving him power above all others (1:21). Paul then cites Psalm 8:6 and concludes that Christ is head over the church, his body. Adamic overtones are clear: Christ is risen bodily and given eschatological dominion as head of those who share in his nature, serving as second Adam.[27] In Philippians 3:20b–21, Paul writes that, "we await a Savior, the Lord Jesus Christ, who will transform our lowly body to be like his glorious body, by the power that enables him even to subject all things to himself." Here again we see the eschatological expec-

---

under the ideas of typology, "christological exegesis," and "*gezerah shavah* (comparing similar expressions)."

25. Psalm 110:3 may also reference the preexistence of Christ, while 110:4 emphasizes priesthood in the order of Melchizedek, with the associated ambiguity of the human/non-human role of this shadowy figure. See Bates, *Birth of the Trinity*, 54–56.

26. See the growing emphasis on Adam's glory before the fall in *Sir.* 49.16; the Greek *Life of Adam and Eve* 20:1–2, 21:2, 6; *2 En.* 30:11–14; *Apoc. Adam* 1:2. Eschatological expectations have been treated in brief above. For further analysis, see: Fletcher-Louis, *Jesus Monotheism*, 250–56; Gabrielson, *Primeval History*, 140–51. Of course one can grant the elevated views of Adam in much Second Temple literature without agreeing with Fletcher-Louis's narrative of how christological monotheism emerged.

27. Bruce, *Colossians, Philemon, and Ephesians*, 274; cf. Lincoln, *Ephesians*, 66.

tation that the Lord will reign as the faithful are conformed to his nature. Outside of Paul, we see Psalm 8 functioning in a similar fashion. The first two chapters of Hebrews emphasize the human reign of Christ by drawing on OT passages emphasizing human viceregency, including Psalm 8:6.[28] In each of these citations, there is a clear emphasis on human dominion.

The citation of Psalm 8:6 is the immediate context of 1 Cor 15:28, and it helps us understand Paul's meaning when he writes, "When all things are subjected to him, then the Son himself will also be subjected to him who put all things in subjection under him, that God may be all in all." All things will be subjected to the one who has just been identified as "the man" who undoes the death brought by the first man (15:22). Paul has in mind the "last Adam" (15:45), the one who is "the firstfruits" of the new humanity (15:20), a human who has risen from the dead as proof of God's plans to overcome death. This risen man, this last Adam, the firstfruits of the general resurrection, will have everything put in subjection under him according to the apocalyptic expectation of a second Adam receiving viceregency with God, which is prophetically announced in Psalm 8:6. Paul has in mind a complete restoration of what was intended for Adam, and if Christ has not been raised, then the Corinthians have no hope for the defeat of death or for the restoration of humanity through a second Adam (15:17). Here Paul adds two important clarifying statements. First, "he is excepted who put all things in subjection under him" (15:27). Grudem sees this as an attempt to safeguard the authority of the Father over the Son, but since the Son as last Adam is in view, it is actually an effort to safeguard the monarchy of God over humanity. Everything is subject to the second man except God. Second, "the Son himself will also be subjected to him who put all things in subjection under him" (15:28). EFS theologians treat this as evidence of the Son's eternal submission, but the entirety of Paul's argument so far has attempted to establish the central importance of the resurrection of Christ due to his status as second Adam. After 15:28, Paul continues to speak of Christ's role as second Adam, explaining how the resurrection body will mirror Christ's risen body for he is the last Adam (15:35–49). This context and the citation of the human-oriented Psalm 8 reveals Paul's intent. Christ will reign as second Adam, the human viceregent with God. Then, at some point, this human reign as second Adam will end, "so that God may be all in all" (15:28b).[29]

---

28. McCartney, "Ecce Homo," 8.

29. Fitzmyer suggests that the final subjection of the Son will be "because Christ's regnal and salvific role will be at an end." Fitzmyer, *First Corinthians*, 574. See also Johnson, *1 Corinthians*, 294; Montague, *First Corinthians*, 274; Ridderbos, *Paul*, 560–61.

What Paul has in mind in verse 28 has nothing to do with the eternal relation between Father and Son, and everything to do with Christ's human status as second Adam, a status that Paul reveals will one day be supplanted by the even greater grace of God's direct rule. Here is where Hamilton's comparison with Revelation does come into play. Paul appears to teach of Christ's reign as second Adam for a time, much akin to the millennial reign in Revelation, but this time will end and there will be a final consummation in which creation can then be directly subject to God without Adamic mediation.[30] Thus, the purpose of creation is fulfilled, not frustrated. This is evident from the fact that Paul is citing Old Testament passages thought to speak of a son of man, an heir of David, and a new Adam. It is evident because the entirety of chapter 15 alludes to various facets of Genesis 1–3 and its account of the creation and fall of humanity.[31] It is evident because Paul's argument hinges on Christ being representative of humanity, the firstfruits, a claim which requires a common humanity between Christ and the church. It is also clear in that the occasion of Paul's writing is a refutation of misunderstandings of human resurrection and afterlife. I can agree with Hamilton that Paul is not explaining how Jesus's humanity and divinity relate; this explanation arose at the Council of Chalcedon through second-order reflection on a range of biblical passages. However, Hamilton is entirely wrong to view this passage as merely focusing on chronology, for he fails to identify fundamental theological themes central to Paul's argument here. Paul is speaking of the second Adam, and hence of a future subjection of the human vicegerent to the direct rule of God. Chalcedonian Christology can later explain that Christ *in his humanity* fulfills this role, and ultimately completes the operation of passing the kingdom to the direct rule of the Father, an operation of submission performed in and through the human nature of Christ, not eternally through the divine nature of the Son. Pro-Nicene trinitarian thought would also add that the inseparable opera-

---

30. In a previous article I offered a similar interpretation of 1 Cor 15:20–28. Unfortunately in the editing process I missed a significant typographical error, and the final publication includes the claim that "the fulfillment of Christ's human role will no longer be *complete*." The intended phrasing was "Christ's human role will no longer be *incomplete*." (This is still poorly worded). I did not and do not intend to point to the undoing of the work of Christ, but rather to its final consummation. Butner, "Eternal Functional Subordination," 145.

31. Wright, *Paul*, 28. Besides the explicit appeal to Adam, Wright notes that Psalm 8 itself was understood to allude to Genesis 1–3. Paul's discussion of the type of resurrected body assumes the creation account of Genesis 1. Wright also argues that the contrast between the earthly and spiritual bodies found in 15:42–49 is rooted in Genesis 2:7. L. J. Kreitzer perhaps goes too far when he argues that Paul is drawing on a midraishic interpretation Genesis 2:7 in his argument in 15:42–49. Kreitzer, "Adam and Christ," 11–12.

tions of the persons *ad extra* entails that the Son will also reign eternally with the Father and Holy Spirit according to their shared divine nature (cf. Luke 1:33, Dan 7:14).

Both the pro-Nicene and the Chalcedonian gloss of 1 Corinthians 15 move beyond mere exegesis; these claims arise from a broad survey of Scripture to develop a trinitarian and christological hermeneutic or rule of faith.[32] It is, of course, theoretically possible that a different hermeneutic rooted in EFS could offer a different reading of 1 Corinthians 15 that suggested eternal submission of the Son. However, that would be a gloss arising from a second-order reflection on the Bible in its entirety, and not a first-order conclusion drawn directly from what Paul intends in this passage. It is certainly not the case that 1 Corinthians 15 demands acceptance of the idea of eternal submission. Nor is it the case that Paul is intending to address the eternal divine relationship between Father and Son in this passage. Moreover, I have argued throughout this book that EFS is an inferior second-order set of doctrines because it fails to answer key questions that the traditional premise of a single divine will is capable of answering. It is also worth noting that in terms of 1 Corinthians 15, there would be a greater gap between the doctrine of EFS and biblical exegesis than between pro-Nicene and Chalcedonian doctrine and biblical exegesis. EFS doctrinal readings emphasize Christ's divinity in this passage, whereas Chalcedonian readings emphasize Christ's humanity, as does Paul. Simply put, the strongest potential candidate for direct scriptural endorsement of EFS fails to prove the eternal obedience of the Son.

Other Purported New Testament Evidence for EFS

While 1 Corinthians 15:28 may be the most important verse in the debate surrounding eternal submission, it is not the only verse cited by EFS theologians to make their case. Even if 1 Corinthians 15:28 does not explicitly teach eternal submission, it is certainly possible that EFS is evident in other biblical passages or tropes. We must therefore consider a number of additional passages from the New Testament to assess adequately the biblical case for eternal submission.

---

32. It is important to note that this interpretation is entirely consistent with the pro-Nicene and dyothelite theologies described above. Another strategy EFS theologians deploy in 1 Corinthians 15 is to accuse a commentator treating 15:28 as referring only to the Son's humanity as a Nestorian, a problematic argument following the same pattern as the accusations of Nestorianism treated in chapter 2. For example see Dahms, "Subordination," 342.

Passages That Speak of the Son's Submission During His Incarnate Life

A number of theologians who affirm EFS point to passages of Scripture that depict the Son having a distinct will and/or submitting to his Father during his incarnate life and ministry as one reason to support eternal submission. John Dahms sees Jesus's claim that "the Father is greater than I" (John 14:28) as pointing not only to Jesus's incarnate status, but also to his eternal status.[33] Though John 8:28–29 is traditionally a text interpreted to reveal the inseparable operations of the Father and Son, Bruce Ware argues that it actually points to eternal submission. When Jesus says, "I do nothing of my own authority, but speak just as the Father taught me," Ware sees evidence that "Jesus's submission to the Father, then, is complete, comprehensive, all-inclusive, and absolute."[34] Michael Ovey points to John 3:34, 7:18, 5:19ff, 8:26, 12:49, and 14:24 as evidence that the Son eternally submits to the Father.[35]

When considering Jesus's claims or acts of obedience during his incarnate life, it is important to recognize that much like Paul, the Gospels present Christ serving as a second Adam, reversing the sin brought about by the first Adam. This is particularly evident at the beginning and end of the Gospel accounts. A number of scholars see the temptation in the wilderness in the Synoptic Gospels as a second Adamic trope, where the Messiah triumphs over temptation where the first Adam failed. In Mark 1:12–13 this parallel is muted, though still suggested from the word *ekballo* being used both in the Septuagint to describe Adam and Even cast from the garden into the wilderness and in Mark to describe Jesus being sent out into the wilderness. Second Temple literature had developed a tradition that Adam had fasted for forty days, much like Christ in the wilderness. Furthermore, Mark's reference to wild animals may imply Jesus, like Adam, has dominion over the animals, though this is contested.[36] The parallel is more evident in Matthew and Luke. Immediately prior to the temptation account, Luke finishes the genealogy by tracing Christ's ancestry all the way back to "son

---

33. Dahms, "Subordination," 358–59.
34. Ware, "Equal in Essence," 20.
35. Ovey, *Your Will be Done*, 89–90.
36. Crowe, *Last Adam*, 24–27. John Paul Heil objects to an Adamic parallel here, arguing that Adam does not fast (here Heil misses the account in *The Life of Adam and Eve*, whose dating is contentious), and that the lack of domestic animals with Christ suggests that wild animals are associated with Satan, not a second Adam figure. Heil's objections do weaken Adamic Christology in Mark 1, though they are not decisive. Heil, "Jesus with the Wild Animals," 68.1, 63–78.

of Adam, son of God" (Luke 3:38), perhaps setting Christ up as a second Adam figure.[37] Luke and Matthew also detail the specific temptations that Christ faces in Adamic terms. Like Adam, Jesus is tempted to eat what is improper (Luke 4:3; Matt 4:3). Adam fails the test but Jesus passes by rightly identifying how humans ought to live—"Man shall not live by bread alone" (Luke 4:4; Matt 4:4).[38] In another temptation the devil quotes Psalm 91:11–12, challenging the Son to throw himself off the temple because God will protect him (Luke 4:9–11; Matt 4:5–7). Interestingly, Psalm 91:13 speaks of trampling the serpent underfoot, an allusion to Genesis 3:15 and the ultimate victory over Satan by the Adamic line.[39] Immediately after the temptation, Luke depicts Jesus preaching a text from Isaiah 61, a passage that references human viceregency intended for humans but lost by Adam.[40]

Adamic overtones are found elsewhere throughout the Synoptic Gospels and John. The first two words in the Gospel of Matthew, *biblos geneseos*, are only found elsewhere in the Bible in the Septuagint in Genesis 2:4 and 5:1. This shared vocabulary leads G. K. Beale to conclude that Matthew sets up the birth narrative in second Adam terms, something also evident in the parallel between the Spirit-born Christ (Matt 1:18–20) and the first man born of the breath/spirit of God (Gen 2:7).[41] Throughout Matthew, Jesus exercises dominion in a manner that not only reflects his divine prerogatives, but that may also depict dominion as intended in the creational Adamic viceregency (Matt 8:27; 9:6–8).[42] In John, we see second Adam allusions most clearly in the passion narrative.[43] In John 19:5, for example, Pilate presents Christ and declares, "Behold the man!" The Hebrew of Genesis 3:22 can also be translated "behold the man has become like one of us!" In Genesis 3, this is an ironic statement, for Adam and Eve are banished from Eden and cursed immediately following this interjection. In the apocryphal *Life of Adam and Eve* 13:3, the angels are told "behold, Adam," and instructed to worship him. In this context, the phrase is also ironic—the scene is a flashback, so the reader is already well aware of the lowly fallen state of Adam in the present. Similar irony and Adamic references appear in John 19:5. The cross is the time when the Son is most glorified (see John

---

37. Crowe, *Last Adam*, 28–29.
38. See the discussion in Kirk, *Man Attested*, 215–28.
39. Ibid., 77.
40. McCartney, "Ecce Homo," 9.
41. Beale, *New Testament Biblical Theology*, 388–89. Beale makes the case with reference to Genesis 1:2, but a parallel is also clearly found with Genesis 2:7, though the verb *gennēthen* in Matthew 1:18 may make an echo of Genesis 1 more apparent.
42. McCartney, "Ecce Homo," 10, 12.
43. What follows is a much distilled summary of Litwa, "Behold Adam," 129–43.

12:23; 13:31; 17:11), but Pilate uses this phrase mockingly. Pilate presents a man, not recognizing that this man is really the second Adam, fulfilling the role intended for Adam because Jesus is strengthened by divine might. This interpretation fits with the wider Christology of John. Adam was ironically called like God (Gen 3:22) because he was an icon now possessing knowledge of good and evil. Jesus is the one who truly sees the Father (John 14:9), the one who knows the very mind of God (John 1:18).

There is a growing body of scholarly literature that suggests that the title "Son of Man" used throughout the Gospels may be connected with a theology of Jesus as second Adam.[44] Joel Marcus makes the case on linguistic grounds. The Septuagint uses the anarthrous "a son of man" (*huios anthropou*), but never the articular *"the* son of *the* man" (*ho huios tou anthropou*), which is how the Greek from throughout the Gospels should be literally translated. Marcus remarks, "The natural question would then be, 'the Son of *which* man?'"[45] After demonstrating that previous theories for the unusual grammatical structure fail, Marcus argues that we must treat the Greek literally and recognize that it points back to Adam, who is simply called "the man" (*ho anthropos*) in the Septuagint (Gen 1:27; 2:7, 8, 15, 18).[46] On this account, the title "the Son of the Man" would "on the analogy of 'the Son of David,' indicate a person who was descended from that first man, but who was also, in a way, on a par with or even greater than him."[47] Even if the linguistic argument does not hold, the fact that both Daniel 7:13–14 and Psalm 8, the texts most likely lying behind the term "Son of Man" in the New Testament, are both shaped by creational and Adamic imagery suggests an overlap between a second Adam and the Son of Man.[48] There

---

44. See the helpful survey article: Street, "From Marginal to Mainstream," 77–98.

45. Marcus, "Son of Man," 41. Emphasis original.

46. Ibid., 42–45. The dominant theory for the unusual construction is that it is a mistranslation of the Aramaic original. Marcus considers this methodologically flawed, as it is always preferable to assume that translation choices are deliberate. Moreover, there may have been multiple translators—could they all have made the same mistake? Finally, the mistranslation claim depends on a disputed chronology concerning the development of Aramaic grammar—the underlying Aramaic base may not have even meant what the dominant theory assumes at this time.

47. Ibid., 45.

48. Beale, *Biblical Theology*, 83–84. Though Daniel 7:13–14 is often seen as the most likely source of the "Son of Man" title in the New Testament, G. K. Beale argues that Daniel itself draws on Psalm 8:6. Beale notes "the following common themes: (1) the defeat or judgment of God's enemies; (2) the rule of the Son of Man; (3) the rule over sea creatures (the Targum of Ps 8 identifies the sea creature as Leviathan); (4) the glory of the Son of Man; (5) allusion to Gen 1:28 in Ps 8 and Dan 7:13–14." Even if Psalm 8 actually draws on Daniel, or if both texts are not theologically interwoven until New Testament times, such an overlap in themes warrants consideration of both when

is also significant overlap between the work, suffering, and coming glory attributed to the Son of Man in the Gospels and to a new Adam in Adamic Christology. This overlap supports connecting Son of Man imagery with the second Adam motif in early Christian thought.[49] In some Second Temple literature, Adam functions similarly to the Son of Man in Daniel 7.[50] This connection is already illustrated with 1 Corinthians 15 above, where Paul's citation of Psalm 8 may imply an attempt to develop a Son-of-Man Christology.[51] Though there is and likely will continue to be debate surrounding the term "son of man" for some time, one strong option is to regard the term as a reference to paradigmatic humanity.

The new Adam typology throughout the Gospels, which itself overlaps with a Christology emphasizing idealized human kingship,[52] coupled with the possibility that the title Son of Man identifies the son of Adam provides *prima facie* warrant for treating New Testament language about the obedience of the Son during the incarnation as a human obedience. His obedience is simply the obedience of the second Adam and Son of Man. A longer treatment of the subject could provide evidence of Jesus as second Moses, or as covenant representative of Israel to make the same point. One

---

treating the development of the idea of the son of man. Daniel 7:13–14 likely alludes to a restoration of Adamic viceregency, filtered through the lens of Genesis 22:18. Daniel 7:2 begins with the work of the wind, which may reference either Genesis 1:2. See also the treatment of son of man as idealized human in Kirk, *Man Attested*, 140–49.

49. Brandon Crowe, *Last Adam*, 43–49; cf. Cullmann, *Christology of the New Testament*, 142–52; Marcus, "Son of Man," 48–49; Kirk, *Man Attested*, 277. Crowe argues that in his work, the Son of Man's authority and sinlessness reflect the original authority and sinlessness of the first Adam. In his sufferings, a representative notion of suffering (see Mark 10:45) ties in well with a covenantal and representative reading of Adam, which may be present in Genesis, but is found more clearly in Paul's treatment of Adam in Romans 5. Crowe sees the coming glory of the Son of Man as perhaps referring to the glory Adam possessed before the fall, though Crowe sees an allusion to divine glory as more likely here. For my part, I do not see why the reference cannot allude to both. Cullmann's treatment extends to Second Temple Jewish literature and concludes that "'Son of Man' and 'Second Adam' are two different developments of the same christological idea" (145).

50. For example, see Hooker, *The Son of Man in Mark*, 49–56. This is particularly clear in 2 Esdras, which draws on ideas from Daniel 7 to depict Adam functioning quite similarly to the son of man figure in Daniel 7. Marcus suggests that there may be direct terminological overlap in 1 Enoch 62:7 and the Syriac of 4 Esdras 8:44. Marcus, "Son of Man," 46.

51. Schelkle comments that Paul may intentionally be developing a Christology focusing on son of man imagery without using the title itself, since it would be meaningless to a Gentile audience. Schelkle, *Theology of the New Testament: II*, 192; cf. Cullmann, *Christology*, 167–70.

52. See Kirk, *Man Attested*, 223–24.

can reasonably read these texts in canonical context to point toward human obedience.

Theological considerations also point in such a direction. Protestants were historically prone to treat Christ's obedience as the "active obedience" of the God-man,[53] whose human obedience was the basis of satisfaction, as explored in chapter 3. We have also encountered this idea in a text treated in chapter 2: Jesus's prayer in Gethsemane in Matthew 26:39-46. The Chalcedonian tradition that developed into dyothelite Christology and which was exemplified by Maximus the Confessor treats Jesus's prayer for the cup to pass, yet "not what I want, but what you want" (26:39b) to be an operation of Jesus's human nature, since both will and operation are proper to nature.[54] This was viewed as an important safeguard to the full humanity of Jesus, and to human sanctification through participation in Christ's humanity. Recall that Michael Ovey argued that this passage must depict joint submission of Jesus's human and divine nature, for if Jesus does not will the same thing in his humanity and divinity, then we purportedly face Nestorianism.[55] Ovey is certainly not arguing based on first-order biblical theology, nor on exegesis that expresses the direct concerns of the text of Matthew. In fact, second Adam imagery within this passage hints at the fact that human obedience is in view. Jesus is dealing with the temptation to turn from his Father's will, but unlike the first Adam, Christ submits to the Father's desires. This temptation occurs in a garden,[56] which brings to mind the Edenic site of the first Adam's failure. Like Paul's contrast between the first fleshly man and the second man as life-giving spirit (1 Cor 15:45-48), Jesus chides his disciples who have fallen asleep with a contrast between the weakness of the flesh and the willingness of the spirit (Matt 26:51). While Adam ate what was forbidden and was punished, Jesus accepts the cup that was offered and will be rewarded. When his time of prayer ends, Jesus proclaims: "the Son of Man is betrayed into the hands of sinners" (Matt 26:45), which may intend an explicit connection to second Adam Christology. Perhaps this claim draws to mind how the first man died for disobedience, while the Son of the first man dies for obedience. None of these New Testament echoes of the

---

53. I treat the problem of satisfaction in terms of active obedience in Butner, "Against Eternal Submission," 16. I opted to avoid emphasizing the terminology in this work to simplify the argument for a wider audience, but the basic idea is found in chapter 3.

54. Maximus the Confessor, *Opusculum 6*, 173-74.

55. Ovey, *Your Will be Done*, 113-14.

56. The Greek can be translated "estate," which probably references a walled piece of land, likely an orchard. This fits with John's description of the place being a garden (John 18:1).

Old conclusively proves dyothelitism, nor pro-Nicene theology. However, it is easy to see that the traditional reading is not against the grain of the Scriptures, and the weight of the biblical evidence may favor the traditional interpretation, albeit inconclusively.

Of course, it may well be that the title Son of Man does not point to a second Adam figure. Perhaps the title refers to a collective people or to an angelic mediator,[57] in which case the Adamic typology in Matthew 26 grows more muted. Perhaps the title is meant to indicate a fully divine figure,[58] in which case there may be some evidence in favor of divine obedience being in view, while other evidence favors obedience of the Son in his humanity. Whatever the case, at least some Adamic imagery remains. There is too little information to draw a first-order biblical conclusion about eternal submission, a question that is peripheral to the concerns of Matthew. However, second Adam imagery is perfectly consistent with interpreting this passage as pointing to Jesus's human obedience, and similar arguments exist for other passages. Consider John 14:28, for example. In the context of teaching that the Father is greater than the Son, Jesus also highlights his mediatorial role between the disciples and the Father. Jesus is the vine in which the branches (i.e., the faithful) remain (John 15:1–5), and because he lives, the faithful will live as well (John 14:19). While Christ's mediatorial role is not explicitly Adamic in these passages, canonically the organic connection between Christ and the church is attributed to Christ's status as the second Adam. John 14:28 can therefore be taken as referring to Christ's human mediatorial status during the incarnation without doing injustice to the text. As John Dahms, who cites this passage as offering a degree of support for eternal subordination, admits, "There is nothing in the saying itself, or in the immediate context, to indicate that the eternal relationship of the Son to the Father is in view."[59] Dahms simply makes an inference, one that can certainly be questioned. The main conclusion to highlight here is, again, that there is nothing in the direct, first-order teaching of Scripture concerning Jesus's incarnate obedience that demands acceptance of eternal functional subordination. There is a strong second-order systematic theological argument against EFS that would call for its rejection.

---

57. Maloney, "Son of Man."
58. For example, see Zehnder, "'Son of Man' is a Divine Being," 331–47.
59. Dahms, "Subordination," 359.

Sending Language in the New Testament

Those who affirm EFS frequently point to the Father sending the Son as evidence that the Son eternally submits to the Father. As Ware notes,

> John's Gospel mentions more than thirty times the fact that Jesus was sent by the Father to accomplish his mission, and in some of these places it is very clear that the sending took place before the Son became incarnate. His very coming to earth was itself in obedience to the Father.[60]

Christopher Cowan argues that the notion of sending relies on the "Jewish institution of 'agency' (*shaliach*)," where "dealing with the agent was considered the same as dealing with the sender. The agent would carry out his mission in obedience to the sender," a claim long debated in New Testament studies.[61] Cowan cites Leon Morris's statement that "the very concept of mission, of being 'sent,' contains within it the thought of doing what the Sender wills."[62] As Jesus himself notes, "a servant is not greater than his master, nor is a messenger greater than the one who sends him" (John 13:16). This leads Cowan to conclude that the concept of sending seems "to imply the Son's subordination to his Father who sent him."[63]

Two important objections undermine Ware, Cowan, and other EFS advocates' arguments concerning sending language in the New Testament. First is the problem of the actual meaning of the word *apostellō*, the word most frequently used to describe the Father sending the Son in the New Testament (Matt 15:24; Luke 4:43; 9:48; John 3:17; 6:29, etc.).[64] The word

---

60. Ware, *Father, Son, and Holy Spirit*, 77. cf. Ovey, *Your Will Be Done*, 79; Grudem, "Biblical Evidence," 243–45.

61. Cowan, "The Father and the Son," 49. For a survey of the debate on the *shaliach* concept, see: Agnew, "NT Apostle-Concept," 75–96. A more updated (but less extensive) survey is found in: Keener, *The Gospel of John*, 311–13. Agnew shows that in the mid-twentieth century consensus moved away from the *shaliach* concept lying behind *apostellō*, before a growing body of literature noted that the two concepts were parallel developments of earlier OT themes. Keener treats the rabbinic idea as analogous, though the Christian notion is distinctive in various ways. In John, Keener sees the notion of sending as implying subordination (316). Kevin Giles, on the other hand, sees the *shaliach* concept as an idea establishing the Son's authority and unity of operation with the Father, without any implication of subordination. See Giles, *Jesus and the Father*, 119–20. Scholars lack sufficient consensus regarding the connection between *apostellō* and the *shaliach* concept to allow the concept to provide much warrant for EFS.

62. Morris, *New Testament Theology*, 251, as cited in Cowan, "Father and Son," 48 n. 5.

63. Cowan, "Father and Son," 49.

64. The word *pempō* is also used, though less frequently. *Pempō* denotes submission

itself need not imply the authoritative sending of one who obeys. In the Septuagint, *apostellō* is used to describe sending inanimate objects like cedar and Cyprus (2 Chr 2:8), wheat, barley, oil, and wine (2 Chr 2:15; Joel 2:19), portions of food (Neh 8:10), the ark of the covenant (1 Sam 6:3), and letters (2 Kgs 5:5). It also describes God sovereignly sending plagues (Exod 8:21; 9:14), fire (Ezek 39:6; Amos 1:4, 2:2), curses (Deut 28:2), or even anger (Exod 15:7). Examples could be multiplied. In each of these instances, the word does not denote submission of the thing sent, except perhaps in a loose metaphorical manner. After all, food, curses, fire, and letters all lack a will with which to submit. It is therefore not the case, as Grudem argues, "if one sends and the other is sent, then one commands and the other obeys."[65]

When EFS theologians interpret such sending language as implying that "the Father wills to send, the Son submits and comes,"[66] or that "He was first 'sent' as Son, and then he obeyed and humbled himself and came,"[67] they move beyond the strict denotation of the word *apostellō*. It is certainly possible that various sending verses in the New Testament imply submission, but it is also possible, as discussed in excursus 1, that sending language merely reflects the divine missions, understood historically to be the processions plus a created term. Sending may simply be the going forth from the Father of the eternally begotten Son into the created order. Again, the latter interpretation is not required by the text, but it is certainly amenable to it. The question here is more a matter of second-order theological reflection than first-order biblical exegesis—is the Son sent in a manner similar to the procession of objects like a letter, or in a manner similar to a submissive servant? The New Testament authors do not focus on such questions, which are the domain of systematic theology. Consider another passage cited by Cowan: where Jesus teaches that one sent is not greater than the sender (John 13:16), a claim intended to compel the disciples to humble themselves and to "wash one another's feet" (John 13:14), Cowan sees this verse establishing "the sent one's subordination to the sender."[68] However, the focus of John 13 is on the call for disciples to humble themselves and serve others, not on the inner relations of the Trinity. Moreover, Jesus states that the sender is not inferior, but he does not state that the one sent must

---

even less clearly than *apostellō*, particularly in John. See Mercer, "*Apostelein* and *Pempein* in John," 619–24.

65. Grudem, "Biblical Evidence," 245.
66. Ware, "Equal in Essence," 17.
67. Grudem, "Biblical Evidence," 244.
68. Cowan, "Father and Son," 49.

be inferior.[69] The meaning of such sending dialogue itself does not require EFS, though it may certainly be compatible with it.

Admittedly, in the *Theological Dictionary of the New Testament* K. H. Rengstorf argues that *apostellō* functions as a technical religious term by the time of the Septuagint and New Testament, referring to the sending of a messenger given a specific task.[70] Such a technical term would imply a hierarchy in authority, and perhaps obedience. However, Rengstorf is careful to qualify this claim when the word is applied to Christ in the Gospel of John. Whereas Epectetus can use this as a technical term denoting exclusive obedience to Zeus by Cynic philosophers, Rengstorf writes,

> This is a thought which necessarily lies outwith the mode of thinking of the Fourth Gospel. It is excluded by the fact that between Jesus and the "Father" is a unity in will and action (10:30, 14:9) which leaves no room for "responsibility." And it is wholly and utterly excluded by the fact that alongside the formula *o pater me apestalken* (5:36) Jesus with equal justification can use the formula *elthon* (10:10, 12:47) or *elelutha* (*eis ton kosmon*) (12:46; 16:28; 18:37), which finds the basis of this unity in the time preceding his earthly life.[71]

Rengstorf sees in John's frequent identification of the Father as *pempas me* ("the one who sends me/Christ") an effort to highlight the unity of action between Father and Son, while the word *apostellō* is used to justify his works by grounding them in the authority of the Father.[72] Rengstorf's understanding of the technical religious meaning in John is therefore not an open endorsement of EFS, and other philologists reject any technical sense for *apostellō* altogether.[73]

The extended quotation from Rengstorf above has already introduced a second important objection to those who would appeal to "sending"

---

69. Certainly the disciples are subordinate to their Lord, but Jesus's intention here is not to establish his own eternal subordination.

70. Rengstorf, "*apostellō (pempō)*," 398–406. Rengstorf writes, "the word simply denotes sending; it acquires a religious connotation only to the extent that the situation is religiously conditioned and the obedience of the one to be sent is seen as a self-evident attitude before God as the one who sends"(402).

71. Ibid., 405.

72. Ibid., 404–5; *pace* Mercer, "*Apostelein* and *Pempein* in John," 619–24. Mercer sees a differing emphasis on commissioning, not an emphasis on authority.

73. The entry in the *New International Dictionary of New Testament Theology and Exegesis* notes, "There is no real evidence that the vb. by itself became a technical term denoting divine authorization . . . but it was certainly natural to use it in such contexts." Silva, ed. "*apostellō*," 366.

language in the New Testament to defend EFS: Jesus also repeatedly speaks of himself having come, as if by his own volition (Matt 5:17; Luke 19:10/Matt 18:11; Mark 10:45/Matt 20:28; John 9:39; 10:10; 18:37, etc.). Bruce Ware treats language of coming as an act of submission, something parallel to the functional subordination he sees implied in sending statements.[74] However, there is a distinction between "I have come" and "I was sent" statements. As Simon Gathercole demonstrates, "I have come" sayings with a conjoined purpose statement highlight "the prior intent and purpose of the Son," so that they place "the emphasis on the action of the envoy rather than on the sender."[75] Unlike sending language, which may or may not imply volition, the "I have come" sayings conjoined with a purpose statement are volitional claims because Jesus is said to come with a purpose. Gathercole claims the "I have come" statements highlight his own actions and purposes.[76] The Son did not come as a "passive envoy," but rather as one who comes of his own will (a will shared jointly with Father and Spirit, pro-Nicene systematic theology would add).[77] By ignoring the distinction between "I have come" statements and sending statements in the New Testament, EFS theologians neglect themes that suggest that the Son entered the world of his own volition with his own purposes. We have already uncovered a similar mistake in how EFS theologians treat John 10:17–18. EFS theologians tend to neglect this passage, but when they address it they highlight that the Son received a

---

74. Ware, "Equal in Essence, Distinct in Roles," 17.

75. Gathercole, *The Preexistent Son*, 290. John Collins and Adela Yarbo Collins argue that Gathercole is mistaken to see "I have come" statements as evidence of pre-existence of the Son, for the phrase could be idiomatic rather than a parallel to statements offered by angels to explain their missions. Furthermore, Qumran sources use "I have come" language without intending to imply a move in location from heaven to an incarnate life. Douglas McCready's analysis of pre-existence motifs in the New Testament provides a helpful starting point for a response to Collins and Yarbo Collins. While sending language and "I have come" statements could be taken to refer to something other than pre-existence (and hence not to the Son's eternal volitional commitment to pursue the divine mission of redemption), one must interpret such statements in the broader context of the New Testament. Such titles as Word, Wisdom, and perhaps Son of Man all suggest pre-existence in such a manner that Gathercole's claims are defensible. Yarbo Collins and Collins's objections arise from an overly low Christology. Yarbo Collins and Collins, *King and Messiah*, 123–26; McCready, *He Came Down from Heaven*, 64–66.

76. Gathercole, *Preexistent Son*, 179, 189. Gathercole argues that sending statements do suggest a kind of subordination, emphasizing that the one sent is under the authority of God. I will argue that an *ordering* is implied in such statements, but *not* submission or subordination, so I am at odds with Gathercole on the sending statements. Despite this disagreement, the distinction he draws between "I have come" and sending statements is helpful and pertinent to this discussion.

77. Ibid., 290.

"charge" from his Father, but not that he laid down his life of his own accord, as Anselm highlighted in developing the doctrine of consequent necessity. Here again, evidence for the Son's initiative in the divine mission is set aside.

EFS advocate J. Scott Horrell argues the fact that the Bible only claims in a fixed order that the Father sent the Son, never that the Son sent the Father, "does not imply that the Son and Spirit do not also come of their own volition."[78] He rightly associates this order with a tradition tracing back to at least Nicaea.[79] While I agree that it is perfectly acceptable—even necessary—to speak of an order in the Trinity, order need not be described in terms of submission or obedience. It may instead be explained as an economic effect of the eternal procession of the Son from the Father. It may also be represented through language of divine operations proceeding from the Father through the Son. After all, biblical language of *apostellō* does not always require submission or obedience by the one sent, and the "I have come" sayings conjoined with a purpose statement in the New Testament imply that the Son willed his own incarnation just as much as the Father. Sending language simply does not require acceptance of EFS.

Ordering in New Testament Trinitarian Descriptions

The issue of sending language in the New Testament is in some respects a subset of the larger issue of the order apparent in the New Testament between the Father, Son, and Spirit. Horrell argues that the patterns of operations *ad extra* that distinguish the Father, Son, and Spirit must reflect something of an order within the divine Trinity, which in turn challenges "the social-model euphoria ... that often emphasizes fully egalitarian divine relations."[80] Much of the scriptural evidence put forward by EFS theologians draws on this order, traditionally called a *taxis*, as evidence of the authority of the Father and obedience or submission of the Son.[81] Wayne Grudem, for example, cites Ephesians 1:3–5, 9–11, 3:9–11, Romans 8:29, 2 Timothy 1:9, 1 Peter 1:19–20, and Revelation 13:8 as evidence of a "unique leadership role for the Father long before the Son came to earth."[82] Robert Letham summarizes the biblical *taxis*: "the Father sends the Son and not vice versa.

---

78. Horrell, "Complementarian Trinitarianism," 362–63.
79. Though his terminology of "role" is an innovation.
80. Ibid., 368.
81. See especially Dahms, "Subordination."
82. Grudem, "Biblical Evidence," 232–35.

... The Son obeys the Father, the Father does not enter into a situation where obedience is owed the Son."[83]

The scriptural evidence for a *taxis* in the Trinity is clear, even if it is not a universal pattern.[84] This *taxis* does not entail eternal obedience because an ordering can be explained in various ways (even "first, second, and third" could qualify). The only place where the Bible uses the word "to submit" (*hypotassō*) of the Son in a context that is clearly either before the incarnation or after the ascension is 1 Corinthians 15:28. As we have seen above, there is strong evidence that Paul has a human role for the last Adam in mind, not the eternal divine relation between Father and Son. When advocates of eternal submission move from the *taxis* evident in the Bible to claims of obedience, however, they are not drawing their ideas directly from the Scriptures, but instead are importing a second-order theological gloss into the text. Consider the example of Ephesians 1:3–5, which reads:

> Blessed be the God and Father of our Lord Jesus Christ, who has blessed us in Christ with every spiritual blessing in the heavenly places, even as he chose us in him before the foundation of the world, that we should be holy and blameless before him. In love he predestined us for adoption to himself as sons through Jesus Christ, according to the purpose of his will.

A pattern is clear: the Father predestines through the Son. This fits well with the pro-Nicene claim that all divine operations are indivisible and proceed from the Father *through* the Son *in* the Spirit, a principle derived from John 5:17–19, but a principle also supported by Paul's language here and elsewhere.[85] Grudem moves beyond this language when he summarizes Ephesians 1 by claiming, "The Father is the one who *chooses* and *predestines*, and the Son is already designated as the one who would come in obedience

---

83. Letham, "Man-Woman Debate," 68.

84. So Kevin Giles notes variance in the order of the divine persons in Paul. Sixteen passages put the Son first (Rom 8:1–1; 15:16, 18–19, 30; 1 Cor 2:2–4; 6:11, 17–20; 2 Cor 1:19–20; 3:3, 16–18; 13:13; Gal 3:1–5; Eph 2:17–18, 20–22; Phil 3:1–5; Col 3:16); nine put the Spirit first (Rom 8:9–11, 16–17; 14:17–18; 1 Cor 12:4–6; Eph 2:18–20; 3:6; 4:4–6; 5:18–20; Phil 3:3), and six put God/Father first (Eph 3:14–17; Col 1:6–8, 1 Thess 1:4–6; 2 Thess 2:13; 2 Tim 1:7–8; Titus 3:4–6). Giles, *Jesus and the Father*, 109–10.

85. Paul teaches that God creates through the Son (Col 1:16; cf. John 1:3). God gives victory through Christ (1 Cor 15:57), reconciles through Christ (2 Cor 5:18), and pours out the Spirit through Christ (Titus 3:6). Paul can even write that "there is one God, the Father, from whom are all things and for whom we exist, and one Lord, Jesus Christ, through whom are all things and through whom we exist" (1 Cor 8:6). The Pro-Nicene explanation of the divine *taxis* is a second-order statement meant to provide conceptual clarity, but it is also one that seeks to make sense of a wide range of scriptural claims.

to the Father."[86] The term "obedience" simply is not present in the text. It is certainly possible that one could draw this theological conclusion in a second-order systematic reading of the text, but I believe the weight of the evidence is against this claim. Given the scriptural warrant for a single will in God and inseparable operations in order to preserve the unity of the divine nature, the fullness of Christ's humanity, the voluntary nature of the atonement, and the compatibility of three divine persons with the divine attributes, it is better to interpret Ephesians 1 in a different manner. Better to use the language deployed by Louis Berkhof: "The decree of predestination is undoubtedly in all its parts the concurrent act of the three persons of the Trinity, who are one in their counsel and will." Nevertheless, "predestination is more particularly attributed to the Father,"[87] an appropriation that fits with scriptural patterns of language and with the personal property of the Father. The Father is the source of the Son and Spirit, so his distinctive subsistence is most clear in divine acts *ad extra* such as predestination that are the source of the divine work of redemption.

Space prevents me from addressing each scriptural passage that displays a *taxis* among the divine persons that EFS theologians have cited in defense of the eternal obedience of the Son. Each passage certainly leads the interpreter to affirm distinctions between the divine persons as well as an ordering among them. None of these passages provides explicit scriptural support for claims of eternal submission. The divine *taxis* does explain why it was the Son who assumed a human nature by which he offered temporary human obedience to the Father. All divine operations proceed from the Father through the Son to the Spirit, as patterned on the eternal procession of the Son from the Father, and of the Spirit from the Father and (or through)[88] the Son. It was fitting according to this *taxis* that the divine act of redemption would be accomplished through the Son incarnate, who was sent from the Father, and who acted in the power of the Holy Spirit.

1 Corinthians 11:3

Beyond 1 Corinthians 15:28, perhaps the most common passage cited in defense of EFS is 1 Corinthians 11:3—"But I want you to understand that

---

86. Grudem, "Biblical Evidence," 232. Emphasis original.

87. Berkhof, *Systematic Theology*, 112–13.

88. The question of the Spirit's procession is heavily contested between the Orthodox, Roman Catholic, and Protestant churches, historically in an East/West division, but more recently Western theologians are divided on the matter as well. For present purposes, the point stands regardless of where the reader may stand on the *filioque*.

the head of every man is Christ, the head of a wife is her husband, and the head of Christ is God." Thomas Schriener interprets this passage as revealing how "the Son willingly submits himself to the Father's authority. The difference between the members of the Trinity is a functional one, not an essential one."[89] Bruce Ware argues that "1 Cor 11:3 offers a truth-claim about the relationship between the Father and the Son that reflects an eternal verity . . . there is a relationship of authority and submission in the very Godhead."[90] God being the head of Christ is thus treated as clear evidence of eternal submission, but such apparent clarity can in fact be misleading.

The main debate surrounding 1 Corinthians 11:3 concerns the meaning of "head" (*kephalē*). Schreiner argues that the term must refer to God having authority over Christ. On this account, when Paul uses *kephalē* in his writings, he is referring to authority. This is also the common meaning in the Septuagint, which would have been the source in Paul's mind. While *kephalē* could mean "source," all instances of this meaning in the New Testament are contested, while there are clear instances where the word refers to an authority relationship. Schriener concludes that Paul is referring to an eternal relationship of authority in the Trinity.[91] Kevin Giles, on the other hand, argues that the actual Lexical evidence that *kephalē* used metaphorically implies authority is actually "very rare." Giles sees 1 Corinthians 11:4–5's argument that men and women can have prophetic authority in the church as contextual evidence that Paul is not seeking to distinguish the authority of men and women in 11:3, but rather uses *kephalē* metaphorically to speak of men as the source of women (see Gen 2:21–23).[92] The debate concerning *kephalē* is quite complex, and no consensus is likely to emerge in the near future.[93] At the very least we can say that the EFS advocates' appeal to 1 Corinthians 11:3 is at most as strong as the case for understanding *kephalē* as referring to authority, a claim that many readers will no doubt evaluate differently.

There is actually a generally neglected deeper issue concerning 1 Corinthians 11:3 in the context of the EFS debate: Does the title "Christ" in the phrase "God is the head of Christ" refer to the Son's humanity or divinity? Of course, if *kephalē* is a metaphor for "source of" then it seems that Christ's humanity is clearly in reference here. Christ would then be the head of man

---

89. Schreiner, "Head Coverings, Prophecies, and the Trinity," 128.
90. Ware, "Equal in Essence," 22.
91. Schreiner, "Head Coverings," 127–28.
92. Giles, "Rise and Fall," 53.
93. Anthony Thiselton surveys pertinent arguments well, and concludes that *kephalē* is best translated as "preeminent" or "foremost." Thiselton, *First Epistle to the Corinthians*, 812–22.

in the sense that Christ is the source of the new birth of men through his mediatorial role as second Adam.[94] If *kephalē* implies authority, there is still good evidence to treat "Christ" as a title of the Son's humanity. Though Paul often used the "Christ" as "a virtual second name," he does not appear to have lost sight of the fact that the word was once a title.[95] In the Old Testament, this title applied to those kings, prophets, or high priests who God anointed for a particular purpose. In other words, insofar as Paul uses Christ as a title and not a second name, it appears to highlight Jesus's human role as prophet, priest and king, even if the title itself focuses more on Jesus's work than nature.[96] Though Paul's intention in 1 Corinthians 11 is not to disclose the eternal relationship between the Father and Son, the second-order theological reading offered by John Calvin seems compatible with the text. Calvin writes, "Let us, therefore, bear it in mind, that this is spoken of Christ as mediator. He is, I say, inferior to the Father, inasmuch as he assumed our nature."[97] Even if we grant that *kephalē* refers to authority, there is simply nothing in the text that entails eternal submission or obedience.

Kyle Claunch is more careful in his exegesis than many EFS advocates. He argues that "Christ is the head of man" is in "reference to Christ's current exalted lordship over the church" because whenever Paul calls Christ the head of something, he is called head of the church (Eph 1:22; 5:23; Col 1:18). Claunch concludes that the parallel headship claim that God is the head of Christ "refers directly to the relationship between the incarnate Son of God and God the Father."[98] Despite the fact that he sees 11:3 referring to the divine economy of redemption, Claunch is confident that what is revealed of the economy in 1 Corinthians 11:3 does provide some insight into the eternal relationship between the Father and the Son in the Trinity. "The revelational correspondence between the immanent and economic Trinity is such that this verse does ground gender complementarity in the immanent Trinity, albeit indirectly." Claunch calls this a "good and necessary inference,"[99] but he overstates the case.

Claunch is dealing with two analogies that do not necessarily overlap. Claunch treats the relationship between the Son's work in the economy of

---

94. Gordon Fee offers a similar reading: Christ is the head of the church because he is "the source of its being." Thus, when he says the Father is the head of Christ "Paul is hardly thinking of the 'eternal generation' of the Son from the Father. Rather, [*kephalē*] refers to the incarnational work of Christ." Fee, *First Epistle to the Corinthians*, 504–5.

95. See the arguments in Ben Witherington III, "Christ," 97.

96. O'Collins, *Christology*, 24–25, 42.

97. Calvin, *Corinthians*, vol. 1, 353.

98. Claunch, "God is the Head of Christ," 81.

99. Ibid., 87.

redemption and the Father/Son relationship as an analogical relationship.[100] The self-revelation of God in Christ truly reveals God, but it does not exhaustively reveal God. The divine economy is only analogically related to the eternal life of the Trinity (as explored in chapter 4). This is the first analogy, which I will call the incarnation/Trinity analogy—somehow the Father/Son relationship in the incarnation is related to the Father's eternal generation of the Son.[101] Second is the analogy found in 1 Corinthians 11:3, where Claunch sees gender roles as analogous to the incarnate submission of the Son to the Father. I will call this the incarnation/gender analogy. All analogies are based on some similarity and some dissimilarity, but there is no guarantee that two different analogies point to the same relationship, even if they share a common term. Thus, a banana is analogous to an orange because both are fruit, while an orange is analogous to a ball because both are circular. Does being a circle necessarily have something to do with being classified as a fruit? Not at all; pears are not circles and marbles are not fruit. Similarly, the incarnation/Trinity analogy and the incarnation/gender analogy both have a common term: the relationship between the Father and the incarnate Son. On the complementarian read of 1 Corinthians 11:3, the incarnation/gender analogy refers to authority and submission, but is it a "good and necessary inference" that the incarnation/Trinity analogy is therefore also constituted by a similarity that relates to authority and submission? Such an inference is no more good or necessary than an inference that being a circle teaches us something about being classified as a fruit. This is in fact good news for Claunch, given that he argues that it is

---

100. Ibid., 86.

101. Claunch assumes that the Son's incarnate obedience must have some analogical comparison to the immanent Trinity because there must be some reason why the Son was incarnate. Here Claunch commits the fallacy of composition—what is true of the whole is not necessarily true of the parts. There is an analogical comparison between the Son's incarnation and the Son's eternal generation that make the incarnation fitting or appropriate. The analogy explains the whole incarnation in terms of a fittingness between the state of being incarnate and eternal generation. There is some relation between these two terms. This fittingness or relation does not pertain to parts of the incarnate life of Christ, for example, why the Son was hungry and thirsty, or why he died. Nor need it explain why the Son submits. The point is clear if we modify Claunch's claim. Assume that it is true that "God the Son was suited to become the incarnate and submissive one" because "any Biblical statement about the economic trinitarian relationships bears revelatory correspondence to the immanent triune being of God" (ibid., 86–87). If this is true, then it is also true that the Spirit leading the Son (i.e., Matt 4:1) must possess a fittingness such that we can conclude that the Son somehow is eternally subordinate to the Spirit. However, the Son also sends the Spirit (John 15:26), so on Claunch's principle it must also be true that the Son sending the Spirit possesses a fittingness that the Spirit is somehow eternally subordinate to the Son. Of course, this is a contradiction, so Claunch's principle must be false.

unacceptable to speak of eternal submission and authority! If there was a necessary and good correlation, this would make a strong case for reading *kephalē* in 1 Corinthians as a metaphor for "source." After all, few dispute that the Father is *fons divinatis,* the source of the Son and Spirit, but Claunch himself denies that terms like authority and submission can apply to the incarnation/Trinity analogy.[102] Once again, an EFS proof text does not in fact require acceptance of EFS and is likely best interpreted referring to Christ's human role.

The Names "Father" and "Son"

Some who affirm eternal submission claim that this notion follows logically from the names "Father" and "Son" used throughout the Bible. Bruce Ware notes, "without question, a central part of the notion of 'Father' is that of fatherly authority." The use of such terms across the Bible of the first two divine persons "marks their relationship as one in which an inherent and eternal authority and submission structure exists."[103] Wayne Grudem notes that the names "Father" and "Son" apply outside of the incarnation (citing Rom 8:29 and Heb 1:2), suggesting that these names point to the eternal relation between the divine persons. Grudem argues that such terms are not deployed in a univocal sense, but that they do intend to describe an analogy between human fatherhood that extends beyond mere likeness. Jesus's teachings across the New Testament that frequently point to his obedience help us understand "that the analogy of a human son's obedience to a human father is in fact very appropriately applied to the relationship between the divine Father and Son."[104] Grudem puts forward the following principle: "What is everywhere true of a father-son relationship in the biblical world, and is not contradicted by any other passages of Scripture, surely should be applied to the relationship between the Father and the Son in the Trinity."[105]

By treating the titles "Father" and "Son" as an analogy, Grudem allows for certain aspects of human sonship that may not apply to the eternal Son—most significantly the idea that fathers exist prior to their sons, which would lead to Arianism. Grudem rightly excludes this on the clear teaching of Scripture. I have argued that there are various patterns of Scripture that lead to doctrines which preclude speaking of eternal submission. For example, dyothelite Christology treats will and operation as proper to nature,

---

102. Ibid., 89.
103. Ware, "Equal in Essence," 17.
104. Grudem, "Biblical Evidence," 227–30.
105. Ibid., 231–32.

so that Christ can be tempted in his human nature but not in his divine nature (see Jas 1:13; Matt 4:1–11 and pars.). Pro-Nicene thought treated will and operations as proper to nature to make sense of the broad scriptural testimony that Father, Son, and Spirit work inseparably (for example in creation—Gen 1:1–2; Ps 33:6; John 1:1). Satisfaction theory develops the concept of a non-obligatory death of the Son arising from consequent necessity to make sense of the numerous biblical passages speaking of the Son offering a payment (1 Cor 6:20; 7:23; 1 John 4:10, etc.) or laying down his life voluntarily (Isa 53:7; John 10:17–18; 15:13, etc.). In the face of such clear teaching of Scripture, based on Grudem's own principle, we can rightly exclude submission from the analogical relationship between human sons and the eternal Son of God.

Grudem might object that what I am presenting is not the explicit teaching of Scripture, but rather doctrines derived from the Bible but one stage removed. Grudem's own theology stands at a distance from the Bible's explicit teachings, as I have shown. However, even granting his objection for the sake of argument, I must note that his particularly maximalist account of the analogy between earthly sons and the divine Son may be flawed. Perhaps the biblical analogy is not intended to apply to all aspects of human sonship to the Father unless explicitly prohibited. Perhaps a minimalist account is superior, such that only a single attribute is in mind. Given that much of the evidence Grudem sees suggesting the Son eternally submits refers to the Son's human role as second Adam, the new Moses, the promised messiah of the Davidic line, and the awaited descendent of Abraham, there is not the scriptural warrant Grudem imagines for projecting submission into the Godhead.

Other EFS Arguments

I have now treated the most common arguments put forward for eternal submission. I will only briefly refer to several additional yet more peripheral arguments put forward in defense of EFS. Denny Burk argues against what he calls the "conventional view" of the use of the articular infinitive in Greek grammar, instead putting forward a novel understanding of the article in infinitives as a mere syntactical marker. As a result, Burk translates Philippians 2:6 as follows: "who, although he existed in the form of God, did not regard equality with God as something he should grasp for."[106] As a result, Burk argues that Paul says Jesus has the form of God by nature, but not equality

---

106. Burk, "Christ's Functional Subordination," 84.

with God.¹⁰⁷ It would be a mistake, however, to abandon pro-Nicene trinitarianism, dyothelitism, satisfaction theory, and classical conceptions of the divine attributes based on a speculative re-envisioning of Greek grammar. In any event, Burk has scaled back his support for EFS.¹⁰⁸ John Dahms treats John 17:24's depiction of the Father as giving glory to the Son before the foundation of the world as evidence of eternal subordination, but the same passage can be explained with reference to eternal generation.¹⁰⁹ He also sees the Son's lack of knowledge of the day and hour of the second coming as possible evidence of eternal subordination.¹¹⁰ Of course, if this refers to Jesus's eternal and not temporal knowledge, then the Son would not be omniscient and hence not *homoousios* with the Father—here the standard *homoousios* objection to EFS succeeds. Michael Ovey argues that John 14:31 connects obedience to love in such a way that it points to eternal obedience, but the same contextual cues discussed above for John 1:28 apply here, suggesting that Jesus's humanity may be in view.¹¹¹ J. Scott Horrell argues that the fact that the Father is repeatedly said to give to the Son and Spirit (i.e., the Father gives authority in Matt 9:6) suggests "unalike" and "nonegalitarian" eternal relationships between the Father, Son, and Spirit. Like we have seen with the example of sending above, Horrell reads subordination and submission into a term—giving—that need not take on this meaning.¹¹² One can find additional peripheral arguments for EFS, but the case against EFS has sufficiently been made.

---

107. Ibid., 104.
108. Burk, "My Take-Aways." See especially point 4.
109. Dahms, "Subordination," 354.
110. Ibid., 356.
111. Ovey, *Your Will Be Done*, 94–100. Ovey denies that the verse could apply to Christ's humanity alone. He thinks this "drives a wedge with regard to the Son's love between economic and immanent trinities" (100). In fact, it only drives a wedge between how the Son's love is known. The world knows that the incarnate Son loves the Father because the incarnate Son obeys the Father. We can then know that the pre-existent Son loves the Father by some other means, without positing a radical break between the economic Trinity and the immanent Trinity. After all, our manner of knowing now differs from our manner of knowing at the final consummation, when we see the immanent Trinity with an unveiled face (1 Cor 13:12), so different ways of knowing are possible.
112. Horrell, "Eternal Son of God," 63–64.

The Fragile New Testament Case for Eternal Submission

I have argued that any theology discussing the eternal submission of the Son, either favoring such submission or rejecting it as implausible, must draw on second-order systematic doctrines drawn from the wide pattern of biblical claims as informed by reason, rather than on first-order conclusions derived from the explicit teaching of the Bible. Chapters 1 through 4 represent my best effort to show that EFS violates such second-order systematic conclusions. In this chapter, I have shown why the dispute over eternal submission cannot be settled through simple appeal to the direct teaching of the Bible.

There is insufficient biblical evidence to require endorsement of EFS as an explicit teaching of Holy Scripture. The only passage that speaks of Jesus submitting outside of the context of his life in first century Judea is 1 Corinthians 15:28. This passage does speak of the Son being subjected to the Father in the future, but in the context of 1 Corinthians 15 it is clear that Paul has in mind some cessation of the need for an Adamic (and hence human) mediator between God and creation at the final consummation. Much of the biblical language of the Son's submission is not written with the intention of exploring the eternal Father/Son relationship. However, given the prevalence of the last Adam motif, it is certainly plausible to interpret language found in such passages as referring to the human obedience of Christ. 1 Corinthians 11:3 is often taken as a proof text for EFS, but the case is weakened by debate surrounding the meaning of *kephalē* and by the fact that the title "Christ" again likely identifies human nature. Neither biblical language of "sending" nor the titles "Father" and "Son" require acceptance of EFS.

Though certain portions of the New Testament may be compatible with EFS, the bulk of the evidence compels us to abandon the idea of eternal submission in the Godhead. EFS, like pro-Nicene accounts of the Trinity, can account for certain patterns in the New Testament such as sending language or ordering of divine actions such as the Father creating through the Son, for example. However, as previous chapters have shown, EFS is incompatible with traditional doctrines developed to make sense of the patterns in Scripture that depict the Son performing both human and divine operations, that depict the Son offering payment to the Father for satisfaction, or that attempt to make sense of biblical language about the nature and character of God. The weight of the biblical evidence is therefore against any claim of eternal submission, obedience, or functional subordination in the Godhead.

Conclusion
The Son Who Learned Obedience

THEOLOGICAL DEBATES ARE RARELY as simple as the slogans associated with them may suggest. The summer of 2016 featured much evangelical debate concerning whether those who accepted the eternal submission of the Son were Arians who deviated from the tradition, or whether those who deny such submission are evangelical feminists who disregarded clear scriptural teaching. In fact, neither caricature is accurate. Those who have historically challenged the idea of eternal submission cannot properly be labeled as feminists, nor is it clear from scriptural teaching that the Son eternally submits to the Father. As I have demonstrated, texts often cited in defense of EFS do not require that we interpret such submission as an eternal reality, and biblical authors certainly were not intending to address such questions. The only explicit reference to submission outside of Christ's incarnate life occurs within the context of second Adam Christology—Paul refers here to a human submission offered through Christ's humanity. Though the biblical authors do not have questions of the eternal intra-trinitarian relations between Father and Son in mind, many texts referring to Christ's submission during his incarnate life are best interpreted in light of such second Adam Christology. They most likely refer to the Son's human obedience. Where EFS advocates appeal to 1 Corinthians 11:3, language of sending, or the titles Father and Son, they do not make such a strong case that one must accept EFS on the basis of exegesis or on the basis of what I have called first-order biblical theology. It simply is not the case that EFS theologians are preserving clear scriptural truth against the supposed threat of feminism.

Because the biblical texts do not offer an explicit teaching concerning the eternal relationship between the Father and the Son, it is necessary to appeal to systematic theology, which I have explained as a second-order reflection on the biblical text. Systematic theology attempts to make reasoned inferences from the broad pattern of scriptural teaching, clarifying important themes by appealing to reason and tradition to provide conceptual clarity. In so doing, systematic theology is scripturally rooted, yet it moves beyond what is clearly taught in any single passage of the Bible. Ultimately, EFS must be judged based on its ability to make sense of the complex accounts found in the Bible, but like any theology of the Trinity, EFS exceeds the explicit biblical witness. The main issue concerns EFS theologians' ability to provide conceptual clarity, to offer a reasoned account of their position, and to make sense of the broad scope of Scripture.

Opponents of EFS have often accused those who support eternal submission of Arianism, and for this reason EFS theologians are accused of offering an inadequate theology. The accusation of Arianism is inaccurate. EFS theologians are quite clear that they are speaking of the divine persons when they speak of eternal submission, so it simply is not the case that they necessarily abandon the *homoousios* when speaking of the Son's submission to the Father. This objection would only work if EFS advocates used categories like *ousia*, nature, person, and *hypostasis* with an identical meaning to pro-Nicene thought. They do not. Therefore, EFS should be seen as one of a number of modern efforts to explain the Trinity in a different manner than the pro-Nicene tradition. In this manner, EFS has more akin to social trinitarianism, for example, than Arianism.

Though EFS is not properly classified as Arianism, the main EFS defense against charges of Arianism does cause substantial problems across important loci of systematic theology. By insisting that submission is predicated of the persons, EFS theologians commit themselves to either insisting that Father and Son have a different will, or claiming that Father and Son have different modes of willing. This is a deviation from pro-Nicene trinitarian theology, whose doctrine of inseparable operations treated both will and operation as proper to the essence such that there was one will, one power, and one operation in the Godhead. The idea of inseparable operations was fundamental to pro-Nicene exegesis, to the pro-Nicene definition of nature and essence, and to the defense of Nicaea in the face of early heresies like Eunomianism and pneumatomachianism. Though tradition is certainly not inerrant, the fact that EFS advocates deviate from such a central plank of pro-Nicene thought should raise concerns regardless of whatever proof texts EFS theologians can provide where patristic authors appear to speak of eternal submission in passing.

Systematic theology is, to speak redundantly, systematic. No doctrine exists in isolation of other doctrines, so it is unsurprising that a shift from pro-Nicene trinitarianism has serious consequences for other theological loci. Claiming that will is a property of the divine persons creates major problems for Christology. Since the seventh century, orthodox theologians have agreed that Christ has two wills, one proper to his divine nature and one proper to his human nature. This dyothelite theology follows logically from Chalcedon's claim that the incarnate Christ is two natures in one person, which on the pro-Nicene account of will and operation as proper to nature requires two wills in Christ. More importantly, dyothelite Christology is the best theological explanation on offer for what Christ is and what Christ does. Without a human will, it is not clear how Christ is fully human, and without two wills and operations, it is not clear how Christ completes both human and divine acts. Despite frequent EFS accusations that dyothelitism leads to Nestorianism, a weak claim with no historical backing, no EFS theologian to my knowledge has adequately explained who the incarnate Son is or what the incarnate Son does if will and operation are proper to the single divine person.

Some theologians may prefer to defend EFS by claiming that will and operation are proper to the divine nature, but each person has a different mode of willing. I have not seen any theologian explain how this would work in terms of Christology in a compelling manner, but even if an EFS supporter produced such an explanation, massive problems remain for the doctrine of atonement. If the Father commands the Son in all divine actions, then the Son is under obligation to obey the Father. Such is the nature of authoritative divine commands—they create an obligation. This obligation exists whether we speak of different wills or different modes of willing. An eternal obligation of this sort would eliminate the logic of satisfaction found in Anselm's satisfaction theory and in penal substitutionary atonement. Traditionally, Christ's death was said to be a supererogatory payment that compensated for human debt precisely because the Son died voluntarily according to consequent necessity—he was under no obligation so his death rendered an honor to God that merited the reward of human salvation. If Christ was obligated to die, he earned nothing but his own status as righteous and the logic of satisfaction theory falls apart. This is an unsurmountable problem that applies whether EFS theologians speak of distinct wills or of distinct modes of willing. In terms of offering a rational explanation of the broad scope of Scripture, EFS is catastrophic.

Systematic theology also pursues conceptual clarity, but the language of eternal submission is anything but clear. Assuming an analogical account of theological language, as all EFS advocates I am aware of appear to do, divine submission must bear some similarity to human submission but an even greater dissimilarity. After qualifying the word "submits" be negating what must be denied as a result of the divine attributes of simplicity, eternality, immutability, omnipotence, and omniscience, it is unclear how the word "submits" contributes any conceptual clarity when applied to the eternal Father/Son relationship. In fact, it is unclear to me how the word "submits" could be used properly of God at all. Traditional language of eternal generation and procession, or even the more obscure language of *taxis*, offer far greater conceptual clarity and with greater exegetical warrant.

A survey of the systematic consequences of EFS reveals the deep and, in my opinion, insurmountable problems facing EFS. The claim that the Son eternally submits to the Father is not explicitly taught in the Bible, and its acceptance offers an inferior second-order explanation of scriptural patterns, undermines rational explanations of Christology, Soteriology, and the doctrine of God, deviates from tradition, and provides little conceptual clarity. Simply put, theologians ought to stop claiming that the Son eternally submits to the Father.

I hope that my arguments concerning EFS will help move the debate past a common stalemate that arises from false accusations of Arianism, feminism, and biblical infidelity. Theologians who insisted that they were not Arian while affirming the eternal submission of the Son have not, as far as I am aware, considered the consequences of their beliefs for their theology as a whole. Perhaps recognizing wider problems will convince them of their error. Many EFS theologians currently accept dyothelitism, satisfaction theory, and relatively traditional accounts of analogy and the divine attributes, despite the logical inconsistency between these positions and EFS. Now that these inconsistencies are clear, perhaps support for EFS will wane. Unfortunately, I fear another possible outcome (should my arguments or similar conclusions reach more than a meager audience). Many EFS theologians have already abandoned inseparable operations, or they have modified classical accounts of the divine attributes. Once the great inconsistencies between other doctrines and EFS is clear, some may choose to further modify and abandon classical accounts of Christology, the doctrine of God, and the atonement. The result would be no less significant of a deviation from historic orthodoxy than is found in process theology or some forms of protestant liberalism. When you modify the fundamental metaphysics of Christian doctrine by changing the meaning of terms like person, nature, and essence and fully work out the consequences, the theological change must be enormous. If nothing else, I hope I have demonstrated how interconnected theological doctrines are and how great the potential ramifications could be once theologians of this or future generations consistently articulate a theology that focuses on the eternal submission of the Son.

I hope that classical perspectives, which offer an alternative interpretation of the Son's submission, will prevail. On this account, when the Son submits to the Father, he does so in his humanity with the human will assumed in the incarnation, so that he may make a human offering to the Father by which we are saved. The only way that we can speak of the Son's submission is by referring to his human nature. The Son assumes a human will in time so that he may submit in time. This occurs without the divine nature undergoing change,[1] so God remains simple, eternal, and immutable, possessing a single omnipotent will shared by Father, Son, and Holy Spirit. The Son does not eternally submit. We would be better off to speak using the language of the author of Hebrews—"Although he was a Son, he learned obedience through what he suffered" (Heb 5:8).

Of course, the author of Hebrews does not explicitly teach a theology explaining Christ's submission as an operation of his human will working what is proper to it in conjunction with the divine will. The author is not concerned to explain the metaphysics of the incarnation any more than he is offering a technical explanation of the eternal relationship between the Father and the Son. Ambiguities in the text remain when it comes to the debate surrounding EFS. Hebrews 5:7's "In the days of his flesh" frames the claim that the Son learns obedience (5:8),[2] and Erickson notes that, "the adversative *kaiper,* 'although,' suggest[s] that obedience was perhaps something unusual or unexpected for a son."[3] This passage may also fit within the last Adam Christology explored in chapter 5. These features of the text suggest that obedience is only proper to the incarnate Christ, but Hebrews 5:8 is not decisive. John Dahms rightly points out that Hebrews 5:8 refers to a specific subset of obedience through suffering, and it is possible to interpret him simply learning "in the conditions of human life on earth" what he eternally knew in different form.[4] Erickson convinces me more than Dahms, but here again, we cannot resolve the EFS debate through a simple proof text.

Given the ambiguities of the text, there is still far greater theological warrant for interpreting Hebrews 5:8 in a manner that is compatible with the claim that the Son only submits through his incarnate humanity, even

---

1. The definition of the Council of Chalcedon claims that the union of human and divine nature are "without confusion, without change, without division, without separation."
2. Giles, *Jesus and the Father,* 116.
3. Erickson, *Who's Tampering?* 121.
4. Dahms, "Subordination," 362.

if this interpretation is not required by pure exegesis. Claiming that the Son only submits through his incarnate humanity fits with pro-Nicene teaching on inseparable operations, with dyothelite Christology, and with satisfaction and penal substitutionary atonement. Therefore, it provides a reasonable explanation of doctrine that makes sense of the numerous texts these second-order reflections attempt to explain. This interpretation also offers conceptual clarity, while freeing us from attempting to explain what eternal submission would mean. Claiming that the Son submits in time through his humanity is the better theological choice, one that can make sense of scriptural patterns including Hebrews 5.

Claiming that the Son first submitted through the incarnation is equally able to deliver powerful devotional insights into the character of God. For all its theological failings, EFS is to be commended for its efforts in trying to live a Christian life informed by doctrine. I disagree with the doctrine EFS presents, and I consider the application of this doctrine misguided, but I hope that theologians who ponder the Son's human submission will produce practical and devotional insights for the benefit of the church just as those who wrote on eternal submission attempted to do. After all, these weighty theological matters are both abstract and capable of fostering deep spiritual insights. The Son learned obedience, taking on that characteristic aspect of humanity that we had forsaken in the Garden of Eden, in order that Christ might restore to us by grace the fittingly human act of submitting to God, an act we can share in as the Spirit conforms us to Christ's humanity. I can think of no better way to conclude my argument than providing space for awe-filled reflection on the benefits Christians receive thanks to the Son who learned obedience.

Bibliography

Abailard, Peter. "Exposition of the Epistle to the Romans (Excerpt from the Second Book)." In *A Scholastic Miscellany: Anselm to Ockham*, edited and translated by Eugene R. Fairweather, 276–87. Philadelphia: Westminster, 1956.
Agatho of Rome. "The Letter of Agatho and of the Roman Synod of 125 Bishops Which Was to Serve as an Instruction to the Legates Sent to Attend the Sixth Synod." In *The Nicene and Post-Nicene Fathers, Vol. XIV—The Seven Ecumenical Councils*, edited by Philip Schaff and Henry Wace, 340–41. Grand Rapids: Eerdmans, 1956.
———. "The Letter of Pope Agatho." In *The Nicene and Post-Nicene Fathers, Vol. XIV—The Seven Ecumenical Councils*, edited by Philip Schaff and Henry Wace, 328–39. Grand Rapids: Eerdmans, 1956.
Agnew, Francis H. "The Origin of the NT Apostle-Concept: A Review of Research." *Journal of Biblical Literature* 105.1 (1986) 75–96.
Allen, Leslie C. *Psalms 101–50*. Rev. ed. Nashville: Thomas Nelson, 2002.
Allen, Michael. "Knowledge of God." In *Christian Dogmatics: Reformed Catholicity for the Church Catholic*, edited by Michael Allen and Scott R. Swain, 7–29. Grand Rapids: Baker, 2016.
Alsford, Sally. "Sin and Atonement in Feminist Perspective." In *Atonement Today*, edited by John Goldingay, 148–65. London: SPCK, 1995.
Ambrose of Milan. *Of the Christian Faith*. In *Nicene and Post-Nicene Fathers: Second Series, Vol. X*, edited by Philip Schaff and Henry Wace, translated by H. de Romestin, 199–314. Grand Rapids: Eerdmans, 1955.
———. *Of the Holy Spirit*. In *Nicene and Post-Nicene Fathers: Second Series, Vol. X*, edited by Philip Schaff and Henry Wace, translated by H. de Romestin, 91–158. Grand Rapids: Eerdmans, 1955.
Ames, William. *The Marrow of Theology*. Translated by John Dykstra Eusden. Durham, NC: Labyrinth, 1968.
Anastasius. "Letter of Anastasius Apocrisarius to Theodosius of Gangra." In *Maximus the Confessor and His Companions: Documents from Exile*, edited and translated by Pauline Allen and Bronwen Neil, 132–47. Oxford: Oxford University Press, 2002.
Anatolios, Khaled. *Retrieving Nicaea: The Development and Meaning of Trinitarian Doctrine*. Grand Rapids: Baker Academic, 2011.
Anselm of Canterbury. *A Meditation on Human Redemption*. In *Anselm of Canterbury*, edited and translated by Jasper Hopkins and Herbert Richardson. 5 vols. Toronto: Mellen, 1974.

———. *On the Incarnation of the Word*. In *Anselm of Canterbury: The Major Works*, edited by Brian Davies and G. R. Evans, 233–59. New York: Oxford University Press, 1998.

———. *On the Procession of the Holy Spirit*. In *Anselm of Canterbury: The Major Works*, edited by Brian Davies and G. R. Evans, 390–434. New York: Oxford University Press, 1998.

———. *On Truth*. In *Anselm of Canterbury: The Major Works*, edited by Brian Davies and G. R. Evans, 151–74. New York: Oxford University Press, 1998.

———. *Why God Became a Man*. In *Anselm of Canterbury: The Major Works*, edited by Brian Davies and G. R. Evans, 260–356. Oxford: Oxford University Press, 1998.

Asiedu-Peprah, Martin. *Johannine Sabbath Conflicts as Juridical Controversy*. Tübingen: Mohr Siebeck, 2001.

Athanasius of Alexandria. *Ad Afros Epistola Synodica*. In *Nicene and Post-Nicene Fathers: Second Series, Vol. IV*, edited by Philip Schaff and Henry Wace, translated by Archibald Robertson, 488–94. Grand Rapids: Eerdmans, 1975.

———. *Letters to Serapion on the Holy Spirit*. In *Works on the Spirit*, translated by Mark DelCogliano, Andrew Radde-Gallwitz, and Lewis Ayres, 51–138. Yonkers, NY: St. Vladimir's Seminary Press, 2011.

———. *Orationes contra Arianos IV*. In *Nicene and Post-Nicene Fathers: Second Series, Vol. IV*, edited by Philip Schaff and Henry Wace, translated by Archibald Robertson, 303–437. Grand Rapids: Eerdmans, 1975.

———. *Tomus ad Antioches*. In *Creeds, Councils, and Controversies*, edited by J. Stevenson, 53–56. London: SPCK, 1966.

Augustine of Hippo. *On Christian Teaching*. Translated by R. P. H. Green. Oxford: Oxford University Press, 1997.

———. "On the Creed." In *Nicene and Post-Nicene Fathers: First Series, Vol. III*, edited by Philip Schaff, translated by C. L. Cornish, 367–75. Grand Rapids: Eerdmans, 1975.

———. *On the Trinity*. In *Nicene and Post-Nicene Fathers, Vol. III*, edited by Philip Schaff, translated by Arthur West Haddon, 1–228. Grand Rapids: Eerdmans, 1956.

———. *Tractates on the Gospel According to St. John*. In *Nicene and Post Nicene Fathers, Vol. VII*, edited by Philip Schaff, 7–452. Peabody, MA: Hendrickson, 1997.

Aulén, Gustaf. *Christus Victor: An Historical Study of the Three Main Types of the Idea of Atonement*. Translated by A. G. Hebert. New York: MacMillan, 1967.

Ayres, Lewis. *Nicaea and its Legacy: An Approach to Fourth-Century Trinitarian Theology*. New York: Oxford University Press, 2004.

Balswick, Jack and Judith Balswick. "A Trinitarian Model of Marriage." In *The New Evangelical Subordinationism? Perspectives on the Equality of God the Father and God the Son*, edited by Dennis W. Jowers and H. Wayne House, 325–37. Eugene, OR: Pickwick, 2012.

Barnes, Michel René. "One Nature, One Power: Consensus Doctrine in Pro-Nicene Polemic." In *Studia Patristica, Vol. XXIX*, edited by Elizabeth A. Livingstone. Leuven: Peeters, 1997.

———. *The Power of God: Dunamis in Gregory of Nyssa's Trinitarian Theology*. Washington, DC: The Catholic University of America Press, 2001.

Barrett, C. K. "'The Father is Greater than I' John 14:28—Subordinationist Christology in the New Testament." In *Essays on John*, 19–36. Philadelphia: Westminster, 1982.

———. *The First Epistle to the Corinthians*. Peabody, MA: Hendrickson, 1968.

Barth, Karl. *Church Dogmatics I.1—The Doctrine of the Word of God*. Translated by G. T. Thomson. Edinburgh: T. & T. Clark, 1936.

Basil of Caesarea. *On the Holy Spirit*. Translated by David Anderson. Crestwood, NY: St. Vladimir's Seminary Press, 1980.

———. "Letter VIII." In *Nicene and Post-Nicene Fathers: Second Series, Vol. VIII*, edited by Philip Schaff and Henry Wace, translated by Blomfield Jackson, 115–22. Grand Rapids: Eerdmans, 1975.

Bates, Matthew W. *The Birth of the Trinity: Jesus, God, and Spirit in New Testament and Early Christian Interpretations of the Old Testament*. Oxford: Oxford University Press, 2015.

Bathrellos, Demetrios. *The Byzantine Christ: Person, Nature, and Will in the Christology of Saint Maximus the Confessor*. Oxford: Oxford University Press, 2004.

Beale, G. K. *A New Testament Biblical Theology: The Unfolding of the Old Testament in the New*. Grand Rapids: Baker, 2011.

Beale, G. K., and D. A. Carson, eds. *Commentary on the New Testament Use of the Old Testament*. Grand Rapids: Baker Academic, 2007.

Beckwith, Carl L. *The Holy Trinity*. Ft. Wayne, IN: The Luther Academy, 2016.

Beeley, Christopher A. *The Unity of Christ: Continuity and Conflict in the Patristic Tradition*. New Haven, CT: Yale University Press, 2011.

Behr, John. "Response to Ayres: The Legacies of Nicaea, East and West." *Harvard Theological Review* 100.2 (2007) 145–52.

Berkhof, Louis. *Systematic Theology*. 4th ed. Grand Rapids: Eerdmans, 1941.

Bilezikian, Gilbert. "Hermeneutical Bungee-Jumping: Subordination in the Godhead." *Journal of the Evangelical Theological Society* 40.1 (1997) 57–68.

Blowers, Paul M. *Maximus the Confessor: Jesus Christ and the Transfiguration of the World*. New York: Oxford University Press, 2016.

Boersma, Hans. *Violence, Hospitality, and the Cross: Reappropriating the Atonement Tradition*. Grand Rapids: Baker, 2004.

Boff, Leonardo. *Trinity and Society*. Translated by Paul Burns. Maryknoll, NY: Orbis, 1988.

Bonaventure. *Disputed Questions on the Mystery of the Trinity*. Translated by Zachary Hayes. New York: The Franciscan Institute of St. Bonaventure University, 1979.

Boyd, Gregory. "Christus Victor Response." In *The Nature of the Atonement*, edited by James Beilby and Paul R. Eddy, 99–105. Downers Grove, IL: InterVarsity, 2006.

Bradshaw, David. "The Concept of Divine Energies." In *Divine Essence and Divine Energies: Ecumenical Reflections on the Presence of God in Eastern Orthodoxy*, edited by Constantinos Athanasopoulos and Christoph Schneider, 27–49. Cambridge: James Clark, 2013.

Brown, Raymond E. *An Introduction to New Testament Christology*. New York: Paulist, 1994.

Bruce, F. F. *The Epistles to the Colossians, to Philemon, and to the Ephesians*. Grand Rapids: Eerdmans, 1984.

Burk, Denny. "Christ's Functional Subordination in Philippians 2:6: A Grammatical Note with Trinitarian Implications." In *The New Evangelical Subordinationism? Perspectives on the Equality of God the Father and God the Son*, edited by Dennis W. Jowers and H. Wayne House, 82–107. Eugene, OR: Pickwick, 2012.

———. "My Take-Aways from the Trinity Debate." Online: http://www.dennyburk.com/my-take-aways-from-the-trinity-debate/. Accessed July 31, 2017.

Butner, Jr., D. Glenn. "Against Eternal Submission: Changing the Doctrine of the Trinity Endangers Salvation and Women." *Priscilla Papers* 31.1 (2017) 15–21.

———. "Eternal Functional Subordination and the Problem of the Divine Will." *Journal of the Evangelical Theological Society* 58.1 (2015) 131–49.

———. "For and Against de Régnon: Trinitarianism East and West." *International Journal of Systematic Theology* 17.4 (2015) 399–412.

Calvin, John. *Institutes of the Christian Religion*. Translated by Henry Beveridge. Peabody, MA: Hendrickson, 2008.

Campbell, Constantine R. *Paul and Union with Christ: An Exegetical Study*. Grand Rapids: Zondervan, 2012.

Carnley, Peter. *Reflections in Glass: Trends and Tensions in the Contemporary Anglican Church*. Sydney: HarperCollins, 2004.

Chemnitz, Martin. *The Two Natures of Christ*. Translated by J. A. O. Preus. St. Louis, MO: Concordia, 1971.

Cheng, Patrick S. "A Three-Part Sinfonia: Queer Asian Reflections on the Trinity." *Journal of Race, Ethnicity, and Religion* 3.2 (2012) 1–23.

Claar, Victor. "What I Wish Theologians Understood about Markets and the Economists Who Study Them." *Faith & Economics* 60 (Fall 2012) 32–39.

Claunch, Kyle. "God is the Head of Christ: 1 Corinthians 11:3." In *One God in Three Persons: Unity of Essence, Distinction of Persons, Implications for Life*, edited by Bruce A. Ware and John Starke, 65–93. Wheaton, IL: Crossway, 2015.

———. "What God Hath Done Together: Defending the Historic Doctrine of the Inseparable Operations of the Trinity." *Journal of the Evangelical Theological Society* 56.4 (2013) 781–800.

Coakley, Sarah. *God, Sexuality, and the Self: An Essay "On the Trinity."* Cambridge: Cambridge University Press, 2013.

———, ed. *Rethinking Gregory of Nyssa*. Malden, MA: Blackwell, 2003.

Coakley, Sarah, and Martin A. Nowak, eds. *Evolution, Games, and God: The Principle of Cooperation*. Cambridge: Harvard University Press, 2013.

Cocceius, Johannes. *The Doctrine of the Covenant and Testament of God*. Translated by Casey Carmichael. Grand Rapids: Reformation Heritage, 2016.

Cortez, Marc. *Theological Anthropology: A Guide for the Perplexed*. London: T. & T. Clark, 2010.

Cowan, Christopher. "The Father and the Son in the Gospel of John." In *One God in Three Persons: Unity of Essence, Distinction of Persons, Implications for Life*, edited by Bruce A. Ware and John Starke, 47–64. Wheaton, IL: Crossway, 2015.

Crisp, Oliver D. *Divinity and Humanity: The Incarnation Reconsidered*. Cambridge: Cambridge University Press, 2007.

Crowe, Brandon D. *The Last Adam: A Theology of the Obedient Life of Jesus in the Gospels*. Grand Rapids: Baker Academic, 2017.

Cullmann, Oscar. *Christology of the New Testament*. Rev. ed. Translated by Shirley C. Guthrie and Charles A. M. Hall. Philadelphia: Westminster, 1963.

Dahms, John V. "The Subordination of the Son." *Journal of the Evangelical Theological Society*. 37.3 (1994) 351–64.

Davies, Brian. *The Thought of Thomas Aquinas*. Oxford: Clarendon, 1992.

Davis, Leo Donald. *The First Seven Ecumenical Councils (325–787): Their History and Theology*. Collegeville, MN: Liturgical, 1983.

Denzinger, Henry. *The Sources of Catholic Dogma*. Translated by Roy J. Deferrari. Fitzwilliam, NH: Loreto, 2001.

Didymus the Blind. *On the Holy Spirit*. In *Works on the Spirit*, translated by Mark DelCogliano, Andrew Radde-Gallwitz, and Lewis Ayres, 143–227. Yonkers, NY: St. Vladimir's Seminary Press, 2011.

Doran, Robert. *The Trinity in History: A Theology of the Divine Missions: Volume 1— Processions*. Toronto: University of Toronto Press, 2012.

Dorner, I. A. *History of the Development of the Doctrine of the Person of Christ, Volume 3*. Translated by D. W. Simon. Edinburgh: T. & T. Clark, 1889.

Dunn, James D. G. *The Theology of Paul the Apostle*. Grand Rapids: Eerdmans, 1998.

Durand, Emmanuel. *La périchorèse des personnes divines: Immanence mutuelle, Réciprocité et communion*. Paris: Cerf, 2005.

Edwards, Jonathan. *A History of the Work of Redemption*. Translated and edited by John F. Wilson. New Haven, CT: Yale University Press, 1989.

Emerson, Matthew Y. "The Role of Proverbs 8: Eternal Generation and Hermeneutics Ancient and Modern." In *Retrieving Eternal Generation*, edited by Fred Sanders and Scott R. Swain, 44–66. Grand Rapids: Zondervan, 2017.

Emery, Giles. *The Trinitarian Theology of St. Thomas Aquinas*. Oxford: Oxford University Press, 2010.

Ephrem the Syrian. *Ephrem the Syrian: Hymns*. Translated by Kathleen E. McVey. New York: Paulist, 1989.

Erickson, Millard. "Language, Logic, and Trinity: A Critical Examination of the Eternal Subordinationist View of the Trinity." *Priscilla Papers* 31.3 (2017) 8–15.

———. *Who's Tampering with the Trinity? An Assessment of the Subordination Debate*. Grand Rapids: Kregal, 2009.

Fairbairn, Donald. *Life in the Trinity: An Introduction to Theology with the Help of the Church Fathers*. Downers Grove, IL: IVP Academic, 2009.

Fee, Gordon D. *The First Epistle to the Corinthians*. Grand Rapids: Eerdmans, 1987.

Feinberg, John S. *No One Like Him: The Doctrine of God*. Wheaton, IL: Crossway, 2001.

Fesko, J. V. *The Trinity and the Covenant of Redemption*. Fearn, UK: Mentor, 2016.

Fletcher-Louis, Crispin. *Jesus Monotheism: Volume 1. Christological Origins: The Emerging Consensus and Beyond*. Eugene, OR: Cascade, 2015.

Frame, John. *Systematic Theology: An Introduction to Christian Belief*. Phillipsburg, NJ: P & R, 2013.

France, R. T. *The Gospel of Matthew*. Grand Rapids: Eerdmans, 2007.

Gabrielson, Timothy. "Primeval History according to Paul: 'In Adam' and 'In Christ' in Romans." PhD diss., Marquette University, 2016.

Garr, W. Randall. *In His Own Image and Likeness: Humanity, Divinity, and Monotheism*. Leiden: Brill, 2003.

Gathercole, Simon J. *The Preexistent Son: Recovering the Christologies of Matthew, Mark, and Luke*. Grand Rapids: Eerdmans, 2006.

Geisler, Norman. *Systematic Theology: Volume Two—God, Creation*. Minneapolis, MN: Bethany House, 2003.

Geisler, Norman L., and Ralph E. MacKenzie. *Roman Catholics and Evangelicals: Agreements and Differences*. Grand Rapids: Baker, 1995.

Gifford, Jr., James D. *Perichoretic Salvation*. Eugene, OR: Wipf & Stock, 2011.

Giles, Kevin. *The Eternal Generation of the Son: Maintaining Orthodoxy in Trinitarian Theology*. Downers Grove, IL: IVP Academic, 2012.

———. *Jesus and the Father: Modern Evangelicals Reinvent the Doctrine of the Trinity*. Grand Rapids: Zondervan, 2006.

———. *The Rise and Fall of the Complementarian Doctrine of the Trinity*. Eugene, OR: Cascade, 2017.

———. *The Trinity and Subordinationism: The Doctrine of God and the Contemporary Gender Debate*. Downers Grove, IL: InterVarsity, 2002.

———. "The Trinity without Tiers." In *The New Evangelical Subordinationism? Perspectives on the Equality of God the Father and God the Son*, edited by Dennis W. Jowers and H. Wayne House, 262–87. Eugene, OR: Pickwick, 2012.

Gilson, Étienne. *The Philosophy of St. Bonaventure*. Translated by Dom Illtyd Trethowan and Frank J. Sheed. Patterson, NJ: St. Anthony Guild Press, 1965.

———. *The Philosophy of St. Thomas Aquinas*. Translated by G. A. Elrington. New York: Arno, 1979.

Goligher, Liam. "Is It Okay to Teach a Complementarianism Based on Eternal Subordination?" Online: http://www.alliancenet.org/mos/housewife-theologian/is-it-okay-to-teach-a-complementarianism-based-on-eternal-subordination#.WYxx32xK3mQ. Accessed August 6, 2017.

———. "Reinventing God." Online: http://www.mortificationofspin.org/mos/housewife-theologian/reinventing-god#.WYxylWxK3mS. Accessed August 6, 2017.

Gons, Philip R., and Andrew David Naselli. "An Examination of Three Recent Philosophical Arguments against Hierarchy in the Immanent Trinity." In *One God in Three Persons: Unity of Essence, Distinction of Persons, Implications for Life*, edited by Bruce Ware and John Starke, 195–213. Wheaton, IL: Crossway, 2015.

Goodwin, Thomas. *Christ the Mediator*. In *The Works of Thomas Goodwin*, edited by Thomas Smith, 3–436. Edinburgh: Nichol, 1863.

Gregory of Nazianzus. "Letters on the Apollinarian Controversy." In *Christology of the Later Fathers*, edited by Edward R. Hardy, 215–24. Louisville, KY: Westminster John Knox, 1954.

———. *The Theological Orations*. In *Christology of the Latter Fathers*, edited by Edward R. Hardy, 128–214. Louisville, KY: Westminster John Knox, 1954.

Gregory of Nyssa. *Against Eunomius*. In *Nicene and Post-Nicene Father, Vol. V*, edited by Philip Schaff and Henry Wace, translated by William Moore and Henry Austin Wilsom, 33–249. Grand Rapids: Eerdmans, 1954.

———. "An Answer to Ablabius: That We Should Not Think of Saying That There are Three Gods." In *Christology of the Later Fathers*, edited by Edward R. Hardy, 256–267. Louisville, KY: Westminster John Knox, 1954.

———. *On the Holy Spirit*. In *Nicene and Post-Nicene Father, Vol. V*, edited by Philip Schaff and Henry Wace, translated by William Moore and Henry Austin Wilsom, 315–25. Grand Rapids: Eerdmans, 1954.

Grotius, Hugo. *A Defense of the Catholic Faith Concerning the Satisfaction of Christ*. Translated by W. H. London: Parkhurst, 1692.

Grudem, Wayne. "Biblical Evidence for the Eternal Submission of the Son to the Father." In *The New Evangelical Subordinationism? Perspectives on the Equality of God the Father and God the Son*, edited by Dennis W. Jowers and H. Wayne House, 223–61. Eugene, OR: Pickwick, 2012.

———. "Doctrinal Deviations in Evangelical-Feminist Arguments." In *One God in Three Persons: Unity of Essence, Distinction of Persons, Implications for Life*, edited by Bruce A. Ware and John Starke, 17–46. Wheaton, IL: Crossway, 2015.

———. *Systematic Theology: An Introduction to Biblical Doctrine*. Grand Rapids: Zondervan, 1994.

Guthrie, Shirley C. *Christian Doctrine*. Rev. ed. Louisville, KY: Westminster John Knox, 1994.

Hamilton, Jr., James M. "That God May Be All in All: The Trinity in 1 Corinthians 15." In *One God in Three Persons: Unity of Essence, Distinction of Persons, Implications for Life*, edited by Bruce A. Ware and John Starke, 95–108. Wheaton, IL: Crossway, 2015.

Hanson, R. P. C. *The Search for the Christian Doctrine of God: The Arian Controversy, 318–381*. Grand Rapids: Baker Academic, 2005.

Harris, Murray J. *Raised Immortal: Resurrection and Immortality in the New Testament*. Grand Rapids: Eerdmans, 1983.

Hedberg, Nancy. "One Essence, One Goodness, One Power." *Priscilla Papers* 25.4 (2011) 6–10.

The Heidelberg Catechism. In *The Creeds of Christendom: Vol. 3—The Evangelical Protestant Creeds*. Edited by Philip Schaff. Grand Rapids: Baker, 2007.

Heil, John Paul. "Jesus with the Wild Animals in Mark 1:13." *Catholic Biblical Quarterly* 68.1 (2006) 63–78.

Henry, Carl. *God, Revelation, and Authority. Vol. I—God Who Speaks and Shows, Preliminary Considerations*. Waco, TX: Word, 1976.

Heppe, Heinrich. *Reformed Dogmatics: Set Out and Illustrated from the Sources*. Translated by G. T. Thomson. Grand Rapids: Baker, 1950.

Hilary of Poitiers. *On the Trinity*. In *Nicene and Post-Nicene Fathers: Second Series, Vol. IX*, edited by Philip Schaff and Henry Wace, 40–233. Grand Rapids: Eerdmans, 1955.

Hinlicky, Paul R. *Divine Complexity: The Rise of Creedal Christianity*. Minneapolis, MN: Fortress, 2011.

Hodge, Archibald Alexander. *The Atonement*. Philadelphia: Presbyterian Board of Publication, 1867.

Hodge, Charles. *Systematic Theology*. 3 vols. Grand Rapids: Eerdmans, 1940.

Holmes, Stephen R. *The Quest for the Trinity: The Doctrine of God in Scripture, History and Modernity*. Downers Grove, IL: InterVarsity, 2012.

———. *The Wondrous Cross: Atonement and Penal Substitution in the Bible and History*. Milton Keynes, UK: Paternoster, 2007.

Hooker, Morna D. *The Son of Man in Mark: A Study of the Background of the Term "Son of Man" and Its Use in St. Mark's Gospel*. Montreal: McGill University Press, 1967.

Horrell, J. Scott. "Complementarian Trinitarianism: Divine Revelation is Finally True to the Eternal Personal Relations." In *The New Evangelical Subordinationism? Perspectives on the Equality of God the Father and God the Son*, edited by Dennis W. Jowers and H. Wayne House, 339–74. Eugene, OR: Pickwick, 2012.

———. "The Eternal Son of God in the Social Trinity." In *Jesus in Trinitarian Perspective*, edited by Fred Sanders and Klaus Issler, 44–79. Nashville, TN: B&H, 2007.

House, H. Wayne. "The Eternal Relational Subordination of the Father to the Son in Patristic Thought." In *The New Evangelical Subordinationism? Perspectives on the*

Equality of God the Father and God the Son, edited by Dennis W. Jowers and H. Wayne House, 133–82. Eugene, OR: Pickwick, 2012.

Hovorun, Cyril. *Will, Action and Freedom: Christological Controversies in the Seventh Century*. Leiden: Brill, 2008.

Hugh of St. Victor. *On the Sacraments of the Christian Faith*. Translated by Roy J. Deferrari. Cambridge, MA: The Mediaeval Academy of America, 1951.

Hussey, J. M. *The Orthodox Church in the Byzantine Empire*. Oxford: Oxford University Press, 1986.

Hütter, Reinhard. *Dust Bound for Heaven: Explorations in the Theology of Thomas Aquinas*. Grand Rapids: Eerdmans, 2012.

Instone-Brewer, David. *Feasts and Sabbaths: Passover and Atonement*. In *Traditions of the Rabbis from the Era of the New Testament, Vol. 2*. Grand Rapids: Eerdmans, 2011.

Jeffery, Steve, Mike Ovey, and Andrew Sach. *Pierced for Our Transgressions: Rediscovering the Glory of Penal Substitution*. Nottingham, UK: InterVarsity, 2007.

Johnson, Elizabeth A. "Redeeming the Name of Christ." In *Freeing Theology: The Essentials of Theology in Feminist Perspective*, edited by Catherine Mowry LaCugna, 115–38. New York: Harper Collins, 1993.

———. *She Who Is: The Mystery of God in Feminist Theological Discourse*. New York: Crossroad, 1992.

Johnson, Keith E. "Penal Substitution as an Undivided Work of the Triune God." *Trinity Journal* 36.1 (2015) 51–67.

———. "Trinitarian Agency and the Eternal Submission of the Son: An Augustinian Perspective." In *The New Evangelical Subordinationism? Perspectives on the Equality of God the Father and God the Son*, edited by Dennis W. Jowers and H. Wayne House, 108–32. Eugene, OR: Pickwick, 2012.

Jones, Paul Dafydd. "Barth and Anselm: God, Christ, and the Atonement." *International Journal of Systematic Theology* 12.3 (July 2010) 257–82.

Jowers, Dennis W. "The Inconceivability of Subordination within a Simple God." In *The New Evangelical Subordinationism? Perspectives on the Equality of God the Father and God the Son*, edited by Dennis W. Jowers and H. Wayne House, 375–410. Eugene, OR: Pickwick, 2012.

Keener, Craig S. *The Gospel of John: A Commentary—Volume 1*. Grand Rapids: Baker, 2003.

———. "Subordination within the Trinity: John 5:18 and 1 Cor 15:28." In *The New Evangelical Subordinationism? Perspectives on the Equality of God the Father and God the Son*, edited by Dennis W. Jowers and H. Wayne House, 39–58. Eugene, OR: Pickwick, 2012.

Kelly, J. N. D. *Early Christian Doctrines*. Rev. ed. San Francisco: HarperSanfrancisco, 1978.

Kirk, J. R. Daniel. *A Man Attested by God: The Human Jesus of the Synoptic Gospels*. Grand Rapids: Eerdmans, 2016.

Köstenberger, Andreas J. *A Theology of John's Gospel and Letters*. Grand Rapids: Zondervan, 2009.

Kovack, Stephen D., and Peter R. Schemm, Jr. "A Defense of the Doctrine of the Eternal Subordination of the Son." *Journal of the Evangelical Theological Society* 42.3 (1999) 461–76.

Kreitzer, L. J. "Adam and Christ." In *Dictionary of Paul and His Letters*, edited by Gerald F. Hawthorne, Ralph P. Martin, and Daniel G. Reid, 9–15. Downers Grove, IL: InterVarsity, 1993.

LaCugna, Catherine Mowry. *God for Us: The Trinity and Christian Life*. New York: HarperSanFrancisco, 1991.

Leo the Great. *The Tome of Leo*. Translated by William Bright. In *Christology of the Later Fathers*, edited by Edward R. Hardy, 359–70. Louisville, KY: Westminster John Knox, 1954.

Letham, Robert. "Eternal Generation in the Church Fathers." In *One God in Three Persons: Unity of Essence, Distinction of Persons, Implications for Life*, edited by Bruce A. Ware and John Starke, 109–26. Wheaton, IL: Crossway, 2015.

———. *The Holy Trinity: In Scripture, History, Theology, and Worship*. Phillipsburg, NJ: P & R, 2004.

———. "The Man-Woman Debate: Theological Comment." *The Westminster Theological Journal* 52.1 (1990) 65–78.

———. "Reply to Kevin Giles." *Evangelical Quarterly* 80.4 (2008) 339–45.

———. *The Work of Christ*. Downers Grove, IL: InterVarsity, 1993.

Letham, Robert, and Kevin Giles. "Is the Son Eternally Submissive to the Father?" *Christian Research Journal* 31.1 (2008) 10–21

Levering, Matthew. *Engaging the Doctrine of the Holy Spirit: Love and Gift in the Trinity and the Church*. Grand Rapids: Baker, 2016.

Lister, Rob. *God Is Impassible and Impassioned: Toward a Theology of Divine Emotion*. Wheaton, IL: Crossway, 2012.

Long, D. Stephen. *The Perfectly Simple Triune God: Aquinas and His Legacy*. Minneapolis, MN: Fortress, 2013.

Maloney, Francis J. "Constructing Jesus and the Son of Man." *Catholic Biblical Quarterly* 75.4 (2013) 719–38.

Marcus, Joel. "The Son of Man as Son of Adam." *Revue Biblique* 110.1 (2003) 38–61.

Marshall, I. Howard. *New Testament Theology: Many Witnesses, One Gospel*. Downers Grove, IL: IVP Academic, 2004.

Matthews, Kenneth A. *Genesis 1—11:26*. Nashville, TN: Broadman and Holman, 2001.

Maximus the Confessor. *Ad Thalassium 21*. In *On the Cosmic Mystery of Jesus Christ*. Translated by Paul M. Blowers and Robert Louis Wilken. Crestwood, NY: St. Vladimir's Seminary Press, 2003.

———. "Dispute at Bizya." In *Maximus the Confessor and His Companions: Documents from Exile*, edited and translated by Pauline Allen and Bronwen Neil, 75–119. Oxford: Oxford University Press, 2002.

———. *The Disputation with Pyrrhus of our Father among the Saints*. Translated by Joseph P. Farrell. South Canaan, PA: St. Tikhon's Seminary Press, 1990.

———. *Opuscule 3*. In *Maximus the Confessor*, translated and edited by Andrew Louth, 192–98. London: Routledge, 1996.

———. *Opusculum 6*. In *On the Cosmic Mystery of Jesus Christ*, edited and translated by Paul M. Blowers and Robert Louis Wilken, 173–76. Crestwood, NY: St. Vladimir's Seminary Press, 2003.

Maxwell, Paul C. "Is There an Authority Analogy between the Trinity and Marriage? Untangling Arguments of Subordination and Ontology in Egalitarian-Complementarian Discourse." *Journal of the Evangelical Theological Society* 59.3 (2016) 541–70.

McCall, Thomas H. *Which Trinity? Whose Monotheism? Philosophical and Systematic Theologians on the Metaphysics of Trinitarian Theology*. Grand Rapids: Eerdmans, 2010.

McCartney, Dan G. "Ecce Homo: The Coming of the Kingdom as the Restoration of Human Viceregency." *Westminster Theological Journal* 56.1 (1994) 1–21.

McCready, Douglas. *He Came Down from Heaven: The Preexistence of Christ and the Christian Faith*. Downers Grove, IL: InterVarsity, 2005.

McGrath, Alister E. "Rectitude: The Moral Foundation of Anselm of Canterbury's Soteriology." *The Downside Review* 99.336 (1981) 204–13.

Meeks, M. Douglas. *God the Economist: The Doctrine of God and Political Economy*. Minneapolis, MN: Fortress, 1989.

Meijering, E. P. "The Fathers and Calvinist Orthodoxy: Systematic Theology." In *The Reception of the Church Fathers in the West: From the Carolingians to the Maurists*. Vol. 2, edited by Irena Backus, 867–87. Leiden: Brill Academic, 2001.

Mercer, Calvin. "*Apostelein* and *Pempein* in John." *New Testament Studies* 36.4 (1990) 619–24.

Meyendorff, John. *Byzantine Theology: Historical Trends and Doctrinal Themes*. New York: Fordham University Press, 1979.

———. *Christ in Eastern Christian Thought*. Washington, DC: Corpus, 1969.

Miller, Rachel. "Eternal Subordination of the Son and the ESV Study Bible." Online: https://adaughterofthereformation.wordpress.com/2016/07/07/eternal-subordination-of-the-son-and-the-esv-study-bible/. Accessed August 10, 2017.

Moltmann, Jürgen. *The Trinity and the Kingdom: The Doctrine of God*. Translated by Margaret Kohl. New York: Harper & Row, 1981.

Moo, Douglas J. *The Epistle to the Romans*. Grand Rapids: Eerdmans, 1996.

———. *The Letters to the Colossians and to Philemon*. Grand Rapids: Eerdmans, 2008.

Morris, Thomas V. *The Logic of God Incarnate*. Eugene, OR: Wipf and Stock, 2001.

Muller, Richard A. *Post Reformation Reformed Dogmatics. Volume Three: The Divine Essence and Attributes*. Grand Rapids: Baker, 2003.

———. *Post Reformation Reformed Dogmatics. Volume Four: The Triunity of God*. Grand Rapids: Baker, 2003.

———. "Toward the *Pactum Salutis*: Locating the Origins of a Concept." *Mid-America Journal of Theology* 18 (2007) 11–65.

"The Nicaeno-Constantinopolitan Creed." In *The Creeds of Christendom—Vol. II: The Greek and Latin Creeds*, edited by Philip Schaff, revised by David S. Schaff, 58–59. Grand Rapids: Baker, 2007.

Novak, Michael. *The Spirit of Democratic Capitalism*. Lanham, MD: Madison, 1991.

———. "Seven Theological Facets." In *Capitalism and Socialism*, edited by Michael Novak, 109–23. Washington, DC: American enterprise Institute for Public Policy Research, 1978.

O'Brien, Peter T. *Colossians, Philemon*. WBC. Waco, TX: Word, 1992.

O'Collins, Gerald. *Christology: A Biblical, Historical, and Systematic Study of Jesus*. 2nd ed. Oxford: Oxford University Press, 2009.

Ovey, Michael J. *Your Will Be Done: Exploring Eternal Subordination, Divine Monarchy, and Divine Humility*. London: The Latimer Trust, 2016.

Owen, John. *The Doctrine of Justification by Faith through the Imputation of the Righteousness of Christ*. Philadelphia: Leighton, 1862.

Pabst, Adrian. *Metaphysics: The Creation of Hierarchy*. Grand Rapids: Eerdmans, 2012.

Petersen, David L. *The Prophetic Literature: An Introduction*. Louisville, KY: Westminster John Knox, 2002.
Peterson, Robert A. *Calvin's Doctrine of the Atonement*. Phillipsburg, NJ: P & R, 1983.
Prestige, G. L. *God in Patristic Thought*. 2nd ed. London: SPCK, 1952.
Rahner, Karl. *The Trinity*. Translated by Joseph Donceel. New York: Seabury, 1974.
Ray, Darby Kathleen. *Deceiving the Devil: Atonement, Abuse, and Ransom*. Cleveland, OH: Pilgrim, 1988.
Rengstorf, K. H. "*apostellō (pempō)*." In *Theological Dictionary of the New Testament*, edited by Gerhard Kittel, translated by Geoffrey W. Bromiley, 1:398–406. Grand Rapids: Eerdmans, 1964.
Reuther, Rosemary R. *Introducing Redemption in Christian Feminism*. Sheffield, UK: Sheffield Academic, 1998.
Richard of St. Victor. *Richard of St. Victor, On the Trinity: English Translation and Commentary*. Translated by Ruben Angelici. Eugene, OR: Cascade, 2011.
Ridderbos, Herman. *Paul: An Outline of His Theology*. Translated by John Richard De Witt. Grand Rapids: Eerdmans, 1975.
Sanders, Fred. *The Deep Things of God: How the Trinity Changes Everything*. Wheaton, IL: Crossway, 2010.
Sanders, John. *The God Who Risks: A Theology of Divine Providence*. Rev. ed. Downers Grove, IL: IVP Academic, 2007.
Schelkle, Karl Herman. *Theology of the New Testament: II—Salvation History and Revalation*. Translated by William A. Jurgens. Collegeville, MN: Liturgical, 1976.
Schnackenburg, Rudolf. *The Gospel According to St John, Vol. 2*. New York: Seabury, 1980.
Schreiner, Thomas R. "Head Coverings, Prophecies, and the Trinity: 1 Corinthians 11:2–16." In *Recovering Biblical Manhood and Womanhood: A Response to Evangelical Feminism*, edited by John Piper and Wayne Grudem, 124–39. Wheaton, IL: Crossway, 2006.
———. *Paul: Apostle of God's Glory in Christ*. Downers Grove, IL: InterVarsity, 2001.
———. "Penal Substitution View." In *The Nature of the Atonement*, edited by James Beilby and Paul R. Eddy, 67–98. Downers Grove, IL: IVP Academic, 2006.
Silva, Moisés, ed. "*apostellō*." In *New International Dictionary of New Testament Theology and Exegesis*, 2nd ed., 1:365–76. Grand Rapids: Zondervan, 2014.
Smail, Tom. *Like Father, Like Son: The Trinity Imaged in Our Humanity*. Grand Rapids: Eerdmans, 2005.
Staniloae, Dumitru. *Orthodox Dogmatic Theology: The Experience of God*. Vol. I. Brookline, MA: Holy Cross Orthodox Press, 1998.
Starke, John. "Augustine and His Interpreters." In *One God in Three Persons: Unity of Essence, Distinction of Persons, Implications for Life*, edited by Bruce A. Ware and John Starke, 155–72. Wheaton, IL: Crossway, 2015.
"The Statement of Faith of the Third Council of Constantinople." In *Christology of the Later Fathers*, edited by Edward R. Hardy, 382–85. Louisville, KY: Westminster John Knox, 1954.
Strachan, Owen, and Gavin Peacock. *Grand Design: Male and Female He Made Them*. Fearn, UK: Christian Focus, 2016.
Street, Andrew D. "From Marginal to Mainstream: The Adamic Son of Man and the Potential of Psalm 80." *Criswell Theological Review* 13.2 (2016) 77–98.

Strom, Mark. *Reframing Paul: Conversations in Grace & Community*. Downers Grove, IL: InterVarsity, 2000.

Swain, Scott, and Michael Allen. "The Obedience of the Eternal Son." *International Journal of Systematic Theology* 15.2 (2013) 114–34.

"The Symbol of Chalcedon." In *The Creeds of Christendom—Vol. II: The Greek and Latin Creeds*, edited by Philip Schaff, revised by David S. Schaff, 62–65. Grand Rapids: Baker, 2007.

Te Velde, Dolf, and Roelf te Velde. *The Doctrine of God in Reformed Orthodoxy, Karl Barth, and the Utrecht School: A Study in Method and Content*. Leiden: Brill, 2013.

The Theology Program: Trinitarianism. Edmund, OK: Credo House, 2011.

Thiselton, Anthony C. *1 Corinthians: A Shorter Exegetical and Pastoral Commentary*. Grand Rapids: Eerdmans, 2006.

———. *The First Epistle to the Corinthians*. Grand Rapids: Eerdmans, 2000.

Torrance, Alan J. *Persons in Communion: Trinitarian Description and Human Participation*. Edinburgh: T. & T. Clark, 1996.

Torrance, Thomas F. *The Christian Doctrine of God: One Being, Three Persons*. London: T. & T. Clark, 1996.

Trueman, Carl. "Fahrenheit 318." Online: http://www.alliancenet.org/mos/postcards-from-palookaville/fahrenheit-381#.WYcoOmxK3mQ. Accessed August 6, 2017.

Turretin, Francis. *The Institutes of Elenctic Theology*. 3 vols. Translated by George Musgrave Giger; edited by James T. Dennison, Jr. Phillipsburg, NJ: P & R, 1992–97.

Ursinus, Zacharias. *The Commentary of Zacharias Ursinus on the Heidelberg Catechism*. Translated by G. W. Williard. Phillipsburg, NJ: P & R, 1852.

Van Dyk, Leanne. "How Does Jesus Make a Difference?" In *Essentials of Christian Theology*, edited by William C. Placher, 205–20. Louisville, KY: Westminster John Knox, 2003.

Vanhoozer, Kevin. "A Drama-of-Redemption Model." In *Four Views on Moving Beyond the Bible to Theology*, edited by Gary T. Meadors, 151–99. Grand Rapids: Zondervan, 2008.

Von Rad, Gerhard. *Old Testament Theology—Vol. 1 The Theology of Israel's Historical Traditions*. Translated by D. M. G. Stalker. New York: Harper & Row, 1962.

Ware, Bruce A. "Does Affirming an Eternal Authority-Submission Relationship in the Trinity Entail a Denial of *Homoousios*?" In *One God in Three Persons: Unity of Essence, Distinction of Persons, Implications for Life*, edited by Bruce A. Ware and John Starke, 237–48. Wheaton, IL: Crossway, 2015.

———. "Equal in Essence, Distinct in Roles." In *The New Evangelical Subordinationism? Perspectives on the Equality of God the Father and God the Son*, edited by Dennis W. Jowers and H. Wayne House, 13–38. Eugene, OR: Pickwick, 2012.

———. *Father, Son & Holy Spirit: Relationships, Roles, & Relevance*. Wheaton, IL: Crossway, 2005.

———. *God's Greater Glory: The Exalted God of Scripture and the Christian Faith*. Wheaton, IL: Crossway, 2004.

———. "How Shall We Think About the Trinity?" In *God Under Fire: Modern Scholarship Reinvents God*, edited by Douglas S. Huffman and Eric L. Johnson, 253–77. Grand Rapids: Zondervan, 2002.

———. "A Modified Calvinist Doctrine of God." In *Perspectives on the Doctrine of God*, edited by Bruce A. Ware, 76–120. Nashville, TN: B & H Academic, 2008.

Ware, Bruce A., and John Starke. "Preface." In *One God in Three Persons: Unity of Essence, Distinction of Persons, Implications for Life*, edited by Bruce A. Ware and John Starke, 11–15. Wheaton, IL: Crossway, 2015.
Warfield, Benjamin Breckinridge. "Atonement." In *Studies in Theology*, 261–82. 1932. Reprint. Grand Rapids: Baker Academic, 2003.
Westcott. B. F. *The Gospel According to St. John*. Grand Rapids: Eerdmans, 1954.
The Westminster Confession. In *The Creeds of Christendom: Vol. 3—The Evangelical Protestant Creeds*, edited by Philip Schaff. Grand Rapids: Baker, 2007.
Wilken, Robert Louis. *The Spirit of Early Christian Thought*. New Haven: Yale University Press, 2003.
Wippel, John F. "Metaphysics." In *The Cambridge Companion to Aquinas*, edited by Norman Kretzmann and Eleonore Stump, 85–127. Cambridge: Cambridge University Press, 1993.
Witherington, III, Ben. *John's Wisdom*. Louisville, KY: Westminster John Knox, 1995.
Witsius, Herman. *The Economy of the Covenants Between God and Man*. Translated by William Crookshank. London: T. Tegg & Son, 1837.
Wollebius, Johannes. *Compendium Theologiae Christianae*. In *Reformed Dogmatics: Seventeenth-Century Reformed Theology Through the Writings of Wollebius, Voetius, and Turretin*, edited and translated by John W. Beardslee III, 26–262. Grand Rapids: Baker, 1965.
Wright, N. T. *The New Testament and the People of God*. Minneapolis, MN: Fortress, 1992.
———. *Paul*. Minneapolis, MN: Fortress, 2005.
———. *The Resurrection of the Son of God*. Minneapolis, MN: Fortress, 2003.
Yandell, Keith. "How Many Times Does Three Go Into One?" In *Philosophical and Theological Essays on the Trinity*, edited by Thomas McCall and Michael C. Rea, 151–70. Oxford: Oxford University Press, 2009.
Yarbo Collins, Adela, and John J. Collins. *King and Messiah as Son of God: Divine, Human, and Angelic Messianic Figures in Biblical and Related Literature*. Grand Rapids: Eerdmans, 2008.
Yee, Gale A. *Jewish Feasts and the Gospel of John*. Wilmington, DE: Glazier, 1989.
Zehnder, Markus. "Why the Danielic 'Son of Man' is a Divine Being." *Bulletin for Biblical Research* 24.3 (2014) 331–47.

Index of Scripture

Apochrypha

2 Maccabees

7	14

Baruch

15:2	14
42:7	14

2 Esdras

	176 n.50
7	14
9:8	14
19:6	14

Pseudepigrapha

1 Enoch

22	14
62:7	176 n.50

2 Enoch

30:11–14	169

4 Esdras

	176 n.50

Apocalypse of Adam

1:2	169n26

Life of Adam and Eve

13:3	174

20:1–2	169n26
21:2	169n26
21:6	169n26

Rabbinic Writings

Exodus Rabbah

30:9	15

Genesis Rabbah

11:10	14

Old Testament

Genesis

1–3	171
1	38
1:1–2	53, 190
1:2	38, 174n41, 176 n.48
1:26–27	153–56, 159, 169
1:26	153
1:27	154, 175
1:27a	153
1:27b	153
1:28	153
1:29–30	167
2:4	174
2:7	171n31, 174, 175
2:8	175
2:15	175
2:18	175
2:21–23	186
3:15	174
3:22	174, 175

Genesis (continued)

5:1	174
5:3	154
17:7	143
18:1–2	155n26
22:18	176n48

Exodus

3:6	122
8:21	180
9:14	180
15:17	180
17:1–7	16
20:2	122
31:18	37

Leviticus

18:5	107
26:12	37

Deuteronomy

6:4	64, 140
16:1–8	15
28:2	180
32:18	158
32:39	140
33:15	143
34:9	37

Judges

21:14	14

1 Samuel

6:3	180

1 Kings

8:27	123

2 Kings

5:5	180
5:7	14

2 Chronicles

2:8	180
2:15	180

Nehemiah

8:10	180
9:6	14

Job

36:6	14

Psalms

2:7	7, 131, 133
8	169, 175
8:6	168–70, 175n48
19:1	155
22:1	158
22:9–10	158
32:11	101
33:6	53, 190
39	71
40:7–8	96
70:20	14
86:8	152
90:2	123
91:11–12	174
91:13	174
102:27	143
102:29	143
110	168
110:1	64, 168
110:3	169n25
115:3	106
135:6	106
147:5	123

Proverbs

8:22–30	133
8:24	131

Ecclesiastes

7:13	14

Isaiah

6:8–11	38
26:19	14
42:14	158
44:6	140
45:23	64
46:10	143

53:4–5	103	1:20	56
53:7	190	3:16	56
55:8–9	152	4:1–11	63, 71, 190
63:13	158	4:1	56
61	174	4:3	174
61:1–2	56	4:4	174
		4:5–7	174
		5:17	96, 104, 182

Jeremiah

23:23–24		7:11	39
		8:27	174

Ezekiel

		9:4	68
		9:6	191
1:28	155	9:6–8	174
8:2	155	11:26	106
10:1–10	155	11:27	64n6
39:6	180	12:28	37, 56
		15:24	179

Daniel

		16:16	65n6
4:35	141	18:11	182
7	167	20:28	182
7:2	176n48	20:34	84
7:13–14	175, 176n48	22:41–46	168
7:14–15	168	26:36–46	87
7:14	172	24:36	68
12:2	14	25:34–40	119
		26:39–46	177

Joel

		26:39	72, 88, 90–91
2:19	180	26:42	99–100
		26:45	177

Amos

		26:51	177
		26:63–64	168
1:4	180		
2:2	180		
3:17	160	## Mark	
		1:12–13	173

Jonah

		4:38	63, 84
		6:48–49	161
3:10	142	8:23	84
		8:33	96

Malachi

		10:31	119
		10:44	114
3:6	123, 136	10:45	182
		11:12	63, 84

New Testament

		12:6	64n6
		12:35–37	168

Matthew

		14:61–62	168
1:1–17	63		
1:1–16	63	## Luke	
1:6	168n23		
1:18–20	174	1:33	172

Luke (continued)

1:35	56
2:47	85
2:52	63, 84
3:23–38	63, 64
3:23	38
3:31	168n23
3:38	154n21, 174
4:1	93
4:1–13	84, 92
4:3	174
4:4	174
4:9–11	174
4:18	56
4:43	179
7:14	84
7:35	134
7:48	63
8:54	84
9:48	179
10:28	107
11:19–20	37
12:11–12	36
13:34	71
19:10	182
20:41–44	168
21:14–15	36
22:67–70	168

John

1:1–18	100n12, 131
1:1	38, 134, 190
1:3	38, 53, 136, 184n85
1:14	63, 161
1:18	175
1:28	191
3:17	179
3:34	173
4:24	136
5–11	15–16
5:1–47	100n12
5:3–16	13
5:17–30	10, 13–15, 160
5:17–19	184
5:17	14
5:18	14
5:19–30	58, 173
5:19	14, 15, 31, 36, 41, 45, 49, 56
5:19–20	16
5:20	15
5:21	14, 39
5:27	14
5:30	114n77
5:36	181
5:42	66
6:1–15	15
6:16–24	15
6:29	179
6:33	39
6:35	15
6:38	79, 99
6:41	15
6:53	15
7:18	173
7:28	144n77
7:37	16
8:12	16
8:26–28	38
8:26	173
8:28–29	173
8:28	114n77
8:42	144n77, 131
9:39	182
10:10	181, 182
10:15	101
10:17–18	99–100, 106, 113, 161, 181, 190
10:17	101
10:18	101, 114n77
10:30	181
10:36	155
11:25	65
11:35	63, 84
12:23	175
12:46	181
12:47	181
12:49	173
13:14	180
13:16	179, 180
13:31	175
13:36	120n99
14:9	175, 180
14:10	114n77
14:19	178
14:21	191
14:24	173

14:26	39
14:28	100n12, 173, 178
15:1–5	178
15:13	190
15:26	39
16:28	181
17	100n12
17:11	174
17:22	153
17:19	66
17:24	191
18:1	177n56
18:37	98n6, 181, 182
19:5	174
20:19	161

Acts

3:15	81
3:17–23	38
4:25	7, 133
6:4	37
7:59–60	39
13:2	37
13:33	7, 133
20:28	81
28:25–26	38

Romans

1:3–4	65
1:3	64, 82
1:7	36
1:18–32	166
1:19	155
1:20	126
3:23	166
5	176n49
5:5	131
5:8	109, 114
5:12–21	165, 166
5:14	166
5:15–19	167
5:15	63
5:19	62, 94, 95, 109, 113
6–8	166
6:6	66
8:1–11	184n84
8:9–11	184n84
8:14	131
8:16–17	184n84
8:29	167n19, 183, 189
11:13	152
11:36	35
12:2	66, 122, 123
13:14	165n10, 166
14:17–18	184n84
15:5	39
15:16	184n84
15:18–19	184n84
15:30	184n84
16:27	37

1 Corinthians

1:2	38
1:24	37, 134
1:30	38, 65
2:2–4	184n84
3:16	37
5:17	81
6:11	184n84
6:17–20	184n84
6:19–20	66
6:20	190
7:23	114, 190
8:4	140
8:6	64, 184n85
11:3	12, 43, 153, 185–89, 192, 193
11:4–5	186
11:7	155
12:4–7	37
12:4–6	184n84
12:11	39
13:12	191n111
15:1–3	109, 114
15:1–19	164
15:5–11	164
15:12–28	163–72
15:12–19	164
15:17	164, 170
15:20–49	66
15:20–28	164, 171n30
15:20	170
15:21–22	165
15:21	168
15:22	165, 170
15:24–28	163

1 Corinthians (continued)

15:24–26	97
15:25–28	64
15:25	165, 168
15:26	165
15:27–28	165
15:27	163, 168
15:28	6, 12, 162–64, 168, 170, 172, 184, 185, 192
15:35–49	170
15:42–49	171n31
15:45–48	177
15:45	63, 166, 170
15:57	184n85

2 Corinthians

1:19–20	184n84
3:3	184n84
3:6	39
3:16–18	184n84
3:18	155
4:4–6	155
4:14	122
5:14	131
5:18	184n85
5:21	103
6:16	37
12:8–9	39
12:9	119
13:13	184n84
13:14	80

Galatians

2:8	37
3:1–5	184n84
3:13	103
4:4–5	104
4:4	161

Ephesians

1:3–5	183, 184
1:8–9	16
1:9–11	183
1:20	169
1:21	169
1:22	187
2:15	165, 166
2:17–18	184n84
2:18–20	184n84
2:20–22	184n84
3:6	184n84
3:9–11	183
3:14–17	184n84
3:16–17	37
4:4–6	184n84
4:18	66
4:22	165, 166
5	118–19
5:18–20	184n84
5:21	118n118
5:23	187
5:25	118

Philippians

2	119
2:6	8, 190
2:7	63, 103, 167
2:8	73, 95, 96
2:8–9	99–100, 102
2:9	167
2:10	64
2:13	66
3:1–5	184n84
3:20b–21	169

Colossians

1:6–8	184n84
1:15	8, 63, 134, 155, 167
1:16	38, 136, 184n85
1:18	187
2:9	155
2:15	97n4
3:3	184n84
3:9–11	165, 166
3:10	66
3:16	184n84

1 Thessalonians

1:4–6	184n84
5:18	16
5:23	38

2 Thessalonians

2:18	184n84

1 Timothy

2:5	140

2 Timothy

1:7–8	184n84
1:9	84, 183
1:10	84
3:3–4	66

Titus

3:4–6	184n84
3:6	184n85

Hebrews

1:2	38, 189
1:3	8, 63, 134
1:5	7, 133
2:14	80, 83
2:17	63
3:1	63
4:14	63
4:15	63
5:7	197
5:8	62, 197
5:8–9	72
6:17	143
8:1–6	63
10:5–10	96, 113
10:29	36

James

1:13	63, 71, 92, 190
1:17	123, 136, 143, 144

1 Peter

1:2	38
1:18–19	114
1:19–20	183
2:11	66
2:21	98n6, 109, 114
3:18	82
4:1	55, 82, 161

2 Peter

1:4	80, 127
1:21	38

1 John

3:16	109, 114
4:7–8	131n40
4:10–13	131n40
4:10	131, 190

Revelation

13:8	183
19–20	166
20:5–6	165
20:13–14	165
22:13	137
22:20	39

Index of Modern Authors

Allen, Michael, 58, 60
Alsford, Sally, 118
Anatolios, Khaled, 33n88, 41n125
Aulén, Gustaf, 97
Ayres, Lewis, 2, 28, 30, 32

Barnes, Michel, 2, 35
Barrett, C. K., 100n12
Barth, Karl, 58, 127n20, 160
Bates, Matthew, 168n24
Bathrellos, Demetrios, 71, 77, 89
Beale, G. K., 169n24, 174
Beely, Christopher, 71
Berkhof, Louis, 111, 185
Bilezikian, Gilbert, 23n39
Boersma, Hans, 114
Boff, Leonardo, 152
Boyd, Gregory, 115
Burk, Denny, 2, 190

Campbell, Constantine, 65n9
Carson, D. A., 169n24
Claar, Victor, 151
Claunch, Kyle, 26, 43–44, 86, 123, 128, 187–88
Coakley, Sarah, 157n38, 158
Collins, Adela Yarbro, 182n75
Collins, John, 182n75
Cowan, Christopher, 179–80
Crisp, Oliver, 82n62
Crowe, Brandon, 176n49

Dahms, John, 173, 178, 191, 197
Daly, Mary, 115
Davies, Brian, 137

Davis, Leo Donald, 70
Doran, Robert, 54–55
Dorner, I. A., 76
Dunn, James D. G., 166

Erickson, Millard, 3, 22–23, 38–39, 47, 164, 197

Fee, Gordon, 187n94
Fesko, J. V., 58
Forsyth, P. T., 23, 25, 85
Frame, John, 3, 24, 128, 135, 138, 140

Gathercole, Simon, 182
Geisler, Norman, 3, 85, 128, 135, 138, 140, 145
Giles, Kevin, 2–4, 26n51, 38, 40, 57, 149, 164, 179n61, 184n84, 186
Goligher, Liam, 1
Gons, Philip, 24
Grudem, Wayne, 1–3, 6, 17, 19–20, 25, 32–34, 45–46, 49–52, 54, 58, 85, 112, 128, 135, 138, 140, 142–43, 145, 148, 164, 183–84, 189–90
Guthrie, Shirley, 117n91

Hamilton, James, 164–66, 170
Hanson, R. P. C., 28
Hedberg, Nancy, 38–39
Holmes, Stephen, 116
Horrell, J. Scott, 24, 26, 44, 58, 86, 93, 123, 128, 183, 191
House, H. Wayne, 29, 53

Johnson, Elizabeth, 114–15, 116, 156–58
Johnson, Keith, 38–39
Johnson, Marcus Peter, 66
Jones, Paul Dafydd, 108

Keener, Craig, 179n61
Kovack, Steven, 29

LaCugna, Catherine M., 49–50, 123n3, 159
Letham, Robert, 3, 5n8, 20, 26, 50–51, 57, 86, 92n106, 135, 149, 156, 183
Levering, Matthew, 129
Long, D. Stephen, 129

Marcus, Joel, 175
McCall, Thomas, 21–22
McCready, Douglas, 182n75
Meeks, M. Douglas, 151
Meyendorff, John, 72
Miller, Rachel, 3n6
Moltmann, Jürgen, 151–52
Moo, Douglas, 167n19
Morris, Leon, 179
Muller, Richard, 59

Naselli, Andrew, 24
Novak, Michael, 151

Ovey, Michael, 3, 17, 25, 58, 87–93, 109–10, 112n73, 135, 173, 177, 191

Peacock, Gavin, 153, 158
Plantinga, Alvin, 21–22, 82n62
Prestige, G. L., 41n126

Rahner, Karl, 123, 131
Ray, Darby Kathleen, 115
Rea, Michael, 82n62
Rengstorf, K. H., 181
Reuther, Rosemary, 115

Schemm, Peter, 29
Schreiner, Thomas, 3, 165, 186
Smail, Tom, 24, 128
Sonderegger, Katherine, 99
Staniloae, Dumitru, 62
Starke, John, 41–42, 114n77, 159n45
Strachan, Owen, 153, 158
Swain, Scott, 58, 60

Trueman, Carl, 1–2

Van Dyk, Leanne, 117

Ware, Bruce, 1–3, 6, 20, 23, 31, 57, 58, 75–76, 85, 89, 108–9, 111, 115–16, 118, 119n98, 121, 135, 141n84, 142–45, 148, 159n45, 163, 164, 173, 179, 181, 186
Weaver, J. Denny, 118
Wright, N. T., 64, 167n21, 170n31

Index of Historical Authors

Abelard, Peter, 98
Agatho, Pope, 75n41, 79
Ambrose of Milan, 34, 35, 37, 40
Ames, William, 40n124, 106
Anastasius, 79
Anselm of Canterbury, 11, 40n124, 56, 98–102, 105, 107, 108, 111, 113, 120, 139, 195
Aquinas, Thomas, 11, 124–27, 129–32, 135, 137, 138, 145–46, 148
Arius of Alexandria, 35, 74, 76, 158
Asterius, 35
Athanasius of Alexandria, 28, 29n74, 34, 35, 40, 158
Augustine of Hippo, 13, 28, 35, 38–39, 40, 41, 49–50, 129, 131, 150, 152

Basil of Ancyra, 158
Basil of Caesarea, 28, 29, 34, 37
Boethius, 144, 145
Bonaventure, 52, 141–42
Bullinger, Heinrich, 40n124

Calvin, John, 102–3, 104, 187
Chemnitz, Martin, 80–84, 89
Cocceius, Johannes, 60
Cyril of Alexandria, 120n99

Didymus the Blind, 36–37, 40

Edwards, Jonathan, 104n30
Epectetus, 180
Ephraim the Syrian, 120
Eunomius of Cyzicus, 35, 41, 158

Goodwin, Thomas, 95
Gregory of Nyssa, 28, 35, 37, 99, 122, 159

Hilary of Poitiers, 28, 29, 32–33, 35, 40
Hodge, Charles, 103, 144–45
Hugh of St. Victor, 40n124, 52

Leo the Great, Pope, 78, 79, 89

Marcellus of Ancyra, 28
Martin I, Pope, 79
Maximus the Confessor, 35, 44, 69–76, 77, 80, 82, 85, 87–91, 99, 110, 146, 177
Melanchthon, Philip, 52

Nazianzus, Gregory, 28, 42, 65, 66, 72, 80

Origen of Alexandria, 31
Owen, John, 40n124, 103, 106, 109, 111–12

Palamas, Gregory, 40n124
Polanus, Amandus, 136, 139
Pyrrhus, 74

Richard of St. Victor, 40n124, 52

Sergius of Constantinople, 69, 89
Sophronius of Jerusalem, 70
Stephen of Dora, 70

Tertullian of Carthage, 18

Theodosius I, 46n146
Turretin, Francis, 11, 81n62, 105, 124–27, 129, 132–35, 137, 140, 143–44, 148

Ursinus, Zacharius, 103, 106, 140

Warfield, B. B., 107
Witsius, Herman, 60, 106, 108–9
Wollebius, Johannes, 56, 106–7, 113n75